CW00606425

THE RAINBOW SHELL:

English Poetry from Rossetti to Kipling

By the same author:

A Modern Approach to Marriage Counselling (Methuen)
Dealing with Delinquents (Methuen)
Probation Officers' Manual (Butterworths)
Marriage Counselling in the Community (Pergamon)
*Advise, Assist and Befriend: History of the Probation
    Service* (NAPO)
*Friend at Court (*Educational Explorers)
Clouds of Glory (Merlin Books)
Burning Bright (Self Publishing Association)

THE RAINBOW SHELL:

English Poetry from Rossetti to Kipling

Frederick Jarvis

My heart is like a rainbow shell
That paddles in a halcyon sea

The Book Guild Ltd.
Sussex, England

The Book Guild Ltd
25 High Street,
Lewes, Sussex

First published 1996
© Frederick Jarvis 1996
Set in Bembo

Typesetting by Wordset
Hassocks, West Sussex

Printed in Great Britain by
Antony Rowe Ltd,
Chippenham, Wiltshire

A catalogue record for this book is
available from the British Library

ISBN 1 85776 063 8

CONTENTS

INTRODUCTION

This book is about the lives and poetry of five poets whose work spanned the late nineteenth and the early twentieth centuries. Their names are Christina Rossetti, Algernon Swinburne, Gerard Manley Hopkins, Thomas Hardy and Rudyard Kipling. Although they were widely different in upbringing and outlook, they reflected significant aspects of their country's cultural development. My aim is to introduce their poetry to the younger generation; but in doing so, I hope that older people too will be helped to discover or rediscover the wonderful literary heritage which is theirs.

For Britain the nineteenth century was one of continuous development. A largely agricultural country with a population of little more than eleven million at the beginning of the century, it had by its end become an industrial nation of over forty million, most of whom were town-dwellers. The century saw the growth of a thrusting manufacturing and trading middle-class whose influence was a dominant one. The aristocratic and land-owning elements still exercised power in government, but they had now been joined by this new class which, through education at the major public schools and the universities of Oxford and Cambridge, claimed the title of gentleman and shared a common outlook.

Furthermore, the working class had not stood still. By 1870, there was compulsory education for all, and with the progressive extension of the franchise, a modern democratic country was in the making. But even at the end of the century there were still enormous disparities in individual fortunes and rigid class distinctions.

Britain's industrial dominance during the nineteenth century had led to the generation of enormous national wealth. The country was rightly termed the workshop of the world, and it exported its manufactured goods, in its own ships, to the ends of the earth. As trade expanded, the nation acquired and governed vast tracts of land and huge populations – almost, it has been said, in a state of absent-mindedness. It was only gradually that these acquisitions came to be regarded as part of something vaster. At its peak, the British Empire comprised some 450 million people, one quarter of the human race at that time, and embraced almost every race and religion in the world. Its area encompassed a quarter of the world's land surface and extended over all five continents. It was an empire on which it was truly said the sun never set, at any hour there being some place in which the Union Jack was being hoisted at dawn.

The jewel in the crown of this mighty empire was the Indian sub-continent, which at the end of the nineteenth century, was inhabited by some 320 million people. Britain was wealthy enough to possess a gigantic navy to defend its overseas territories, and it followed a policy of having double the number of warships of any other nation.

It was against this background that our five poets lived and wrote. At the centre of this vast empire was London, which, with a population of some eight million, was at that time the largest city in the world. The manufacturing and trading classes had a reputation for philistinism, but sufficient money spilled over to sustain artistic and cultural groupings which were centred largely in the metropolis. Three of our five poets – Rossetti, Swinburne and Hopkins – were born in London, and the two others – Hardy and Kipling – spent some years there. All were products of the culture of a rich industrial country with a long literary heritage. Swinburne and Hopkins experienced the classical education enjoyed by the governing elite of the society of their time, both going to Oxford University, and indeed attending the same College. Christina Rossetti was a cultured woman, but never went to school, being educated at home largely by her mother. Hardy was the product of provincial grammar school and never went to university, his formal education ending at sixteen. Kipling was in a similar situation. All three extended their education by wide reading.

Every one of the five poets was strongly influenced by the Christian religion. Christina Rossetti was brought up as a devout Anglo-Catholic, and Christianity was the mainspring of her life and of her poetry. Indeed, she sacrificed her hope of happiness in this world for her belief in the next. As a Jesuit priest, Gerard Hopkins placed Christianity at the absolute centre of his poetic inspiration: he wrote his poetry to the glory of God. Hardy had a devout upbringing, centred round the Church of England, and like Rossetti and Hopkins, he had a deep knowledge of the Bible. Only reluctantly was his faith prised from him by experience, and he ended his life as an agnostic, dismayed at the inconsequential cruelty of the world.

Kipling's faith was a broad one. Both his grandfathers were Christian ministers and he had a profound knowledge of the Bible; but his wide travels led him to a sympathy with most of the world religions and some of his work reveals an underlying mysticism. Swinburne too had an encyclopaedic knowledge of the Bible, but he used it to refute its teachings. He saw the Christian religion as usurping the pagan traditions of ancient Greece and Rome and imposing restrictions on the natural joy of life.

It is helpful to come to these poets with some knowledge of the scriptures and of the classics, but it is not essential. Christina Rosssetti, particularly, can be read without any preparation. Her poetry makes clear her intense religious faith. The pleasure of Swinburne's work is enhanced by some knowledge of the classical world, but his splendid rhymes and rhythms are a joy to all lovers of poetry. Hardy speaks to the condition of modern man, and his poetry is readily understood. He uses simple words and images to express his sadness in the face of a changing world and the erosion of time.

Hopkins's approach is a Catholic one. He brings to us an intense happiness in the presence of God, but he also expresses a profound despair when the face of the Almighty is seemingly turned away. The language he uses is admittedly difficult, but it becomes less opaque the more it is read. No other poet has ever expressed such exaltation at the presence of God in nature. In contrast, Rudyard Kipling wrote in plain language for the ordinary man, and probably no English poet has ever been so widely read amongst all classes and all age groups. Rhythm and rhyme came as naturally to him as prose. He could command great religious and political themes in verse as easily as he could write humorous poems for children. Consequently, much of his poetry is a joy to recite or sing.

All of our poets were aware to some extent of the tumultuous events around them. Christina Rossetti, like the rest of her family, was a supporter of Italian independence. She was also aware of the sufferings of the lowest classes in England and tried to help through voluntary social work. Hopkins worked as a priest amongst the poorest denizens of our great industrial cities. He was patriotic, and he looked to the extension of the British Empire as a means of spreading the Catholic faith to the rest of the world. Swinburne was very much at home in European culture. He abhorred tyranny and attacked it wherever he saw it. But as he grew older he became more right-wing and insular. Hardy's poetry was rooted in the rural west-country, but he recognized great universal themes, as in his epic poem on the Napoleonic wars. Kipling, of course, was more widely travelled and open to the world than any of the others. He was immensely patriotic, and foresaw a tremendous future for the British Empire, which he hoped would bring peace and prosperity and good government to the world. His political views can seem outdated, even racist to many people today, but this need not come between the reader and the enjoyment of much of his poetry. Indeed, the circulation of many of his books has scarcely diminished since the day they were written.

In the 1890s, the concept of a world-wide empire had taken root in the consciousness of the British nation. Many people in all classes had developed an exaggerated pride in the expansion of British rule. But at the heart of this empire – in London itself – there was a cultural movement which was at odds with what was seen as the noble ideals of Christian ethics and world hegemony. It had its roots in the doctine of aestheticism: the idea that art was an end in itself and did not need any ethical justification. This movement, which was accepted by many of the avant-garde writers and artists in France, carried with it the elements of a revolt against middle-class morality. If beauty mattered more than morality, then sexual license generally became acceptable. Self-indulgence and the pursuit of pleasure rather than duty was a proper pursuit for the artist and the poet. The French poets Gautier, Baudelaire, and Verlaine became influential amongst the intelligentsia of London. The artist James Whistler, Oscar Wilde and other intellectuals advanced their ideas and based their lifestyles upon them. Algernon Swinburne in his youth was a forerunner of this so-called Decadent movement, and it gathered momentum towards the end of the nineteenth century. The *fin de siècle* man of the metropolis must have his fling, and in this febrile, pleasure-loving atmosphere, vice tended to thrive and decadence to be admired. Art for art's sake, art for the glory of God and verse for the glory of the Empire: these tendencies mingled with each other as the Victorian era drew to a close. It was amidst this tumult of outlook and ideas that our five poets wrote, with Hardy and Kipling living on in the shadow of the First World War and its aftermath.

Despite the many quotations given here, there is no substitute for reading the entire poem, and to enjoy this book to the full, access to the poetry discussed is essential. Collected works and anthologies are readily obtainable in bookshops and libraries, and at the end of the book I have listed some publications which are particularly interesting and helpful. I have also included a list of literary and poetical terms and provided some brief biographical notes on notable men and women mentioned in the text.

Acquaintance with great poetry widens emotional experience and uplifts the spirit. A tremendous pleasure awaits those readers who are coming to these poets for the first time; and there is an even greater delight for those who are rediscovering them.

CHRISTINA ROSSETTI

Remember me when I am gone away,
Gone far away into the silent land;
When you can no more hold me by the hand,
Nor I half turn to go yet turning stay.

CHRISTINA ROSSETTI

Writing poetry was not expected of women in the Victorian age. Those who did it, like Christina Rossetti and Elizabeth Barrett Browning, had to be exceptionally talented and very determined. Christina always insisted that she spent her life trying not to be assertive; but her genius thrust her into the front rank of the later Victorian poets. Her work is not to everyone's taste, because she is a melancholy poet, dealing much with parting and death and unrequited love. Overall, she had an unhappy life, being unmarried and childless and suffering long periods of illness. But there are flashes of gaiety in her poetry, and when she is melancholy she reflects the sadness of the human situation in a universal way.

She never earned her own living, and depended on her family not only financially but also for company and emotional support. She was the youngest of four gifted children whose father, Gabriele Rossetti, was an Italian political refugee and whose mother, Frances, was half-Italian and half of English middle-class stock. Gabriele was a clever, talented child of working-class parents. A wealthy benefactor paid for his education at Naples university after which he went to work at the Naples museum. He also wrote opera librettos and patriotic verse. His intense desire for Italian unity and freedom led him into conflict with the authorities and he fled, first to Malta and then to England, reaching London in 1824 where he lived in exile for the rest of his life. In London he met and married Frances Polidori, eighteen years his junior, whose father was also a political refugee from Italy. She was an educated, cultured woman, calm and imperturbable in contrast to her volatile husband.

Such a parentage produced four children of differing temperaments. Maria was their eldest. She was intelligent and hard-working but plain and lacking in sparkle. Sparkle was provided by her brother, the second eldest, christened Gabriel Charles Dante and called Dante Gabriel by people outside the family. He was good-looking, vivacious and immensely artistically talented. He outshone his brother William who came next, and William, who was dutiful and responsible, made no attempt to compete with him. Christina Georgina, the youngest, was born on 5 December 1830. She was a pretty, passionate child who was very much the centre of attraction. In temperament she was as akin to Gabriel as Maria was to William. Almost inevitably, she and Gabriel were nicknamed 'the storms' and Maria and William 'the calms'.

The Rossettis lived in Charlotte Street, now called Hallam Street, near Regent's Park. At that time it was an unfashionable part of London, and number 50, where they lived after 1836, was close to a rowdy public house. Gabriele obtained the grand-sounding post of Professor of Italian at King's College, but he was poorly paid and even with the private tuition he undertook, he seldom earned more than £300 a year. He and his family lived very simply. The children had no nursery or nanny and they spent a lot of time with their parents. They grew up bilingual, speaking Italian with their father and English with their mother. Their father was obsessed with the great. fourteenth-century Italian poet, Dante Alighieri, and it was after him that he named his eldest son. He pored over Dante's mighty poem *The Divine Comedy*, searching it for hidden, esoteric meanings, so much so that it became something of a joke with the children. They loved their father but scarcely respected him, and thought more of their mother. Nevertheless, he doted on them and was miserable if they were ill or away from home.

The early education of the children was the responsibility of their mother, and Frances Rossetti was well fitted for it, being an intelligent, capable teacher. In due course, the boys were sent to a day school, but the girls continued to be taught by their mother. She encouraged them to read widely, not only in English but in Italian and German too. They enjoyed occasional country holidays at the home of their maternal grandparents, who lived near Amersham in Buckinghamshire. It was here, where she was able to wander about alone in the large garden, that Christina first began to think about poetry. She also began to think about death, for she loved playing at funerals with small dead animals. Once she dug up

4

a mouse a few days after burial and was shocked at its putrefied body, the memory haunting her for years.

One of her first poems was composed when she was twelve, and she presented it to her mother as a birthday present with a bunch of flowers:

Today's your natal day;
Sweet flowers I bring;
Mother, accept I pray
My offering.

And may you happy live
And long us bless;
Receiving as you give
Great happiness.

Puberty affected Christina greatly. At the age of eleven she was a lively, active girl, attractive and full of confidence. But gradually her self-assurance diminished and by the time she was sixteen she was shy and withdrawn. It seems that in her early teens she suffered some form of nervous breakdown associated with religious mania. As were the other children, she was considerably affected by changes in the family's circumstances. In 1843, her father became very ill and was soon a bed-ridden invalid, querulous and partially blind. He had to give up his lecturing post and his private pupils, and the family was reduced to real poverty. By good management, Frances kept things going. She gave private tuition and Maria obtained employment as a governess. William, just fifteen, became a clerk in the Excise Office, now the Inland Revenue; but Gabriel was allowed to continue at the school of art where he had just started. Christina's youth and ill-health spared her from making any contribution to the family's finances. But she had to keep her father company, and this was no easy task in view of his enfeebled condition and fear of blindness.

Her father was a Roman Catholic, but she, like her brothers and sister was brought up by her mother as an Anglo-Catholic, with adherence to the Church of England. This faith was to become the consuming passion of her life. She was taught self-control and self-sacrifice and was always setting herself high standards of conduct and blaming herself for not reaching them.

All four Rossetti children wrote poetry. They excelled at a parlour game in which a number of rhyme endings were given to each of them in turn, which they had to use in the composition of a sonnet. Writing poetry was an escape and a release for Christina. Grandfather Polidori had a small printing press and he produced a slim volume of her poetry. Her poems were concerned with romantic love and romantic death, but early on they were distinguished by the use of a varied and highly original metre. For example, *The Martyr:*

> *See, the sun has risen —*
> *Lead her from the prison;*
> *She is young and tender — lead her tenderly;*
> *May no fear subdue her,*
> *Lest the saints be fewer —*
> *Lest her place in Heaven be lost eternally.*

Gabriel had announced from an early age that he intended to be an artist, and despite the family's straitened circumstances, he continued to study at Sass's Art School for the next four years before going on to the Royal Academy School. In 1848, he shared a studio with William Holman Hunt, a young artist of about the same age. Hunt introduced him to John Everett Millais, another young painter of great talent, and it was from their friendship that the Pre-Raphaelite Brotherhood developed.

In youthful fashion, they derided established artistic standards of the time. They felt that Raphael, the great Italian Renaissance painter, was vastly over-rated, and the work of Sir Joshua Reynolds, the renowned English portrait painter, was worthless. They looked for inspiration to the pre-Renaissance painters and favoured a more detailed attention to nature. Their own styles of painting had little in common, but they were bound together for the moment by their enthusiasm and rebellion. The Brotherhood of three was joined by four more members, one of whom was James Collinson, a professional painter with only a moderate talent. He was short and plump, but Christina was nevertheless attracted to him.

The Brotherhood was initially a secret society, and its members signed their pictures with the mysterious letters PRB. At first their

6

work was widely dismissed, but after John Ruskin, the pre-eminent art critic of the day, had praised it, opinion grew more favourable. Although he was barely twenty, Dante Gabriel soon became the dominant personality of the group. He firmly believed that art and literature have the same roots and should be linked. Thus he began to accompany each of his pictures with a sonnet. An early venture of his was a journal called *The Germ,* which was to be a vehicle for the literary work of the Brotherhood. William Rossetti was its editor and the first number appeared on New Year's Day 1850. It included a poem by Gabriel, *My Sister's Sleep,* and two poems by Christina called *Dreamland* and *An End,* both of which were melancholy and romantically unreal. *Dreamland* concerns a woman from a distant country who lies peacefully in a charmed sleep. In *An End,* the poet mourns the passing of a love afair.

The second issue of *The Germ* contained more of her verses, one of them a long religious poem, and another expressing sorrow at the passing of time and of love:

> *Oh roses for the flush of youth,*
> *And laurel for the perfect prime;*
> *But pluck an ivy branch for me*
> *Grown old before my time.*
>
> *Oh violets for the grave of youth,*
> *And bay for those dead in their prime;*
> *Give me the withered leaves I chose*
> *Before in the old time.*

Christina withheld from publication any poem which seemed too personal, but it does appear that renunciation of love had already become part of her character.

Despite the inclusion of Gabriel's poem, *The Blessed Damozel,* which in due course was recognised as one of his major works, *The Germ* did not prosper, and after two more issues collapsed leaving considerable debts. One revealing poem which Christina did not offer for publication then, but has since been widely acclaimed, was:

7

When I am dead, my dearest,
Sing no sad songs for me;
Plant thou no roses at my head,
Nor shady cypress tree:
Be the green grass above me
With showers and dewdrops wet;
And if thou wilt, remember,
And if thou wilt, forget.
I shall not see the shadows,
I shall not feel the rain,
I shall not hear the nightingale
Sing on as if in pain:
And dreaming through the twilight
That does not rise nor set,
Haply I may remember,
And haply may forget.

Christina found her association with the Pre-Raphaelite Brotherhood very thrilling. At the age of seventeen, she was ready for love,
and James Collinson, artist and aspiring poet seemed a suitable man
to fall for. One problem was that he had only a small allowance from
his father and was in no position to marry; but this did not worry
her. She loved her home and family and was in no hurry to leave it.
Collinson dithered between the Anglican and the Roman Catholic
churches. For a time he accepted the Anglo-Catholic persuasion to
please her, and in the autumn of 1848 they became engaged, settling
down to a long period of waiting to get married.

She visited his family in the summer of the following year, oddly
enough without him, and stayed for some weeks. She did not find
them very congenial. Perhaps they knew that he was contemplating
returning to the Roman Catholic faith, for this he did in 1850. She
immediately broke off the engagement and he resigned from the
Brotherhood. She went off to Brighton, depressed and physically
exhausted, writing occasional letters to brother William asking for
news of Collinson, but nevertheless sure she had done the right
thing in sacrificing personal happiness for her religious beliefs.

Just before she got engaged to James Collinson, she had met
another man who was to play a longer part in her life. •This was

William Bell Scott, a Scotsman who too was both an artist and a minor poet. Her brother Gabriel had written to Scott, who lived in Newcastle, praising one of his poems, and Scott on a visit to London called on the Rossetti household to find only Christina at home with her sick father. This was the beginning of a lifetime friendship with the whole Rossetti family. Although Scott was a married man, Christina became very fond of him. There are some who think they enjoyed a secret love affair, but there is no evidence for this; and in view of Christina's strong religious scruples, it is most unlikely that she ever did more than pine for him and admire him from a distance.

Her brother William, as editor of *The Germ*, had been asked to undertake art criticism and literary reviews for other journals, and this brought him into contact with painters and writers. Gabriel too had many acquaintances in this field, and thus Christina had the chance of meeting interesting and cultured people. She already knew the artist Ford Madox Brown because Gabriel had been a pupil of his for a short time, and she got to know him better by attending an art class he ran for working men. She was friendly too with Holman Hunt, Gabriel's great friend, and she sat for him as a model, chaperoned discreetly by her mother. She won the admiration of one well-known artist, John Brett, but spurned his advances, expressing her distaste in a poem called *No Thank-You John*, the last verse of which runs tartly:

> *Let bygones be bygones:*
> *Don't call me false, who owed not to be true:*
> *I'd rather answer 'no' to fifty Johns*
> *Than answer 'yes' to you.*

The Rossettis moved in 1851 from Charlotte Street to 28 Arlington Street, off Piccadilly, where Frances started a small school for girls, Christina being pressed into helping her. It was not a success, and in March 1853, they moved the school to Frome in Somerset. The school was under the supervision of an Anglo-Catholic clergyman, a protégé of Lady Bath, to whom Frances's sister Charlotte acted as companion. With them went Christina's bed-ridden father, but Maria and William remained in London and Christina greatly missed them. Her grandmother Polidori died and her beloved grandfather soon followed. They left some money to Frances, and this made it possible for her to give up teaching. She and Christina returned to London to live with Maria and William in William's house at 45 Upper Albany Street, Camden Town.

Christina had not neglected her poetry. In a poem called *A Bruised Reed shall He not Break*, she envisages a dialogue between her soul and the Almighty. He tells her that He is unable to make her love Him; it must be by her own desire. But if she does not choose to accept His love, He will still strive to win her. This was one of her many religious poems. Another written at about this time was one of her few joyous ones. It was called *Paradise: In a Dream* and was an attempt to imagine what heaven is like. She describes it in terms of birds, which she always loved:

> *I heard the songs of Paradise;*
> *Each bird sat singing in his place;*
> *A tender song so full of grace*
> *It soared like incense to the skies.*
> *Each bird sat singing to his mate*
> *Soft cooing notes among the trees:*
> *The nightingale herself were cold*
> *To such as these.*

A fad of the Pre-Raphaelite Brotherhood was a fascination for beautiful girls with red-gold hair. If they saw a girl like this they would ask her to sit as a model. They knew such girls as 'stunners', and it was in this way that Gabriel met a russet-haired 'stunner' called Elizabeth Siddall, who was a milliner's apprentice, the daughter of a working cutler. He persuaded her to drop the second 'l' of her name, calling her Lizzie Siddal, or more playfully El Cid. She went to live with him in his picturesque house overlooking the Thames near Blackfriars Bridge, and although she disliked the idea of an illicit love affair and longed for marriage, she was content enough at the beginning. He was infatuated with her and they played together like children, calling each other Gug and Guggums. She inspired his artistic talent, and he was forever drawing and painting her in an endless variety of characters and poses. He encouraged her to paint and to write poetry and she revealed talent in both.

Christina's relationship with Lizzie was cool. Probably she would not have considered any woman good enough for her brilliant brother; but certainly Lizzie with her humble background was not her idea of a suitable wife. Christina's poem *In an Artist's Studio* accurately describes the obsessiveness with which her brother painted his model, who came to represent the idealised Pre-Raphaelite woman:

> *One face looks out from all his canvases,*
> *One selfsame figure sits or walks or leans . . .*
> *A queen in opal or in ruby dress,*
> *A nameless girl in freshest summer-greens,*
> *A saint, an angel – every canvas means*
> *The same one meaning, neither more than less.*
> *He feeds upon her face by day and night . . .*

In April 1854, Christina's father died. His last literary effort was a collection of Italian hymns, some of which Christina translated into English. She confessed later that the death of her grandfather a year before had meant much more to her.

In March 1855 she experienced one of her serious but un-diagnosed illnesses, which doctors thought might be angina but then again could be consumption. She was sent to Hastings to convalesce. When she had recovered a little she attempted to work as a gover-ness, but it was too much for her and she became ill again. From then on she gave up all idea of working outside the home. She did her best to earn some money from doing Italian translations, but was listless and depressed.

The Pre-Raphaelite Brotherhood was breaking up. Collinson had resigned, Holman Hunt was painting bibilical scenes in the Middle East and Millais had, as Gabriel saw it, gone over to the enemy by getting himself elected an Associate of the Royal Academy. William was acting the dutiful son by accommodating both Christina and his mother in his Camden Town house. By now the Pre-Raphaelite school had drifted into a dreamy medievalism, turning their eyes from the realities of industrial Britain. Christina tended to cultivate the antiquated and archaic in her poetry. At this time she was more pessimistic in outlook than Gabriel, and whilst he still retained some gaiety and wit, her mind was full of death and desolation.

Both Maria and William had their heartaches. Maria had met John Ruskin and had mistaken his kindly interest in her for something more. She resigned her hopes quickly and turned her mind ever more intently to her religion, as Christina also was to do. William got engaged to Henrietta Rintoul, daughter of the editor of *The Spectator*, only for her to break it off after four years. He was puzzled and hurt and remained a bachelor for another twelve years. He was a modest, conscientious man and Christina depended upon him all her life. In his own way, Gabriel relied on him too, for he was forever borrowing money from him.

In May 1860, after ten years of prolonged courtship, Gabriel eventually married Lizzie Siddal. She had ailed and wailed for much of this time, intermittently leaving and returning to him, always hoping he would marry her. Within a year of the wedding she gave birth to a still-born child. He had never been faithful to her. His streak of sensuality conflicted with the chivalrous idealism of the Brotherhood, and he was increasingly consumed by guilt. In 1862, already heavily dependent on laudanum, Lizzie died from an overdose. The coroner's verdict was accidental death, but Gabriel knew it was suicide and his burden of guilt was even heavier.

Christina had been very unhappy at her brother's marriage, but at the time she herself had been falling in love again. The object of her affection was a young man called Charles Cayley whom she had first met when he was taking Italian lessons from her father. He was a civil servant who had given up his career to concentrate on literary work, from which he earned very little. He was a brilliant linguist and highly intelligent but utterly unworldly. Her love for him developed slowly and she told no-one about it, least of all Cayley himself. The only hint she gave was in two poems about women with mysterious secrets, written in 1857. One verse gives the flavour of them:

> *I tell my secret? No, indeed, not I:*
> *Perhaps some day, who knows?*
> *But not today; it froze and blows and snows,*
> *And you're too curious: fie!*
> *You want to hear it? well:*
> *Only my secret's mine, and I won't tell . . .*

There was nothing in Cayley's outward appearance to attract a woman. He tended to wear a rumpled shirt with no collar and an old tail-coat. He was shy and inarticulate and often deep in his own thoughts. He had little money of his own and relied on hand-outs from his well-to-do family. He was always the perfect gentleman, meticulous about the social conventions – when he remembered them.

If Cayley did not dress to attract the opposite sex, neither did Christina. Increasingly she arrayed herself in black. Her dress fell to the floor and she usually wore a black poke bonnet. In common with many Victorian middle-class women, she took up charity work, concerning herself particularly with the welfare of young prostitutes. For some years she worked in a home for so-called fallen women run by Anglican nuns. In one poem she puts herself in the position of one of the inmates, causing her to say:

> *Take counsel, sever from my lot your lot,*
> *Dwell in your pleasant places, hoard your gold;*
> *Lest you with me should shiver in the world,*
> *Athirst and hungering on a barren spot.*

Gabriel encouraged his sister's poetry and wanted to get it published. He showed some of her work to John Ruskin who criticised the irregular metre, which was in fact one of its remarkable features. Eventually, a young publisher called Alexander Macmillan agreed to print one of her poems in his house journal, *Macmillan's Magazine*. The poem was *Up-Hill*, which has been a popular anthology piece ever since:

> *Does the road wind up-hill all the way?*
> *Yes, to the very end.*
> *Will the day's journey take the whole long day?*
> *From morn to night, my friend.*
>
> *But is there for the night a resting-place?*
> *A roof for when the dark slow hours begin.*
> *May not the darkness hide it from my face?*
> *You cannot miss that inn.*

13

Shall I meet other wayfarers at night?
Those who have gone before.
Then must I knock, or call when just in sight?
They will not keep you standing at that door.

Shall I find comfort, travel-sore and weak?
Of labour you shall find the sum.
Will there be beds for me and all who seek?
Yea, beds for all who come.

Her brother mocked the poem as *your lively little song of the tomb*, and, as if in response to this jibe, an issue of the magazine two months later carried the happiest poem she ever wrote. It dealt not with blighted affections but with love fulfilled, and was called *A Birthday*:

My heart is like a singing bird
Whose nest is in a watered shoot;
My heart is like an apple-tree
Whose boughs are bent with thick-set fruit;
My heart is like a rainbow shell
That paddles in a halcyon sea;
My heart is gladder than all these
Because my love is come to me.

Raise me a dais of silk and down;
Hang it with vair and purple dyes;
Carve it in doves, and pomegranates,
And peacocks with a hundred eyes;
Work it in gold and silver grapes,
In leaves, and silver fleur-de-lys;
Because the birthday of my life
Is come, my love is come to me.

But there was always melancholy in Christina's heart. About the same time, she wrote a sad and bitter poem called *Today and Tomorrow* in which she laments the lack of love in her life:

14

All the world is making love:
Bird to bird in bushes,
Beast to beast in glades and frog
To frog among the rushes:
Wake O south wind sweet with spice,
Wake the rose to blushes.

She concluded the poem with a wish for death:

I wish I were dead, my foe,
My friend, I wish I were dead,
With a stone at my tired feet
And a stone at my tired head.

Things brightened up for her later in 1861 when she visited France with William and her mother, and ended even more sweetly with Macmillan's decision to publish a book of her poems, which Gabriel was to illustrate. The book was entitled *Goblin Market and other Poems*, and it appeared in the bookshops in March 1862. It contained some of her finest lyrics; but it was the title poem which attracted most attention, and it has continued to fascinate poetry-lovers ever since. Written in a deceptively simple but uneven metrical rhythm, it could be mistaken for a fairy tale for children; but it is far more than this. Sexually repressed and inhibited – as so many Victorian gentle-women were – Christina allowed her unconscious feelings full rein. Readers may interpret the story as they wish, but there is no denying the sexually passionate undertones. The poem concerns two young sisters, Lizzie and Laura, who live together and are seemingly devoted to each other and are depicted in close embrace.

In the evenings by a stream, they lie close together while strange-looking goblins, half-men and half-beasts, pass by, crying as they go:

'Come buy our orchard fruits,
Come buy, come buy:
Apples and quinces,
Lemons and oranges,
Plump unpecked cherries,
Melons and raspberries,

Bloom-down-cheeked peaches,
Swart-headed mulberries,
Wild free-born cranberries,
Crab-apples, dewberries,
Pine-apples, blackberries,
Apricots, strawberries; –
All ripe together
In summer weather, –
Morns that pass by,
Fair eves that fly;
Come buy, come buy.'

One evening, Lizzie runs away to avoid temptation, but Laura cannot resist the fruit. Having no money, she buys some of it with a lock of her golden hair, and sucks the sweet juices until her lips are sore. When eventually she arrives home, Lizzie scolds her, but Laura is unrepentant, saying:

'You cannot think what figs
My teeth have met in,
What melons, icy-cold
Piled on a dish of gold
Too huge for me to hold,
What peaches with a velvet nap,
Pellucid grapes without one seed:
Odorous indeed must be the mead
Whereon they grow, and pure the wave they drink
With lilies at the brink,
And sugar-sweet their sap.'

The sisters fall asleep,

Cheek to cheek and breast to breast
Locked together in one nest.

The next evening, Lizzie sees and hears the goblin-men, but Laura cannot. She yearns for their fruit and cannot sleep for desire. Day after day she watches for them but they do not come. As she pines, she dwindles in stature and her hair grows thin and grey. She sits idly by the fire and eats nothing, and soon she is near death. Unable to bear her sister's misery any longer, Lizzie resolves to get some of the goblin fruit in the hope that it will restore Laura to health. One evening she goes to the stream, sees the goblins and begs them to sell her their fruit. They try to make her eat some but she refuses. They coax, beseech, bully and maul her, but she remains adamant:

> *White and golden Lizzie stood,*
> *Like a lily in a flood, –*
> *Like a rock of blue-veined stone*
> *Lashed by tides obstreperously, –*
> *Like a beacon left lone*
> *In a hoary roaring sea.*

They crush their fruits against her mouth, but she will not open it, glorying in the juices which syrup all her face. Eventually, they leave her and she hurries home, running up the garden to Laura, crying:

> *'Did you miss me?*
> *Come and kiss me.*
> *Never mind my bruises,*
> *Hug me, kiss me, suck my juices*
> *Squeezed from goblin fruits for you,*
> *Goblin pulp and goblin dew.*
> *Eat me, drink me, love me;'*

Whereupon, Laura:

> *. . . clung abour her sister,*
> *Kissed and kissed and kissed her.*

Fire spreads through her veins and knocks at her heart until:

Like a foam-topped waterspout
Cast down headlong in the sea,
She fell at last;
Pleasure past and anguish past,
Is it death or is it life?

She sleeps, and in the morning wakes refreshed, her hair golden again, her eyes dancing and her breath as sweet as May. Years afterwards, Laura would tell her children how Lizzie had stood in deadly peril to *win the fiery antidote* which had saved her life. Moralistically, in the Victorian manner, she would add that there is no friend like a sister.

The poem can be read at several levels: as a fairy story, as a parable extolling self-sacrifice, as a tract praising women – for the men in the story, albeit goblin-men, are cruel, whilst the women are kind and loving. The poem in part reads like a sexual fantasy. The passion with which the sisters embrace and kiss and the fire which surges through Laura's veins as she sucks the juices from her sister's mouth are like a sexual consummation. The 'no friend like a sister' ending brings the reader down to earth. It is as if the poet is saying that she does not mean the poem to be anything more than a moral tale for children. Christina had revealed the sexual passion burning beneath her prim exterior and then was concerned to smother and conceal it.

The other poems in the book were divided into two sections: secular and religious. A sonnet in the secular group that reaches all hearts is *Remember*:

Remember me when I am gone away,
Gone far away into the silent land;
When you can no more hold me by the hand,
Nor I half turn to go yet turning stay.
Remember me when no more day by day
You tell me of our future that you planned:
Only remember me; you understand
It will be late to counsel then or pray.
Yet if you should forget me for a while
And afterwards remember, do not grieve:
For if the darkness and corruption leave

> *A vestige of the thoughts that once I had.*
> *Better by far you should forget and smile*
> *Than that you should remember and be sad.*

Another, called *After Death*, has an even more sombre theme. The dead poet is awaiting burial, and as the man she had loved contemplates her corpse, she muses:

> *He did not touch the shroud, or raise the fold*
> *That hid my face, or take my hand in his,*
> *Or ruffle the smooth pillows for my head:*
> *He did not love me living; but once dead*
> *He pitied me; and very sweet it is*
> *To know he still is warm though I am cold.*

One of the poems, *My Dream*, is particularly bizarre. The poet dreams of standing by the river Euphrates watching young crocodiles swiming. One crocodile grow bigger and stronger than the rest and begins to eat the others:

> *He battened on them, crunched and sucked them in.*
> *He knew no law, he feared no binding law,*
> *But bound them with inexorable jaw:*
> *The luscious fat distilled upon his chin,*
> *Exuded from his nostrils and his eyes,*
> *While still like hungry death he fed his maw;*
> *Till every minor crocodile being dead*
> *And buried too, himself gorged to the full,*
> *He slept with breath oppressed and unstrung claw.*

In sleep he dwindles to normal size. A ship glides towards him like an avenging ghost, and he rises to his feet, cries and wrings his hands. The poet cannot explain her dream; she is as mystified as the reader:

> *What can it mean? you ask, I answer not*
> *For meaning, but myself must echo, what?*

19

If dreams have underlying meanings, then perhaps we must see in this a repressed sexual desire expressed in the more acceptable form of eating, with guilt and repentance following satiation. The suppression of sexual feelings demanded of respectable Victorian womanhood exacted quite terrible tolls, and some modern observers see in Christina's continual, often unexplained ill-health, the price she herself had to pay. She found some emotional ease by sublimating sexual desire into love of God; but this consummation could not be achieved in this world, and here may lie a cause of her persistent preoccupation with death. However, too much weight must not rest on this explanation, since she had been interested in death since her early childhood. Nevertheless, one of the poems in the religious section of the *Goblin Market* volume illustrates starkly and pathetically her linking of death with the final consummation of love. It is called *A Better Resurrection*:

> *I have no wit, no words, no tears;*
> *My heart within me like a stone*
> *Is numbed too much for hopes or fears;*
> *Look right, look left, I dwell alone;*
> *I lift mine eyes, but dimmed with grief*
> *No everlasting hills I see;*
> *My life is in the falling leaf:*
> *O Jesus, quicken me.*
>
> *My life is like a faded leaf,*
> *My harvest dwindled to a husk;*
> *Truly my life is void and brief*
> *And tedious in the barren dusk;*
> *My life is like a frozen thing,*
> *No bud nor greenness can I see:*
> *Yet rise it shall – the sap of Spring;*
> *O Jesus, rise in me.*
>
> *My life is like a broken bowl,*
> *A broken bowl that cannot hold*
> *One drop of water for my soul*

Or cordial in the searching cold;
Cast in the fire the perished thing,
Melt and remould it, till it be
A royal cup for Him, my King:
O Jesus, drink of me.

Gabriel was pleased at the success of his sister's book, and he
wanted her to publish another as soon as possible. But she was in
no hurry. During 1864 she was ill again and went to Hastings to
recover, staying there till the spring of 1865, working at her
brother's suggestion, though rather unwillingly, on another long
poem. This was called *The Prince's Progress*, which became the title
poem of her second collection of verses, published in 1866.
Though he had urged haste, publication was somewhat delayed by
Gabriel's tardiness in producing the illustrative woodcuts.

The poem *The Prince's Progress* did not make the same impact as
Goblin Market. It was a fairy story again, but there was little
variation of metre and less ambiguity of meaning. The prince sets
out on a journey to claim his bride, but is delayed by obstacles and
distractions on his way. When he eventually reaches the princess's
palace, he is too late:

What is this that comes through the door,
The face covered, the feet before?
This that cometh takes his breath
This Bride not seen, to be seen no more
Save of Bridegroom Death?

The dallying of the prince appears to parallel Gabriel's ten-year
courtship of Lizzie Siddal. Of course, he did marry her in the end,
but it could be said to have been too late. The description of the
prince is almost a portrait of Christina's brother, for she gives him a
curly black beard like silk and describes him as *of purpose weak*. It is
unlikely that Gabriel failed to recongnise it, and it must have added
to his feelings of guilt.

With her health improved from her stay in Hastings, Christina
made another trip to the Continent with William and their mother.
They went to Paris first, and then to Switzerland and on to Milan,

Como, Verona and Bergamo. In Italy she blossomed as never before, feeling it to be her true home. She returned to London with a heavy heart, and wrote:

To come back from the sweet South to the North
Where I was born, bred and look to die;
Come back to my day's work in its day,
Play out my play –
Amen, amen, say I.

To see no more the country half my own,
Nor hear the half-familiar speech,
Amen, I say: I turn to the bleak North
Whence I came forth –
The South lies out of reach.

It might have been thought that she would have been happy to return to England, because her love affair with Charles Cayley was beginning to bloom again. In August 1864 she had written a poem calling him a mole and implying that he was dilatory in love because he was blind to the obvious – that she loved him. In fact she was uncertain and dilatory too. Eventually, he brought himself to propose to her, probably in the early summer of 1866, and at last she was at the point of decision.

In June 1866 she went to stay with William Bell Scott at his country home, Penkill Castle in Ayrshire. She was not unchaperoned, since he was as usual spending the summer there with his mistress, Alice Boyd. His wife, who preferred London, accepted the situation and visited him in Scotland for short spells. If Christina was aware that the relationship between Scott and Alice Boyd was a sexual one, she turned a blind eye to it, her affectionate feelings for him apparently unaffected. The castle was an old converted Peel Tower and Christina had a room in the turret, where she spent much time gazing out to sea towards the isle of Ailsa Crag and composing poetry. She was also presumably thinking about Charles Cayley and his proposal of marriage.

She was thirty-five years of age by now and this would probably be her last chance of marriage. She loved Cayley, but there were drawbacks: he had little money of his own; but much more important than this, he had no religious belief, and belief in God was of the utmost importance to her. Moreover, though she had a great need to give and receive love, there may have been deep down an aversion to sexual contact. Whatever her reasons and whatever her feelings, we know the outcome: she refused him, and by mid-September the decision was irrevocably made. William, knowing that Cayley had little money, generously offered to have the couple living with him, but this did not sway Christina. She was fond of Charles, she hoped they would remain friends and still see each other, but, as for marriage, that was out of the question. She let it be known that only in God could she find truly satisfying love and that the ephemeral relationships of this world were no substitute. In an earlier poem, *The Heart Knoweth its Own Bitterness*, she had stated this powerfully:

> Not in this world of hope deferred,
> This world of perishable stuff –
> Eye hath not seen nor ear hath heard
> Not heart conceived that full enough:
> Here moans the separating sea,
> Here harvests fail, here breaks the heart:
> There God shall join and no man part,
> I full of Christ and Christ of me.

During the 1860s, Christina produced a cycle of fourteen sonnets with the title of *Monna Innominata* which were not published until 1881. They were written as if by a medieval lady to a troubadour whom she admirees, and the unnamed subject was certainly Charles Cayley. One of the sonnets indicates the strength of her feelings for him:

> Come back to me who wait and watch for you:
> Or come not yet, for it is over then,
> And long it is before you come again.
> So far between my pleasures are and few.
> While when you come not, what I do I do
> Thinking 'Now when he comes', my sweetest 'when':

For one man is my world of all the men
This wide world holds: O love my world is you.
Howbeit, to meet you grows almost a pang
Because the pang of parting comes so soon;
My hope hangs waning, waxing, like a moon
Between the heavenly days on which we meet:
Ah me, but where are now the songs I sang
When life was sweet because you called them sweet?

Gradually Christina drifted into the life of a spinster, focussing on her family, particularly her mother. She could have had a wider field of social contacts. She occasionally accompanied Gabriel to parties given by Ford Madox Brown and there met such luminaries as James Whistler, the artist, Charles Dodgson, who, as Lewis Carroll, wrote *Alice in Wonderland*, and Algernon Swinburne, who had a great admiration for her poetry. When she could overcome her shyness, she was an amusing conversationalist, but she never went out of her way to develop her friendships – even with female poets like Jean Ingelow and Dora Greenwell whom she met and whose work she liked.

Christina met Gerard Manley Hopkins on one occasion in 1864. He enjoyed her writing, one of her poems making a particularly deep impression on him. This was *The Convent Threshold*, written towards the end of 1859. It is about a young woman who has taken the veil to escape from a love affair with a man who, for some unspecified family reason, she is forbidden to love. Racked by guilt, she wrestles in an agony of unfulfilled desire. She suffers terrible nightmares, and one night dreams that her lover visits her in her grave:

I tell you what I dreamed last night:
It was not dark, it was not light,
Cold dews had drenched my plenteous hair;
Through clay; you came to seek me there.
And 'Do you dream of me?' you said.
My heart was dust that used to leap
To you; I answered half asleep:
'My pillow is damp, my sheets are red,
There's a leaden tester to my bed:

24

Find you a warmer playfellow,
A warmer pillow for your head,
A kinder love to love than mine.'
You wrung your hands, while I like lead
Crushed downwards through the sodden earth:
You smote your hands but not in mirth
And reeled but were not drunk with wine.

The 'tester' in line nine is the canopy of a four-poster bed, and it is 'leaden' because the coffin is lined with lead. The poem is suffused with a sexual passion and an erotic energy which Christina normally had under firm control. Hopkins responded to it with a poem from the lover's viewpoint and has him crying out for *wounded love*. In life neither poet was ever to enjoy a sexual relationship.

Another literary contact of Christina's which budded but never blossomed was with Anne Gilchrist, a poet and biographer whose husband was a friend of Gabriel's. She invited Christina and brother William to stay with her at her home near Haslemere in Surrey in the summer of 1863. While she was there, Christina wrote her popular poem *Maiden Song*, of which it is said the Prime Minister, William Gladstone, was particularly fond. It is written in ballad form and concerns three sisters who attract three lovers by their lovely singing. Margaret, the one with the finest voice, wins herself a *golden-bearded King* who kneels at her feet in *eager anguish sweet*. It is a happy fairy tale in complete contrast to the frenzied yearnings of *The Convent Threshold*.

Following the death of her aunt, Margaret Polidori, who had lived with them for some time, Christina moved in June 1867 with her mother and her sister Maria to a rented house in Euston Square, not far from William in Camden Town. For a long period she suffered an unexplained malaise, involving as she put it, 'persistent weariness without exertion'. She maintained her relationship with Charles Cayley, corresponding with him and occasionally inviting him for a game of whist – with her mother in attendance. He seems to have accepted this distant friendship without rancour, writing to her and making her small gifts. We do not know what he said to her in his letters since, as she neared death, she had them destroyed. He sometimes sent her one of his poems, and once gave her a sea mouse preserved in a bottle. In thanking him, she asserted that the creature kept house not in a bottle but in her heart. It was all rather quaint and sad.

Her feelings of weakness persisted. The doctors tried rests in bed and visits to the seaside but to no avail. Eventually, in November 1871, she developed a throat swelling, and Grave's Disease, a form of goitre, was diagnosed. She, who had once been a dainty, active young woman, was now stout and lethargic. Anne Gilchrist's daughter had described her some eight years before as a *dark-eyed slender lady . . . with olive complexion and deep hazel eyes*; but now her skin was discoloured, her eyes protruding and her fine black hair greying and thinning. From time to time she suffered choking and vomiting spasms and fainting fits.

One bright spot in her melancholy invalid's world was the publication early in 1872 of her book of children's poems, *Sing Song*, which was beautifully illustrated by Arthur Hughes, one of the members of the long-dead Pre-Raphaelite Brotherhood. Even in verses for children, Christina did not desert the central themes of her poetry: death and parting and blighted love. For example:

> Good-bye in fear, good-bye in sorrow,
> Good-bye and all in vain,
> Never to meet again my dear –
> Never to part again.
> Good-bye today, good-bye tomorrow,
> Good-bye till earth shall wane,
> Never to meet again, my dear –
> Never to part again.

She gave rein to her quirky sense of humour in poems like *The Ferryman*:

> 'Ferry me across the water,
> Do, boatman, do!'
> 'If you've a penny in your purse
> I'll ferry you'.

'I have a penny in my purse
And my eyes are blue,
So ferry me across the water,
Do, boatman, do'.

'Step into my ferry-boat,
Be they black or blue,
And for the penny in your purse
I'll ferry you'.

One may detect the pathos of spinsterhood and childlessness in such lines as:

I'll nurse you on my knee, my knee
My own little son;
I'll rock you, rock you in my arms,
My least little one.

Commendably, the poems held no moral lessons, the bane of books for Victorian children. Angels are referred to, but no effort is made to force religion on young readers. The critics liked the poems, sales recovered from a slow start, and Christina had something to be happy about.

But her pleasure was marred by increasing anxiety over her brother. Over the years, Gabriel's interest in poetry grew at the expense of his painting. He wrote many sonnets, completing eventually a cycle of more than a hundred. In April 1870 a collection of his poetry was published under the title of *Poems*, and initially it was favourably reviewed. But later in the year a fierce attack on his work appeared in a literary journal, accusing him of being of the 'fleshly' school of poetry, full of sensuality and 'sickly animalism'. The theme of his sonnet-cycle was love between men and women; not just physical passion but love in all its forms, and the criticism was disproportionate and unfair. But, normally cheerful and impervious to critical spleen, he was unable on this occasion to cope with the attack.

On Lizzie's death some eight years previously, he had, as a gesture of contrition, had his poems buried with her, swearing that they would never be printed. As the years pased, he became obsessed with these, and in 1869, he had Lizzie's body exhumed and the manuscript removed. Already remorseful over her suicide, he felt additionally guilty at publishing the poems he had buried with her, and the critical attack upon him was sufficient to push him into depression and paranoia. He fell prey to paranoid delusions, believing that everyone was against him, and that he deserved their contempt.

The insomnia which plagued him, for which he took increasing doses of chloral, an addictive pain-killer, added to his emotional turmoil. Eventually, he overdosed on laudanum in what appears to have been a genuine suicide attempt. Christina was never told of this occurrence, but she worried deeply about him, fearing for his sanity. In due course his mental health improved, but he was never again the same cheerful, sanguine man. Since Lizzie's death, he had been renting a large old house in Cheyne Walk, Chelsea, called Tudor House, sharing it with friends who included Algernon Swinburne and the poet and novelist George Meredith. In those days, life had been relatively happy, with occasional jolly parties, for which his mistress Fanny Cornforth, whom he jokingly called 'Dear Elephant', acted as hostess. Christina, in later life, wrote nostalgically of friendly family parties at Tudor House with Gabriel playing the genial host. No doubt she did not hear of the wild behaviour at the bachelor gatherings, with Swinburne leaping on the furniture and sliding naked down the bannisters. She was well aware, however, of the menagerie of animals that Gabriel kept in the garden, which included a rabbit, wombats, a wallaby, deer and chameleons and armadillos. She, too, was very fond of animals, and was a frequent visitor to Regent's Park Zoo.

Christina's own health improved slowly. She was profoundly grateful to her faithful brother William, who stood by her during her long illness. William felt responsible for his mother and his sister Maria too, and also for Gabriel, who was always in financial difficulties. At long last, he too fell victim to depression, but, thanks to his equable temperament, not for long. Christina drew strength from her Christian faith, though her hope lay not in this world but the next. In one of her poems of this period, Christ is speaking:

> *'Yes, I have sought thee, yea, I have found thee,*
> *Yea, I have thirsted for thee,*

Yea, long ago with love's hands I have found thee:
Now the Everlasting Arms surround thee –
Through death's darkness I look and see
And clasp thee to Me.'

As Gabriel's health improved, he began painting again. As well as supporting a mistress he was deeply in love with Janey Morris, the wife of one of his Pre-Raphaelite friends, William Morris. Christina used to stay at their house, Kelmscott Manor, and came to know Janey very well. William Morris was abroad for long periods, and Christina must have known of or least suspected her brother's adultery, though she never seems to have mentioned it. In any case, she would probably have thought that lack of religious faith was a far greater sin than sexual irregularities. Certainly she was able to sustain a friendship with Janey with no hint of criticism or rebuke.

It was in the summer of 1873 that William became engaged again. His fiancée was Lucy Madox Brown, the daughter of Ford Madox Brown, Gabriel's early teacher and great friend. Maria responded by announcing that she was joining an Anglican sister-hood, taking the veil in the autumn of 1873. Christina approved of William's engagement, and she wrote a letter welcoming Lucy into the family as a dear sister and friend. William brought his young bride to live in the Rossetti home in Euston Square. This proved a mistake, as Christina said it would be. She knew her persistent cough would irritate Lucy, who was twenty years her junior; and she no doubt realised that her pernickety religious observances would eventually prove too much for her free-thinking sister-in-law. In 1876 Christina and her mother moved to another house not far away, in Torrington Square, and were joined by her mother's sisters, Charlotte and Eliza.

Within three years, Maria had died of cancer. Christina mourned her death but was not unduly upset, envying the certainty of her sister's Christian faith. She wrote a commemorative poem of which the last verse reads:

Now keeps she tryst beyond earth's utmost sea,
Wholly at rest, tho' storms should toss and rend her;
And still she keeps my heart and keeps its key,
My love whose heart is tender.

29

Christina continued her circumscribed existence, broken by occasional visits to the seaside or country, but always in the company of her aged mother and her two elderly aunts. She published three books in prose concerned with Christianity and its festivals and prayers. In 1881, she published a volume of poetry called *A Pageant and Other Poems*. This included the *Monna Innominata* sonnets and another sonnet sequence, together with the *Pageant* of the book's title, which was concerned with the months of the year and was intended to be performed by children. The critics commended the work and it enjoyed good sales. She was by now an established poet. She had not discussed the book with Gabriel, feeling he was not well enough to concentrate on it. However, she did send him a copy, telling him in the accompanying letter that she was staying at Sevenoaks with her mother, and was glad to be out of London because she had put on weight and 'a fat poetess' looked incongruous.

After a minor operation, Gabriel fell into deep depression again. He had fallen out with most of his old friends, even banning Fanny Cornforth from the house. He was living alone with a young writer, Thomas Hall Caine, who nobly volunteered to act as his companion and stayed with him for the rest of his life. They lived in the Cheyne Walk house in an atmosphere of gloom and squalor. A short break in the Lake District did Gabriel no good, and after a paralytic seizure in December, he moved with Hall Caine to a house in the village of Birchington on the Kentish coast. William urged him to use his will to cure himself, which of course he could not do. Christina advised penitence, confession and absolution, which she said had helped her during a period of spiritual desolation. The doctors seemed helpless apart from advising him to reduce his intake of chloral and whisky and to take up some occupation. He had his painting equipment with him but the motivation had gone. Christina and her mother visited him in March 1882. Kidney failure was diagnosed. Christina sat up with him through the night, but he was past help and on 9 April he died. He was buried in the churchyard at Birchington, and Christina decorated his grave with a bunch of woodspurge and forget-me-nots. Gabriel had once written a sonnet about gazing down on a woodspurge plant during a period of depression, of which the last lines ran:

> From perfect grief there need not be
> Wisdom or even memory:
> One thing then learnt remains to me –
> The woodspurge has a cup of three.

Another grievous loss came the following year when Charles Cayley was found dead in his bed one morning in December 1883. He left Christina his writing desk. In it were the letters she had written to him, which she destroyed at once. He was buried at Hastings and, the following January, she made a special visit to his grave. In April she composed a poem, *One Sea-Side Grave*, which was surely intended for him, though she never actually said so:

> Unmindful of the roses,
> Unmindful of the thorn,
> A reaper tired reposes
> Among his gathered corn;
> So might I till the morn!
>
> Cold as the cold Decembers.
> Past as the days that set,
> While only one remembers
> And all the rest forget –
> But one remembers yet.

By now Christina's poetic muse had all but deserted her. She lived another twelve years, but wrote little poetry. She produced more religious prose, which she seemed to regard as a duty, but the only poetry she published was a collection of her poems in some of which she addresses God. For example, in *The Lowest Place*, she entreats Him:

> Give me the lowest place: not that I dare
> Ask for that lowest place, but Thou has died
> That I may live and share
> Thy glory by Thy side.

31

> *Give the lowest place: or if for me*
> *That lowest place too high, make one more low*
> *Where I may sit and see*
> *My God and love Thee so.*

She frequently laments that her life is sad and dreary and she looks for happiness after death; and if not happiness, at least rest and peace. In *Life and Death*, she says:

> *Life is not good. One day it will be good*
> *To die, then live again;*
> *To sleep meanwhile; so not to feel the wane*
> *Of shrunk leaves dropping in the wood,*
> *Nor hear the foamy lashing of the main,*
> *Nor mark the blackened bean-fields, nor where stood*
> *Rich ranks of golden grain*
> *Only dead refuse stubble clothe the plain:*
> *Asleep from risk, asleep from pain.*

Sometimes she engages in dialogue with God, as in *Despised and Rejected*:

> *My sun has set, I dwell*
> *In darkness as a dead man out of sight;*
> *And none remains, not one, that I should tell*
> *To him mine evil plight*
> *This bitter night.*
> *I will make fast my door*
> *That hollow friends may trouble me no more.*

But God responds: *Friend open to Me,* and He pleads with her all night: '*Open to Me that I may come to thee*'. In another poem called *Dost Thou Not Care?* she challenges Jesus to show His love for her:

> *I love and love not: Lord it breaks my heart*
> *To love and not love.*
> *Thou veiled within Thy glory, gone apart*
> *Into Thy shrine, which is above,*
> *Dost Thou not love me, Lord, or care*
> *For this mine ill?*

And He answers her:

> *I love thee here or there*
> *I will accept thy broken heart, lie still.*

Amongst the few friends who kept in touch with her was Algernon
Swinburne. He had been dismayed when her brother broke off their
friendship during his period of depression in which he had thought
that everyone was against him. Despite this breach, Swinburne kept
up a correspondence with Christina. It was an odd relationship
between the high-minded, obsessively religious woman and the
heavy-drinking atheist, but they had a great admiration for each
other's poetry and this was their bond. In 1883, Swinburne sent her
and her mother copies of his book, *A Century of Roundels*, which he
dedicated to Christina. She did not object to this although she was
aware of his reputation as a libertine and militant atheist. He mocked
the Christian religion, but he never mocked her poetry. He said of
her poem, *Passing Away*, that he placed it at the head of all the
religious poetry in any language. On her death, her posthumous
book, *New Poems*, was dedicated to him.

On 8 April 1886, Christina's mother died peacefully in her bed.
For Christina the central focus of her life had gone. She was left in a
large, dark house with two elderly invalid aunts to look after. Of
course there were servants to do the work, but the responsibility
was hers. William was now the one member of the family she really
cared about, and her mind was centred strongly on him. In a letter
to his wife Lucy, she called him 'My dear, delightful William'. She
had been working for several years on a meditation on the Book of
Revelation. Its subject, the Day of Judgment, was one of absorbing
interest to her. She was tortured by fear that for past misdemeanours
she would be denied an entry into heaven, and she constantly
searched her mind for sins she might have committed.

In 1890, Aunt Charlotte died and two years later, Aunt Eliza
followed her. Both of them left Christina money, and for the short
time remaining, she was quite a wealthy woman. One of her first
acts was to increase her bequest to William, who had done so much
for her.

The last of her books appeared in 1893. It was a collection of religious verses that had previously been included in her works of prose. It was called *Verses* and included the well-known carol *In the Bleak Midwinter*. She wanted to dedicate the book to William, but, because of his agnosticism, he would not agree to it.

Her health had been steadily deteriorating, and in the spring of 1892, it became clear that an operation for cancer of the breast was necessary. The operation at the end of May appeared successful but in fact did little to check the disease, and in the summer of the following year she took permanently to a bed in her drawing-room. Towards the end, she became very depressed, her mind haunted by religious doubts and her expectation of salvation almost non-existent. During her life, she had written much about heaven, her imagination filling it with flowers and gaily coloured birds. In her poem, *Paradise: In a Dream*, she says:

> *Once in a dream I saw the flowers*
> *That bud and bloom in Paradise;*
> *More fair they are than waking eyes*
> *Have seen in all this world of ours.*
> *And faint the perfume-bearing rose,*
> *And faint the lily on its stem,*
> *And faint the perfect violet*
> *Compared with them.*

In her *Birds of Paradise*, she gives us another vision of heaven:

> *Golden-winged, silver-winged,*
> *Winged with flashing flame,*
> *Such a flight of birds I saw,*
> *Birds without a name:*
> *Singing songs in their own tongue –*
> *Song of songs – they came . . .*

Christina Rossetti died on 29 December 1894 at the age of sixty-four. Amongst the manuscripts she left was a poem – perhaps the last she wrote – which spoke of death as *sleeping at last in a dreamless sleep locked fast*. But it is to be hoped that her mind was filled with visions of lovely flowers and flame-flashed birds when death came to her that cold winter's morning before the sun had risen.

She was buried at Highgate Cemetery with her parents, and later a memorial service was held at Christ Church, Woburn Square. Her brother William published, some two years after her death, a collection of more than 230 of the poems – of varying quality – found amongst her papers, under the title of *New Poems*. In 1906 he produced two volumes of reminiscences of his sister, which empahsised her goodness and kindness and religious faith, and confirmed the image created by other writers of the perfect daughter and sister. It fitted the role assigned to middle-class women of the time: one of modesty, self-sacrifice and concern for others. Christina cared about the poor, about fatherless children and deserted mothers and the evils of vivisection; but strong political views were not encouraged in women of her station. However talented they were, they were expected to be decorative and subservient, and Christina endeavoured all her life to curb her personal ambition, as her Church required her to.

William wrote in his reminiscences that *she had been personally known to few, understood by still fewer and silent to almost all*. Perhaps this is how Victorian society wished its women of genius to be remembered; but modern literary critics think otherwise. In heaven, she sought *the lowest place*; but in this world she ranks among the greatest of Victorian poets.

ALGERNON SWINBURNE

I will go back to the great sweet mother,
Mother and lover of men, the sea.
I will go down to her, I and none other,
Close with her, kiss her and mix her with me.

ALGERNON SWINBURNE

Algernon Charles Swinburne was born in the same year that Queen Victoria came to the throne. He lived for seventy-two years and wrote copiously for most of his life. A classical scholar, he was a novelist and critic as well as a prolific poet. Despite an aristocratic background, he was a republican and an atheist. He rebelled fiercely against Victorian sexual morality and hypocrisy, and for many years he lived a life involving alcoholic excess and perverted sex.

His facility in rhyme and rhythm was in the Tennyson tradition. Tennyson said of him that he was a *reed through which all things blow into music*, and there was no doubt that he carried melodious verse to its ultimate conclusion. His early poetry, which evoked the sexual vices of classical Greece and Rome, took the educated youth of his time by storm. What was lascivious obscenity to the older generation was a marvellous, miraculous release to their children. He gloried in rejecting the religious and moral inhibitions of his fellow Victorians, and for a time he enjoyed an enormous fashionable success. He was a forerunner of end-of-the-century decadence.

But his popularity did not last. His poems were over-long, it was said; his rhythms were monotonous; his verse was beautiful but lacking in content. Today, however, after decades of blank verse, we value again his flights of musical harmony, verbal exuberance and splendid rhyming and are immensely grateful for his major contribution to English poetry.

He was born in London on 5 April 1837 at 7 Chester Street, Grosvenor Square, while his parents were on a visit to the capital. His father, who was eventually to become an admiral, was at that time a captain in the Royal Navy. He came from a wealthy family of landowners who had a large estate in the valley of the North Tyne in Northumberland with a magnificent house called Capheaton

Hall. Coal had been found on the land at the end of the eighteenth century, so the family had become very prosperous. Algernon's mother, Lady Jane Henrietta, was even better connected, being the daughter of the Earl of Ashburnham with a country seat in Sussex.

On their marriage they acquired a fine house at East Dene on the south-east coast of the Isle of Wight, which had become a fashionable place for the wealthy to live and visit. His grandfather, Sir John Swinburne, lived at Capheaton Hall, and until Algernon went to Eton at the age of twelve, his time was divided equally between his parents and his grandparents.

In view of his aristocratic lineage, it may seem strange that Algernon grew up to become not only a dedicated poet, but a drunkard, libertine and militant atheist. He could point out, however, that his grandfather had been a radical MP who had made fierce attacks on the Prince Regent, and that both sides of his family had a history of military prowess: on his mother's side against the Normans and on his father's against the marauding Scots. In later years he said with pride that when at last the family produced a poet, it was unlikely that he would write nothing but hymns for clergymen and idylls for young ladies.

The birth of Algernon was followed in time by that of four sisters, Alice, Edith, Charlotte and Isabel, and a brother, Edward, who was the youngest. Algernon grew up in an extended family group of uncles, aunts and cousins, and his early life was very happy. On holiday with his grandparents at Capheaton, he had access to a magnificent library and the opportunity to ride horses whenever he wished. At both Capheaton and East Dene he had sea bathing on his doorstep, and this was his greatest love. One of his earliest memories was of being held naked by his father and thrown shouting and laughing into the waves.

His parents were caring and indulgent. They encouraged his reading and sent him regularly to church. They were Anglo-Catholics by persuasion and he was given a thorough grounding in biblical studies. His mother introduced him to French and Italian and this later stimulated his interest in European literature. He and his parents had nicknames for each other. Algernon was Hadji, his father Pino and his mother Mimmie, and they used these in their letters to each other throughout their lives. In adulthood,

Algernon wrote two novels, *Love's Cross-Currents* and *Lesbia Brandon* in which he portrayed cruel and sadistic parents, but they cannot be related in any way to his own.

Nevertheless, the beating of children was common enough in those days, and Algernon's highly imaginative young mind was undoubtedly excited by thoughts of corporal punishment. In this he had a fellow enthusiast in his cousin, Mary Gordon, who was three years younger and lived in a village near East Dene. In childhood and in adulthood too, he and Mary shared their fantasies, the central one of which was of a school where the boys were birched. Incestuous love between brother and sister also formed part of their day-dreams, as did love between two girls. At eleven, Algernon was sent to a small private school close to the Gordons' house and there he met Mary frequently. He learnt the rudiments of Latin and Greek in preparation for his forthcoming education at a public school.

At the age of twelve he was sent away to Eton. In such schools at that time a small group of masters taught a large number of boys. Control was maintained by the older boys acting as prefects and by a severe regime of corporal punishment. Flogging was considered normal in the army and navy and it had a regular place in boarding school life. So too did bullying, which the fagging system by which young boys had to perform menial tasks for the older ones, did little to allay. In such a society homosexuality was rife, the staff doing little to monitor or prevent it. Living conditions were relatively grim. The boys were no strangers to cold and dirt and their diet left much to be desired. Nevertheless the masters were scholars and there were genuine opportunities for study.

Algernon was small and delicately built and had a large head with unruly red hair standing up almost vertically. Inevitably he was a target for bullying and for sexual play. He was afforded some protection from an older cousin at the school, and was fortunate also in his housemaster who encouraged his reading which was his greatest consolation. As he grew older he read widely in French and Italian literature as well as in the English classics. According to Swinburne, his housemaster enjoyed caning him as well as educating him, but he was much given to fantasy so it is hard to know what genuinely to believe. There is no doubt that, good scholar as he was, he did not escape the birch and that quite often he saw other boys birched. It can be understood that this experience fed his fascination with corporal punishment and may have contributed to the flagellation perversions of his adulthood.

He soon became recognised as an oddity and a swot. He had a prodigious memory and was much given to reciting poetry. He excelled in Latin and Greek and won a school prize in modern languages. Early in his school career he wrote a play which was full of murders and rapes. He was a solitary lad, living for much of his time in a literary dream world, and as he developed he increasingly resented the discipline imposed upon him. He was very excitable and gradually developed nervous mannerisms, which involved rapid shaking of his hands and an involuntary kicking and twisting of his feet. His contemporaries pronounced him mad, and at the age of seventeen his parents were persuaded by the headmaster to withdraw him from the school. Whatever Captain and Lady Swinburne felt, Algernon bore no animosity towards Eton and always maintained a dreamy affection for it.

The Crimean War broke out in 1854, ranging Britain and France against Russia in defence of the Turks. The country was consumed by war fever and this fuelled Swinburne's desire to become a cavalry officer. Small and slight as he was, he was an intrepid if unorthodox horseman, so that his ambition was not wholly unreasonable. He dreamed of taking part in a military folly like the Charge of the Light Brigade – immortalised by Tennyson – when the cavalry rode straight towards the barrels of the Russian guns. His parents, however, would not hear of a military career, so he had to find some other way of proving his courage. This he did in an extraordinary escapade on the eastern headland of the Isle of Wight. After a swim, he set himself the challenge of scaling the overhanging face of Culver Cliff. He achieved it, even after losing his footing, hanging by his hands and swinging his feet to an adjoining ledge. His manhood vindicated, he felt himself fit to go up to Oxford University, and he entered Balliol College in January 1856.

Very soon he came under the influence of a remarkable man, Benjamin Jowett, who was appointed his tutor. At that time Jowett was Professor of Greek, but later he was to become Master of the College. He exercised a major influence over Swinburne for many years. At first he thought little of his slightly-built, effeminate-looking, squeaky-voiced student, observing that his essays were all language and no thought. But relationships between them slowly improved as Swinburne's academic ability became apparent. One of the most important things that Jowett taught Swinburne was the value and habit of hard work. Swinburne became a poet by his own genius, but that he also became a learned and industrious one was due to Jowett.

In the autumn of 1856, Swinburne became a founder member of a literary society of undergraduates called Old Mortality, so called, its members said, in recognition of the brevity of life and their own poor health. In this company he developed his love of both literature and brandy. He also learnt to abominate autocrats and tyrants, particularly advocating revolutionary violence against Napoleon III, who had just made himself Emperor of France. He expressed his feelings vehemently in verse:

When the devil's riddle is mastered
And the galley-bench creaks with a Pope,
We shall see Bonaparte the bastard
Click heels with his throat in a rope.

It was in the autumn of 1857 that Swinburne first met members of the Pre-Raphaelite Brotherhood in the persons of the young artists William Morris, Edward Burne-Jones and the moving spirit of the movement, Dante Gabriel Rossetti. Rossetti had arranged to decorate the walls of the newly-completed debating chamber of the Oxford Union with the help of his fellow artists, in return for their artistic materials and their keep. It was whilst they were engaged on this task that Swinburne was introduced to them, and he took to them at once and they to him. They were full of song, laughter and enthusiasm and Swinburne's excitable vivacity joined easily with theirs. Burne-Jones particularly became a firm friend at once, nicknaming him 'Little Carrots'. Swinburne admired the poetry of Rossetti and Morris as well as their painting, and in due course lasting friendship grew up with all three. 'We were three,' said Burne-Jones, 'and now we are four.'

While he was at Oxford, Swinburne continued to read widely. He developed a deep love for the literature of ancient Greece and Rome. The work of the Greek dramatist Aeschylus and the female poet Sappho particularly delighted him. Of the Romans he had a special regard for the love poetry of Catullus. He read widely in English sixteenth- and seventeenth-century drama, and modern French literature also held a continual fascination. The dominant literary cults of the French intelligentsia of the time were lesbianism and bisexualism and these fed Swinburne's sexual fantasies. He was strongly attracted to a novel by Théophile Gautier called *Mademoiselle de Maupin*, which developed both themes in a polished erotic manner. The pageboy of the hero, Theodore, turns out to be a girl in disguise; but Theodore is revealed to be none other than Mademoiselle de Maupin, and they are in love with each other. Later in life, Swinburne was to become drawn to the work of the French poet Charles Baudelaire, in whose collection, *Les Fleurs du Mal* such themes are expounded.

Swinburne entered a university poetry competition on the subject of the search for a north-west passage to the far east. His poem was called *The Death of Sir John Franklin* and was concerned with Franklin's unsuccessful expedition which led to his death and the loss of all his crew. He only gained second prize, but he showed an impressive skill in evoking the Arctic scene:

> *And a sad touch of sun scores the sea-line*
> *Right at the middle motion of the noon,*
> *And then fades sharply back, and the cliffs shine*
> *Fierce with keen snows against the kindled moon,*
> *In the hard purple of the bitter sky.*

Whilst enjoying the drinking and companionship at Balliol, he became increasingly disenchanted with the rules with which he was required to conform. He refused to attend chapel regularly and was punished by being confined to the College grounds. He ranted and raved at this, and Jowett kindly suggested that he leave Balliol for a time. When he returned, he went into lodgings where there were fewer restrictions. But he could not accept even these and, eventually, rather than be expelled from the University, he left of his own accord, returning to his parents at East Dene without a degree and with no means of earning a living.

His parents, of course, could not see him without an income, so they made him an allowance of £400 a year, which was four times the current wage of a working man. They were proud of his literary endeavours and his father was prepared to pay for the publication of his poetry and his verse dramas. Whilst he was at Oxford there had been an expectation that he might make a career as a barrister, but the drudgery of poring over legal tomes was too much for him. Once away from the University he was content to extend his already wide reading and to write. He wanted to be a poet and thought that this was a noble enough ambition.

He stayed from time to time with his grandfather at Capheaton Hall. Whilst there, he was a frequent visitor at nearby Wallington Hall, a handsome country house owned by Sir Walter Trevelyan, a wealthy amateur scientist. It was not Sir Walter that he wished to see but his wife, Lady Pauline, a cultured woman who enjoyed playing hostess to artists and literary men. She was in her early forties and she and Swinburne became very fond of each other. She painted portraits of him and listened to him reading his poems, and smiled indulgently at his radical political views. He wrote with great affection of her after her death, extolling her 'grave-eyed mirth on wings'.

His parents took him on holiday with them to Mentone in the south of France. He hated the dried-up treeless scenery there and spent his time writing a verse drama called *Chastelard*, which was the first of three plays about Mary Queen of Scots. For his own amusement he also wrote a farcical novel in French about a revolt of Prince Albert against his wife, Queen Victoria. In February 1861 he visited Italy, a country much more to his taste. Italy was on the point of gaining its independence and a national identity, and Swinburne strongly supported this. Furthermore French women had disgusted him, with, as he saw it, their 'hunched bodies and crooked necks, carrying tons on their heads and looking like death taken sick'; but Italian women were far different. In Venice, he saw a girl like a goddess, and in Genoa and Ventimiglia too he saw similar girls. He did not speak to any of them but he remembered them all his life as exemplars of female beauty.

Towards the end of 1860, subsidised by his father, he published two of his verse dramas, *Rosamund* and *The Queen Mother*, in a single volume. *Rosamund* is about the mistress of Henry II and the revenge wreaked on her by his jealous queen, Eleanor. The Queen Mother of the second drama is Catherine de' Medici, the mother of Charles IX of France who encouraged him to massacre the French Protestants on St Bartholomew's Day in 1572. If either drama had any literary merit it was not observed by the critics who largely ignored them.

In May 1861, Swinburne took lodgings in London and mixed with his artist friends. He also made a new and significant friend in Richard Monckton Milnes, who later became Lord Houghton. He was a wealthy, well-connected, sophisticated man who dabbled both in politics and literature. He also dabbled in pornography. It was Monckton Milnes who arranged the first commercial publication of poems by Swinburne. Seven of them appeared in *The Spectator* in 1862, together with several essays, one of them on Baudelaire, whose collection of poems he so much admired.

Richard Burton, the Arabic scholar and African explorer, was a friend of Milnes and he too became a close companion of Swinburne, and it was to him that Algernon dedicated his second collection of poems. As well as translating into English the celebrated *Arabian Nights*, Burton was the author of *The Perfumed Garden*, which revealed to Victorian England the sexual delights of the Arabian world.

In such company, the sexual fantasies of the young Swinburne had full rein, as he gloried in offending the religious and moral susceptibilities of the middle classes. Some of his poems of this time even shocked his friends. Dante Gabriel Rossetti, for example, urged him to temper his work to the tastes of his readers and critics. Rossetti had married his model Lizzie Siddal and she fascinated Swinburne. They looked alike, both of them having crops of red hair, and they also shared the same nervous energy and zany humour. He used to read Dickens to her and they had many noisy romps together. Rossetti, by now plump and bearded and sober in manner, did not disapprove of this. He was well aware of his wife's depressive phases and was glad to see her taken out of herself. He knew also that Algernon had no real sexual intentions. Michael and Christina Rossetti, Gabriel's brother and sister, were also close friends of

Swinburne, as was William Morris. After Morris's marriage to Jane Burden, Swinburne was a frequent visitor to their home and came to love Janey as much as he did Lizzie. He could always love women who were safely out of his reach. He had a similar relationship with Burne-Jones's young wife, Georgina. (In later life Georgie would write a marvellous description of him, depicting his red hair, green eyes, restless manner, dancing walk, courtesy and innocent affection and kindness to friends.) Swinburne was a great support to the distraught Gabriel after the death of the latter's wife, and in the autumn of 1862 he moved in with him along with other friends when he occupied a house in Cheyne Walk, Chelsea.

However, he did not stay at Cheyne Walk very long and he was often away visiting friends and travelling on the Continent. Some time in 1862 he became friendly with a young girl called Boo, who was not yet in her teens. She was an adopted daughter of a friend of Burne-Jones's and Swinburne is said to have made some advance to her, possibly even proposing marriage. How serious this was is not known, but the inevitable rejection sent him away to his grand-father's house in Northumberland. There, in between swimming in rough seas, he poured out his heart in a poem called *The Triumph of Time*, in which he played the rejected lover to the hilt:

> O all fair lovers about the world,
> There is none of you, none, that shall comfort me.
> My thoughts are as dead things, wrecked and whirled
> Round and round in a gulf of the sea;
> And still through the sound and the straining stream,
> Through the coil and chafe they gleam in a dream,
> The bright fine lips so cruelly curled,
> And strange swift eyes where the soul sits free.
>
> Free, without pity, withheld from woe,
> Ignorant; fair as the eyes are fair.
> Would I have you change now, change at a blow,
> Startled and stricken, awake and aware?
> Yea, if I could, would I have you see
> My very love of you filling me,
> And know my soul to the quick, as I know
> The likeness and look of your throat and hair?

He will, he says, keep his soul out of sight:

> Far off it walks in a bleak, blown space,
> Full of the sound of the sorrow of years.
> I have woven a veil for the weeping face,
> Whose lips have drunken the wine of tears;
> I have found a way for the failing feet,
> A place for slumber and sorrow to meet;
> There is no rumour about the place,
> Nor light, nor any that sees or hears.
>
> I will go back to the great sweet mother,
> Mother and lover of men, the sea.
> I will go down to her, I and none other,
>
> Close with her, kiss her and mix her with me;
> Cling to her, strive with her, hold her fast;
> O fair white mother, in days long past
> Born without sister, born without brother,
> Set my soul free as thy soul is free.

Friends, and enemies too, joked that Algernon, having been rejected, had run back to his mother; but the consolation of the sea was real, for he loved the rough water, swimming without fear and revelling in its cold embrace. He could say with hyperbole but without irony:

> O fair green-girdled mother of mine,
> Sea, that art clothed with the sun and the rain,
> Thy sweet hard kisses are strong like wine,
> Thy large embraces are keen like pain.
> Save me and hide me with all thy waves,
> Find me one grave of thy thousand graves,
> Those pure cold populous graves of thine
> Wrought without hand in a world without stain.

He soon recovered from his unrequited love, for he had real events to lament, principally the death of his elder sister, Edith. He then

48

travelled to Florence to visit an old poetic idol, Walter Savage Landor, now 90 years old. Swinburne had a gift for hero-worship and asserted that he would give his life to playing valet to Landor. Of course he didn't; but at Fiesole, just outside Florence, the sound of nightingales singing in a walled garden inspired him to write a lyric poem which has become famous. It is *Itylus*, and ostensibly concerns a nightingale upbraiding a swallow for migrating southwards. What was really in Swinburne's mind was the gruesome myth of Tereus, King of Thrace who raped his wife's sister, Philomela and then cut out her tongue so that she could not betray him. On learning of this, his wife Procne revenged herself by killing their son and serving him up for dinner to his unwitting father. As a punishment, Procne was changed by the gods into a swallow and Philomela into a nightingale. The poem really concerns Philomela's grief that her sister has forgotten her sinful deed. The last verse of the poem reveals everything – but only to those familiar with the myths of ancient Greece as recounted by the Roman poet Ovid:

> *O sister, sister, thy first-begotten!*
> *The hands that cling and the feet that follow,*
> *The voice of the child's blood crying yet,*
> *'Who hath remembered me? Who hath forgotten?'*
> *Thou has forgotten, O summer swallow,*
> *But the world shall end when I forget.*

It must have tickled Swinburne to have his poem read in family gatherings by worthy Victorian fathers, unaware of its true significance.

In 1865, Swinburne's verse play *Atalanta in Calydon* appeared in the bookshops, published by Moxon, Tennyson's publisher. It appealed to the classically educated middle classes and met with instant success. It tells the story of Queen Althea of Calydon whose son, Meleager, is fated to die if a brand burning in the grate at his birth is consumed by the fire. She snatches the brand from the fire and keeps it. He grows up to become a warrior. The goddess Artemis, at war with Calydon, releases a wild boar to ravage the country. She relents out of sympathy with a young virgin Atalanta, with whom Meleager has fallen in love, and permits him to kill the

49

the boar, which he does. But he then goes on to murder his mother's brothers who try to rob Atalanta of her inheritance. Enraged at the murder of her brothers, Althea throws the brand into the fire. It is burnt up and Meleager dies.

The vigour and variety of the poem's rhythms and the beauty of its language entranced the critics. John Ruskin, the major art and literary critic of the day, pronounced it the grandest thing ever written by a youth, albeit, he added, a demonic youth. There was indeed a touch of the demon in Swinburne: he revelled in mocking the Christian God, but in *Atalanta in Calydon* his worst excesses were in check. He appealed to younger readers as a new and equally melodious successor to Tennyson, and his poetic future seemed assured. Who could resist such lines as:

> *When the hounds of spring are in winter's traces,*
> *The mother of months in meadow or plain*
> *Fills the shadows and windy places*
> *With lisp of leaves and ripple of rain.*

Swinburne's verse drama *Chastelard* was his next work to be published by Moxon and, although it was admired, there was disapproval at some of the sexual references. When in 1886 his first collection, entitled *Poems and Ballads*, reached the public, approval turned to dislike and anger. The collection contained sixty-two poems, the output of the first thirty years of his life. Some of the poems were lyrics of the highest order, but others, though they were only a minority, were salacious in the extreme, celebrating incest, bisexualism, lesbianism, sadism and pagan passion. The language was exuberant, the rhythms intoxicating and the rhymes magnificent; but to the older generation the subject matter was intolerable. The views of older people clashed with those of the young. To the undergraduates in the universities, the poems were a revelation. Here was poetry which did not preach but excited, which did not deny life but exalted it. It marked a return to the energy of the early Greeks. As one critic put it, it was as if the satyrs, the goat-like followers of Dionysus, the ancient Greek god of wine and fruitfulness, were dancing on the vicarage lawn.

Modern readers of the poems may wonder what all the fuss was about. After the licentiousness of the Regency times the Victorian era was one of probity and hypocrisy. The wilder shores of sexuality were well enough known to the worldly-wise, but they were never discussed openly in genteel society. The daughters of the poor might be debauched, but their middle- and upper-class sisters were shielded from the barest hint of impropriety. What a release it was for genteel and edu-cated young men and women to read of violence and eroticism wrapped up in lovely words and enchanting rhythms!

Moxon was understandably cautious about publishing such poetry. As a trial venture in January 1866, he printed one poem in pamphlet form. This was *Laus Veneris*, or 'in praise of Venus', the Roman goddess of love, known to the ancient Greeks as Aphrodite. Though he risks the wrath of the Christian God, the poet in the poem seeks and finds her:

> *Fair still, but fair for no man saving me,*
> *As when she came out of the naked sea*
> *Making the foam as fire whereon she trod*
> *And as the inner flower of fire was she.*
>
> *Yea she laid hold upon me, and her mouth*
> *Clove unto mine as soul to body doth,*
> *And, laughing, made her lips luxurious;*
> *Her hair had smells of all the sunburnt south.*
>
> *And I forgot fear and all weary things*
> *All ended prayers and perished thanksgivings,*
> *Feeling her face with all her eager hair*
> *Cleave to me, clinging as a fire that clings*
>
> *To the body and to the raiment, burning them;*
> *As after death I know that such-like flame*
> *Shall cleave to me forever; yea what care,*
> *Albeit I burn then, having felt the same?*

The poem expresses the lust of the body. It was an earnest expression too of the contempt for Christianity which burned in Swinburne's mind. But it aroused no anger in the minds of those who read it, for it was lengthy and convoluted and at least conveyed a proper fear of the wrath to come for those who worship pagan goddesses.

In July the same year, Moxon risked his reputation further by publishing *Poems and Ballads* in full. Swinburne read the first review of the book whilst walking along Piccadilly. Within seconds he was dancing with rage and swearing horribly. Friends led him to a café and, thinking it would give less offence, urged him to blaspheme in French, which being bilingual, he proceeded to do. The review he had read was written by John Morley, a youngish and not unenlightened man who yet was so angry and disgusted at the poems that he called their author the *libidinous laureate of a pack of satyrs* and described his work as a mixture of vileness and childishness. Another critic asserted that the poems were morally repulsive and that their author had no talent.

When later there were hints that the publisher might be prosecuted for obscene libel, Moxon got cold feet and withdrew the book from his list. Swinburne received threats on his person and indeed on his life, but he was unabashed. He found another publisher, John Camden Hotten, whose standards were not quite so high as Moxon's, and the book continued to sell well. It was particularly appreciated by younger readers. For them it was the poetry of sexual release and revolt. It swept through the universities, with undergraduates chanting in groups its intoxicating verses.

To those without an education in the classics, the poems were largely inexplicable. That Swinburne was looking with fresh eyes at the sexual aberrations of ancient Greece and Rome was lost on them without knowledge of the great classical poets. The lesbianism with which Swinburne was so intrigued was celebrated by Sappho, the female poet who lived on the Isle of Lesbos in the seventh century BC; thus they were unlikely to appreciate that his poem *Anactoria* was the voice of Sappho addressing one of her female lovers:

> *My life is bitter with thy love; thine eyes*
> *Blind me, thy tresses burn me, thy sharp sighs*
> *Divide my flesh and spirit with soft sound,*
> *And my blood strengthens, and my veins abound.*

I pray thee sigh not, speak not, draw not breath;
Let life burn down, and dream it is not death.

That I could drink thy veins as wine, and eat
Thy breasts like honey! that from face to feet
Thy body were abolished and consumed
And in my flesh thy very flesh entombed!
Ah, ah thy beauty! like a beast it bites,
Stings like an adder, like an arrow smites.

Swinburne's poem *Dolores*, greatly enjoyed by undergraduates at the time, was a hymn of praise to a sado-masochistic anti-Madonna whom he called Our Lady of Pain. He describes her thus:

Cold eyelids, that hide like a jewel,
Hard eyes that grow soft for an hour;
The heavy white limbs, and the cruel
Red mouth like a venomous flower;
When these are gone by with their glories
What shall rest of thee then, what remain,
O mystic and sombre Dolores,
Our Lady of Pain.

Ah beautiful, passionate body
That never has ached with a heart!
On thy mouth though the kisses are bloody,
Though they sting till it shudder and smart,
More kind than the love we adore is,
They hurt not the heart or the brain,
O bitter and tender Dolores,
Our Lady of Pain.

He tells us in the poem that Libitina is Dolores' mother and Priapus her father; but only a student of the classics would be aware that Libitina is the Greek goddess of the dead and the Priapus is a Greek fertility god symbolised by the penis.

It has been said that *Poems and Ballads* took the whole lettered youth of England by storm with its audacity and melody. *Dolores* was particularly popular, and we read of undergraduates at Oxford marching arm-in-arm round their college quadrangles chanting the verse which runs:

> *Could you hurt me, sweet lips, though I hurt you?*
> *Men touch them and change in a thrice*
> *The lilies and languors of virtue*
> *For the raptures and roses of vice.*

Vice was becoming the rage among educated youth. Swinburne was at the head of the new move movement of the 1860s which was to lead on to the decadence of the end of the century. He was a *fin de siècle* man a little before his time. His appearance and behaviour and his self-advertisement seemed to indicate that he welcomed this.

The poem *Hermaphrodites*, inspired by a famous statue in the Louvre in Paris, celebrates bisexualism. Another notable poem in *Poems and Ballads* called *Phaedra* is concerned with the incestuous passion of Phaedra for her step-son. A number of poems in the collection express Swinburne's contempt for Christianity, and none more than *Hymn to Proserpine*. Proserpine in the Greek legend is the daughter of Zeus and Demeter, and she was much worshipped in Rome during the last days before the Roman Emperor accepted the Christian faith. The speaker in the poem laments the eclipse of the old gods and goddesses. Calling Christ *the Galilean*, he cries:

> *Thou has conquered O pale Galilean; the world has grown grey*
> *from thy breath;*
> *We have drunken things Lethean, and fed on the fullness of death.*
> *Laurel is green for a season, and love is sweet for a day;*
> *But love grows bitter with treason, and laurel outlives not May.*
> *Sleep, shall we sleep after all? for the world is not sweet in the end;*
> *For the old faiths loosen and fall, the new years ruin and rend.*

The kingdom of Jesus the Galilean will pass in its turn, he tells us, and with it the *ghastly glories of saints, dead limbs of gibbeted Gods!*

In poem after poem, Swinburne exhibited his extraordinary facility for rhyme and metre, sometimes even losing the message in the music. One poem which, though rhythmically fascinating,

54

emphasises the music rather than the meaning, is *The Garden of Proserpine*. Here are three of its verses:

I am tired of tears and laughter,
And men that laugh and weep;
Of what may come hereafter
For men that sow to reap:
I am weary of days and hours,
Blown buds of barren flowers,
Desires and dreams and powers
And everything but sleep.

From too much love of living,
From hope and fear set free,
We thank with brief thanksgiving
Whatever gods may be
That no life lives for ever;
That dead men rise up never;
That even the weariest river
Winds somewhere safe to sea.

Then star nor sun shall waken,
Nor any change of light:
Nor sound of waters shaken,
Nor any sound or sight:
Nor wintry leaves nor vernal,
Nor days nor things diurnal;
Only things eternal
In an eternal night.

And there are many more verses with the same beguiling rhythm and rhyme sequence, not expressing very much apart from a languid world-weariness and a sense that, once he has started, Swinburne does not know quite where to stop. Nevertheless, for a time after the publication of *Poems and Ballads*, he was regarded by many as the most exciting poet of his generation. His poem *Faustine*, a celebration of lust and cruelty spoken by a gladiator about to die, was much admired by Ruskin who said it made him feel hot to read it, like *pies with the devil's finger in them.* The youthful Thomas Hardy confessed that he was so overwhelmed by Swinburne's poetry that, at the risk of being knocked down by the traffic, he would read it walking along the street.

Although he wrote poems of great length, Swinburne's published work was the outcome of brief periods of frenzied activity interspersed with long periods of lethargy. *Faustine*, for example, was written at tremendous speed, its 164 lines being produced during the short train journey between Waterloo and Hampton Court. He claimed that he wrote thirteen stanzas of Laus Veneris in an hour in his bedroom after having had dinner with a friend. But even his phenomenal poetic talents were challenged by his way of life; for he was drinking ever more heavily. By his early thirties, he was an alcoholic, drinking to excess at every opportunity. He normally drank brandy, and when intoxicated he would screech out his by now well-known views on homosexuality and flagellation, to the amusement but growing contempt of all who heard him. His belching out of blasphemy and bawdry, as one of his associates put it, was a common sight in London's clubland scene.

He suffered from diarrhoea, bilious attacks and fainting fits and was clearly killing himself. If it had not been for his parents, he would have done so. It was their practice to come up to London when they heard of a particularly distressing incident and take their son from his lodgings in Portman Square to their new home in Holmwood, Oxfordshire. There, they gave him a quiet life and a regular diet until his health was restored. He would then return to London and events would be repeated all over again. His behaviour towards his parents was gentle and respectful, and he was courteous and well-mannered with their neighbours and friends, who found it hard to imagine what he got up to in London. He also convalesced occasionally with his Gordon cousins on the Isle of Wight. After collapsing sensationally in the library of the British Museum, he went to France to convalesce, staying at Etretat in Normandy. Whilst sea-bathing there he was carried out to sea by an off-shore current and was luckily rescued by some fishermen. He rewarded them, so he said, by reciting some of the poems of Victor Hugo, the revered French poet and novelist, as they brought him ashore.

One of the literary influences on Swinburne was the work of the

Marquis de Sade, from whose name the word sadist is derived. He was able to read the Frenchman's banned books at Fryston, the country mansion of his friend Monkton Milnes. de Sade's four-volume novel *La Nouvelle Justine* particularly fascinated him. de Sade was eventually detained in a mental hospital where he died, and Swinburne regarded him as a hero who had been martyred by the respectable, hypocritical middle-class. His and other pornographic writings of a sado-masochistic nature, sharpened Swinburne's appetite for sexual stimulation by beating.

In 1865 his cousin Mary Gordon married a professional soldier, by whom she had five children. She was apparently happily married, but she nevertheless retained her interest in corporal punishment and was much entertained by Swinburne reading to her from his novel Lesbia Brandon, which concerned the beating of children by sadistic parents. The book, being considered unfit for publication, did not appear until 1952, long after his death. His earlier novel *Love's Cross-Currents* did appear under a pseudonym in a popular journal, but was not published in book form till 1905. He had a gift for creating characters, and had his subject matter conformed more with current notions of respectability, he might have made a career as a novelist.

Swinburne could only find sexual satisfaction in brothels catering for his taste for flagellation. He befriended a boy of sixteen called John Thomson who had an encyclopaedic knowledge of English poetry and who eventually became a literary journalist. Thomson had some connection with a brothel in St John's Wood in London which met Swinburne's needs, and he became a frequent visitor there. Erotic games were played which culminated in the customer being birched by a young woman, perhaps playing the role of a strict governess or school-mistress. Such establishments were not un-common in Victorian London: they were part of the underside of big city life.

Swinburne's friends were aware of course of his perversions, and, in an attempt to raise his sexual behaviour to a more mature level, Dante Gabriel Rossetti and Richard Burton arranged for an older sexually active woman to introduce herself to him. The woman concerned was a well-known actress called Adah Menken who had been married several times before. She was currently performing a circus act in which she enacted the part of the hero of Byron's poem *Mazeppo* who, as punishment, was tied naked to a wild horse which was let loose. She wrote poetry herself and was intrigued at the idea of seducing so famous a poet. She stayed the night with him on several occasions, but reportedly was never able to persuade him to do more than a little sadistic biting. Nevertheless, Swinburne enjoyed her friendship, and was quite happy to pose for a photograph with her for publicity purposes, which displayed him in a frock-coat gazing adoringly down at her as she sat holding his arm.

But Swinburne could not be simply dismissed as a drunkard and pervert: he was a major poet and a considerable scholar. John Ruskin refused to join in the criticism of *Poems and Ballads*, asserting that Swinburne was above him in knowledge and was in fact the mightiest classical scholar of the age. Benjamin Jowett solicited Swinburne's aid in translating Plato's *Symposium* and also sought his help in revising a children's Bible; for though an atheist, Swinburne's biblical knowledge was encyclopaedic.

He was also a fanatical lover of freedom, political as well as personal. His hatred of the autocratic Napoleon III, Emperor of France from 1852 to 1870, was matched by his near idolatry for Giuseppe Mazzini, the chief architect of Italy's liberation from foreign domination. Mazzini had been in exile in England for a time during his political struggle and had contributed articles to literary journals. The combination of political leader and man of letters was for Swinburne irresistible. Some of Swinburne's friends arranged for him to meet Mazzini, thinking it good for the poet to have a great cause to espouse. The two met in 1867, and Mazzini encouraged Swinburne to use his pen in aid of freedom. Swinburne recognised Mazzini as a born leader, and from then on persisted in calling him 'my chief', and saying he was ready to die for him and for the cause of Italian unity and independence. He was not prepared to give up drinking, however, though Mazzini urged him to do so. He found the composing of freedom poems to order was almost beyond him, but he did his best. In 1871 he published a collection of poems called *Songs before Sunrise*, which included much of his political verse.

Like Tennyson, Swinburne greatly enjoyed reading his own poetry aloud, and he particularly liked declaiming his liberty poetry to his friends. His favourite poem, *The Eve of Revolution*, is lengthy and contains much windy rhetoric; but to hear him recite it in his excited, high-pitched voice was a splendid experience, particularly to someone like Dante Gabriel Rossetti who had Italian freedom so much at heart. The poet in the poem turns in order to each point of the compass, blowing a trumpet:

I set the trumpet to my lips and blow.
The height of night is shaken, the skies break,
The winds and stars and waters come and go. . . .

A cynic observed that the weather was clearly affected by the trumpet-blowing, but any influence on the countries concerned seemed non-existent. Another listener said that it felt like a whirlwind let loose in a vacuum, and this just about sums it up for the modern reader. However, some of his contemporaries saw it differently. For them, Swinburne was the outstanding poet of both sexual and political liberation. Rossetti, on first hearing readings from *Songs before Sunrise*, acclaimed its 'glorious poetry and literary splendour'.

By now he had an appreciative readership not only in Britain but in France, Germany and the United States too. He had an outlet for his poetry and prose in a number of literary journals and had also established a formidable reputation as a literary critic. He had been working for a long time on a sequel to his verse drama *Chastelard*, and in 1874 it was published under the title *Bothwell*. It was an enormous tribute to his capacity for hard work, being fifteen thousand lines in length and many times longer than any play by Shakespeare. It was quite unstageable, for uncut, it would have lasted some twelve hours. Even so, his poetic reputation was such that it found a small readership of enthusiasts.

At this time his relationship with Benjamin Jowett was increasingly close. He joined his summer parties at Pitlochrie in Scotland and stayed with him in Oxford too, where at dinner parties he met Tennyson, Browning, Matthew Arnold and other literary luminaries. Jowett had sufficient control over him to check his excessive drinking. He also encouraged his light-hearted gaiety, and his high spirits usually made him the life and soul of any party. He welcomed Jowett's advice on his literary work but found it difficult to follow. Jowett, for example, suggested the cutting of the first scene of *Bothwell*, only to find that Swinburne's re-write was even longer.

At this time, Swinburne could often manage a hundred lines of poetry a day; but these periods of intense inspiration were interrupted by many days of idleness, when he drank heavily and his life seemed purposeless.

In 1876, he produced a verse play called *Erectheus*, which was a sequel to *Atalanta in Calydon* and was a work of scholarship rather than great poetry. He was also working at the same time on a long poem concerned with the legends of King Arthur called *Tristram of Lyonesse*, which was not published until 1882. His aim was to outshine Tennyson, who had written on the same subject, and there are some who think he succeeded.

In the meantime, however, he was extremely hard-up. His parents still made him an annual allowance, but it did not cover the cost of his heavy drinking and his sexual indulgences, and payment for his literary work scarcely met the balance. He depended upon periods of rest and recuperation at his parents' home, and during 1876 he stayed there for several months. But this refuge could not be there for ever. Early in 1877 his father died and it was necessary to sell their house to provide an income for his mother. There was nothing for Algernon to do but return to his lodgings in London, which were now in Great James Street, Holborn, and try to stand on his own feet. He was 40 years old, and his long years of dependency were apparently over.

Although his life was dissolute in the extreme, he did not neglect his poetry. In 1878 he published another collection of poems, entitled *Poems and Ballads, Second Series*, which he dedicated to Richard Burton. It contained some lovely verse, but was very different from his first collection, there being little sensuality to which the prudish could object. Its general tenor was one of serenity tempered with regret. The regret, as ever, was for the passing of the old gods of ancient Greece and their replacement by the Christian god who, in dying yet had conquered. He lamented the death of his father in a poem called *Inferiae* (rites to honour the dead), intoning sonorously:

> *Fourscore years since, and come but one month more*
> *The count were perfect of his mortal score*
> *Whose sail went seaward yesterday from shore*
> *To cross the last of many an unsailed sea.*

He lamented too the death of Charles Baudelaire in *Ave Atque Vale* (Hail and Farewell), saying:

> *Sleep; and if life was bitter to thee, pardon,*
> *If sweet, give thanks; thou hast no more to live;*
> *And to give thanks is good, and to forgive.*

And he added:

> *There lies not any troublous thing before,*
> *Nor sight nor sound to war against thee more,*
> *For whom all winds are quiet as the sun,*
> *All waters as the shore.*

Perhaps the most compelling poem of the whole collection is *A Forsaken Garden*, which was written after a return visit to East Dene in 1876. All the wizardry of rhythm is there:

> *In a coign of the cliff between lowland and highland,*
> *At the sea-down's edge between windward and lee,*
> *Walled round with rocks as an inland island,*
> *The ghost of a garden fronts the sea.*
> *A girdle of brushwood and thorn encloses*
> *The steep square slope of the blossomless bed*
> *Where the weeds that grew green from the graves of its roses*
> *Now lie dead.*

The poet imagines the lovers who walked there once:

> *Heart handfast in heart as they stood, 'Look thither',*
> *Did he whisper? 'look forth from the flowers to the sea*
> *For the foam-flowers endure when the rose-blossoms wither,*
> *And men that love lightly may die — but we?*
> *And the same wind sang and the same waves whitened,*
> *And or ever the garden's last petals were shed,*
> *In the lips that had whispered, the eyes that had lightened,*
> *Love was dead.*

> Or they loved their life through, and then went whither?
> And were one to the end — but what end who knows?
> Love deep as the sea as a rose must wither,
> As the rose-red seaweed that mocks the rose.
> Shall the dead take thought for the dead to love them?
> What love was ever as deep as the grave?
> They are loveless now as the grass above them
> Or the wave.
>
> All are at one now, roses and lovers,
> Not known of the cliffs and the fields and the sea.
> Not a breath of the time that has been hovers
> In the air now soft with a summer to be.
> Not a breath shall there sweeten the seasons hereafter
> Of the flowers or the lovers that laugh now or weep,
> When as they that are free now of weeping and laughter
> We shall sleep.

In the last verse the poet tells us:

> Till the slow sea rise and the sheer cliff crumble,
> Till terrace and meadow the deep gulfs drink,
> Till the strength of the waves of the high tides humble
> The fields that lessen, the rocks that shrink,
> Here now in his triumph where all things falter,
> Stretched out on the spoils that his own hand spread,
> As a god self-slain on his own strange altar
> Death lies dead.

In another poem, *At a Month's End*, Swinburne evokes with a different rhythm the same sense of sadness and loss:

> Silent we went an hour together,
> Under grey skies by waters white.
> Our hearts were full of windy weather,
> Clouds and blown stars and broken light.
>
> Full of cold clouds and moonbeams drifted
> And streaming storms and straying fires,
> Our souls in us were stirred and shifted
> By doubts and dreams and foiled desires.

Nothing of Swinburne's disturbed and disreputable life was reflected in his poems. Living in London, first at Great James Street and later in Guildford Street nearby, he was lonely and isolated and drinking very heavily. He suffered frequent bouts of influenza and liver trouble and was looking increasingly thin and old. By the winter of 1877, he was complaining that he was too ill to hold a pen. A friend described him as like an old man, needing a hand to help him up and down stairs.

His mother was still at Holmwood, waiting for the house to be sold, but he refused to join her there. He did at last acknowledge that he needed help when he wrote to his solicitor friend, Theodore Watts-Dunton, asking him to call. Watts-Dunton was a literary man himself and had been a good friend to Swinburne ever since he had helped him in a legal dispute with his publisher John Hotten, some six years before. He was shocked at Swinburne's appearance: the spruce, lively little poet had changed into a tottering invalid. He got in touch with Lady Swinburne, who despite all her efforts, had not seen Algernon for over a year. She was only too willing to help her son, and with her agreement, Watts-Dunton descended upon the ailing poet early one morning and carried him off, first to his own married sister in Putney and then on to Holmwood, where he stayed with his mother until the sale of her house was completed. Meanwhile, Watts-Dunton took a lease of 2, The Pines, a new, large house in Putney and in 1879 persuaded Swinburne to join him there. Putney in those days was a pleasantly rural outer suburb of London, and Swinburne seems to have been quite happy with the arrangement. His mother was happy with it too, for she paid Watts-Dunton £200 a year for accommodating her son.

Two extreme aspects of Algernon Swinburne's character were rebelliousness on the one hand and submissiveness on the other; and the latter predominated in his relationship with Watts-Dunton. Watts-Dunton was no father-figure, being only five years older than Algernon. He was a bachelor with drooping moustache, a bald head and above all, a determined personality. He had set himself the task of rehabilitating his poet friend and he persisted in it for the next thirty years. That Swinburne, the vivacious, dissolute man about town, should have become the patient, if not the prisoner, of a serious-minded middle-class solicitor was a source of amusement to some of their acquaintances. But the poet was a willing, grateful participant, and there is little doubt that his stern, somewhat dour companion, who admired his poetry so much, literally saved his life.

The two men did not live completely in each other's pockets. They shared the house, with Swinburne occupying the upper half, and they breakfasted separately. Most mornings, Swinburne took a walk on his own across Putney Heath and Wimbledon Common. He lunched with Watts-Dunton and his family, which initially included his two sisters and the young son of one of them. In the afternoons he worked industriously at his writing; his evenings were usually spent with Watts-Dunton, who enjoyed hearing him read his work. His life was as ordered as it had once been chaotic. The routine was broken by occasional visits from friends from the literary world, and sometimes he stayed with his mother; but his health came first and Watts-Dunton saw to that.

His method was to reduce Algernon's alcohol intake by stages, and he did so by influence and encouragement rather than diktat. The brandy-drinking had to be stopped first, and he accomplished this be speaking slightingly of it, and at the same time praising port as the true drink of poets. From port, he moved Swinburne on to claret as being lighter and healthier for him; and the final move was to beer, which was, he said, the love of Shakespeare's England. Swinburne went on to a regimen of a daily bottle of beer at the Rose and Crown in Wimbledon half-way through his morning walk, and another bottle with his lunch; and for the next thirty years he rarely deviated from this routine. His health responded dramatically to regularity and moderation and he continued spry and spruce until his death at 72. There are some who accuse Watts-Dunton of destroying his friend's poetic genius; but it is likely that his powers were on the decline anyway. He reviewed books and wrote literary articles and maintained a lively correspondence with acquaintances in the world of letters. He continued to write a lot of poetry too. A friend and critic, Sir Edmund Gosse, accused him of pouring forth stanzas in which there were occasional luminous passages, but the total effect of which was 'foggy and fatiguing'. Nevertheless, many poets would have been proud of an output like his.

In 1880 three volumes of poetry bearing his name appeared in the bookshops: *Songs of the Springtides, Studies in Song* and *The Heptologia.* The first of these included one notable poem of self-absorption. It was entitled *On the Cliffs*, and was written before he came to live in Putney. The poet is standing on the cliffs overlooking the North Sea in the evening, and is listening to the song of a nightingale. He is reflecting on his past youth and his thoughts are sad and bitter:

> *In fruitless years of youth dead long ago*
> *And deep beneath their own dead leaves and snow*
> *Buried, I heard with bitter heart and sere*
> *The same sea's words unchangeable, nor knew*
> *But that mine own life-days were changeless too*
> *And sharp and salt with unshed tear on tear*
> *And cold and fierce and barren; and my soul,*
> *Sickening, swam weakly with bated breath*
> *In a deep sea like death,*
> *And felt the wind buffet her face with brine*
> *Hard, and harsh thought on thought in long bleak roll*
> *Blown by keen gusts of memory sad as thine*
> *Heap the weight up of pain, and break, and leave*
> *Strength scarce enough to grieve*
> *In the sick heavy spirit, unmanned with strife*
> *Of waves that beat at the tired lips of life.*

But Swinburne is not depressed for long and recognises that, like the nightingale, he is not born for sorrow, nor indeed for joy. He does not strive to attain like other men:

> *. . . the best of all my days*
> *Have been as those fair, fruitless summer strays,*
> *Those water-waifs that but the sea-wind steers,*
> *Flakes of glad foam or flowers on footless ways*
> *That take the wind in season and the sun,*
> *And when the wind wills is their season done.*

The major poem in *Studies in Song* is *By the North Sea.* It is a descriptive seascape composed in the same metre as *Dolores* but utterly different in content. Swinburne is writing about Dunwich on the east coast of Suffolk, a buried town of salt marshes with ruins and crumbling sandbanks. The rhythm of the poem is as monotonous as the placid sea itself:

> *A land that is lonelier than ruin;*
> *A sea that is stranger than death:*
> *Far fields that a rose never blew in,*
> *Wan waste where the winds lacks breath;*
> *Waste endless and boundless and flowerless*
> *But of marsh-blossoms fruitless as free:*
> *Where earth lies exhausted, as powerless*
> *To strive with the sea.*
>
> *The pastures are herdless and sheepless,*
> *No pasture or shelter for herds:*
> *The wind is relentless and sleepless,*
> *And restless and songless the birds;*
> *Their cries from afar fall breathless,*
> *Their wings are lightnings that flee;*
> *For the land has two lords that are deathless:*
> *Death's self, and the sea.*

He keeps the poem going for fifty or so verses, emphasizing remorselessly the bleak monotony of the scene.

The third of the three books published that year, *The Heptologia* (literally the seven sayings), contained parodies of poets including Tennyson and Browning. The most masterly of these was *Nephelidia* (little clouds), which was a self-parody:

> *From the depth of the dreamy decline of the dawn through a*
> *   notable nimbus of nebulus moonshine,*
> *Palid and pink as the palm of the flag-flower that flickers with*
> *   fear of the flies as thy float,*
> *Are the looks of our lovers that lustrously lean from a marvel of*
> *   mystic miraculous moonshine,*
> *These that we feel in the blood of our blushes that thicken and*
> *   threaten with throbs through the throat?*

He published the book anonymously, so there was much speculation in the literary world as to who the author was. Swinburne enjoyed this sort of literary hoax and perpetrated quite a few in his time.

In October 1881 Swinburne completed the third of his enormous trilogy on Mary Queen of Scots, which ends with the Queen's execution. It is long and tedious and was not widely read, but it nevertheless added to his literary reputation. In 1882 came the publication of *Tristram of Lyonesse*, which was in a different class altogether. Tennyson had written of the love between Tristram and Iseult in his version of the legends of King Arthur, *Idylls of the King*, but Swinburne thought the love scenes too dull. Certainly his own exposition of the lovers' passion for each other is dramatically expressed:

> *Only with stress of soft fierce hands she prest*
> *Between the throbbing blossoms of her breast*
> *His ardent face, and through his hair her breath*
> *And with strong trembling fingers she strained fast*
> *His head into her bosom; till at last*
> *Satiate with sweetness of that burning bed*
> *His eyes afire with tears, he raised his head*
> *And laughed into her lips, and all his heart*
> *Filled hers; then face from face fell, and apart*
> *Each hung on each with panting lips, and felt*
> *Sense into sense and spirit into spirit melt.*

Much of Swinburne's poetry expresses his love for the sea, and in his account of Tristram's tremendous struggle with the stormy waters, this passion is splendidly evoked:

> *So for an hour they fought the storm out still,*
> *The keel sprang from the wave-ridge, and the sky*
> *Glared at them for a breath's space through the rain;*
> *Then the bows with a sharp shock plunged again*
> *Down, and the sea clashed on them, and so rose*
> *The bright stern like one panting from swift blows,*
> *And as a swimmer's joyous beaten head*
> *Rears itself laughing, so in that sharp stead*

The light ship lifted her long quivering bows
As might the man his buffeted strong brows
Out of the wave-breach; for with one stroke yet
Went all men's oars together, strongly set
As to loud music, and with hearts uplift
They smote their strong way through the drench and drift.

His friend William Morris's criticism of Swinburne's poetry was that it was founded on literature rather than nature; but this seems empty indeed in the face of these lines and of his many other descriptions of the sea in all its moods.

A number of Swinburne's lesser poems were included in the *Tristram of Lyonesse* volume and among them were absurdly sentimental tributes to infants. Increasingly, he loved babies. During his daily walks he would meet nursemaids with their prams, and he loved to pat the heads of the infants inside and to describe their charms to Watts-Dunton in the evening. He was not a sexual menace. The mothers and nursemaids recognised his emotional senility and were amused rather than fearful. He dressed for his walks in a frock-coat and a black felt hat and was an object of derision to the street urchins he passed. To avoid attention he used to drink his beer on his own in the coffee-room at the Rose and Crown in Wimbledon at the half-way point of his morning walk. His over-fondness for Watts-Dunton's six-year-old nephew Bertie, who was part of the household for a time, was so embarrassingly intense that it was thought wise to send the boy away for six months, and Swinburne felt his absence keenly.

In 1883 his book *A Century of Roundels*, which he dedicated to Christina Rossetti, reached the bookshops. A roundel is a poem of three verses consisting of three lines each. The first and third verse is followed by a short refrain. There was something of a craze for the roundel form at the time and Swinburne wrote a lot of them, as did Christina Rossetti. Both poets were very complimentary about each other's work, though Christina could never stomach Algernon's atheism. As Swinburne grew older he increasingly lamented the passing years, and the roundel was an excellent channel for expressing this sadness. For example:

Had I wist, when life was like a warm wind playing
Light and loud through sundawn and the dew's bright mist,
How the time would come for hearts to sigh in saying
'Had I wist' —

Surely not the roses, laughing as they kissed,
Not the lovelier laugh of seas in sunshine swaying,
Should have lured my soul to look thereon and list.

Now the wind is like a soul cast out and praying
Vainly, prayers that pierce not ears when hearts resist:
Now mine own soul sighs, adrift as wind and straying,
'Had I wist',

As he grew older he turned balder and his beard was more voluminous. He became more patriotic, more reactionary and a good deal deafer. It seemed on the death of Tennyson in 1892 that he might be offered the position of Poet Laureate; but his wild youth and erotic poetry had not been forgotten and the mantle was passed to Alfred Austin, much the lesser poet. People he had known for a great part of his life began to die. He mourned the passing of Dante Gabriel Rossetti in 1882. Never bearing malice at the way Rossetti had cut him out of his life after the death of his wife, he wrote a sonnet which spoke of him as *a light more bright than ever bathed the skies.* On William Morris's death in 1896, he described him as one of the best men who ever lived. An even more poignant grief was reserved for Edward Burne-Jones, his *beloved friend of more than forty years* when he died in 1898. Swinburne's mother had died two years before, and he had felt this to be the beginning of the end for him, cleaving closer to his sisters until they too began to pre-decease him.

One consolation was his continued close relationship with his cousin Mary, who had been Mrs Leith for many years and was now Colonel Leith's widow. He and Mary saw a lot of each other and corresponded frequently, writing their letters in a childish code which pleased them but deceived few people. They retained their mutual interest in flagellation, though writing about it was Swinburne's only sexual outlet now. There are suggestions that he might have contrubuted verse to pornographic journals, but if he did it would have been without the knowledge of Watts-Dunton, who controlled his friend's life in nearly every detail.

In 1905, at the age of seventy-three and a life-long bachelor, Theodore Watts-Dunton surprised everyone by getting married. His bride was Clara Reich, a 21-year-old girl, who had first visited The Pines at the age of sixteen, when she had been brought there to meet the famous poet Algernon Swinburne. This marriage between May and December, as Clara put it, turned out very well, and Swinburne was as happy as her husband at her presence in the house.

Swinburne continued healthy and active until 1 April 1909 when he went out for his morning walk without his overcoat, much to Watts-Dunton's irritation. The morning was cold and rainy and he got very wet. His friend saw that he changed his clothes, but by the next day he was confined to his bed with a bad cold which turned to pneumonia. His bed was moved to the library downstairs and two nurses were installed. Oxygen was administered, but, as there were no effective drugs in those days, double pneumonia could be a sentence of death for the elderly. On 10 April 1909, five days after his seventy-second birthday, Swinburne died — with a smile on his lips, according to Watts-Dunton. In his youth he had not feared the high cliffs of East Dene; he had revelled in reckless horse-riding and tussles with stormy seas; he had stood firm against the ferocity of censorious critics; and he did not fear death. He still considered himself an atheist, and yet he felt a faint hope that there was an after-life, and said it would be rather jolly if there were one.

It was agreed between Watts-Dunton and Swinburne's surviving sister Isabel that he should be buried with his mother and dead sisters at the church in East Dene. Watts-Dunton undertook that there would be no Christian burial service. The ceremony took place five days later on the fifteenth, but the vicar could not resist saying a few liturgical words, such as 'earth to earth and dust to dust', which Swinburne would have probably smiled at. Isabel and his cousin Mary did what they could to conceal from posterity his sexual tastes and his years of heavy drinking. It was not until 1959 when his collected letters were published that the general public knew everything. Few people were shocked at the letters, and many were amused and surprised at the rich vein of humour he possessed, which was not apparent in his poetry.

Swinburne recognised the restricting hypocrisy of the Victorian Christian ethic, but what were his positive beliefs? He had romantic ideas about liberty, but seemed to care little about the great industrial changes through which his country was passing and the suffering of the working class. He valued beauty, even above scholarship, and he cared deeply about sexual liberation. He helped the youth of his generation cast off the inhibitions of Victorian morality. Recalling the sexual aberrations of classical Greece and Rome, he burnished them with a renewed sparkle and evoked them in verse of an intoxicating loveliness. His feeling for rhythm has never been surpassed, nor has the brilliance of his rhyming. Perhaps he wrote too much that was mediocre and monotonous, but he will always be remembered and revered as a brilliant flash of colour across the industrial gloom of his time.

He wrote a suitable epitaph for himself in the closing lines of his poem, *Hymn to Proserpine*:

> *For the glass of the years is brittle wherein we gaze for a span;*
> *A little soul for a little bears up this corpse, which is man.*
> *For long I endure, no longer; and laugh not again, neither weep.*
> *For there is no God found stronger than death; and death is a sleep.*

GERARD MANLEY HOPKINS

Summer ends now; now barbarous in beauty, the stooks arise
Around; up above, what wind-walks! what lovely behaviour
Of silk-sack clouds! has wilder, wilful-wavier
Meal-drift moulded ever and melted across skies?

GERARD MANLEY HOPKINS

Gerard Manley Hopkins did not, like Swinburne, come from the land-owning classes; nor did he as a child know the genteel poverty of the Rossettis. His family's position in the class-conscious society of mid-nineteenth-century England was among the prosperous middle-classes. He attended a minor public school and, being academically gifted, the path seemed clear for a successful professional or academic career. That he was instead to become a Jesuit priest and live a life of poverty, chastity and obedience would have astonished anyone who knew his parents. That he was to have had a leaning towards poetry would have seemed less remarkable for both his parents had literary talents; but the extent of his poetic genius could never have been forseen.

He wrote for future generations, not for his own. Not one of the poems of his maturity was published during his lifetime. Even his closest friend, Robert Bridges, himself a gifted poet, found much of his work incomprehensible. The priests amongst whom he lived and worked knew nothing of his extraordinary talent, and none of the few words written at his death mentioned that he wrote poetry. It was nearly thirty years after he died that a collection of his poems was first published, and several years after that that the quality of his work began to be recognized. His personality was as obscure as his poetry, and it was only gradually that the literary world comprehended his true genius.

Hopkins was born at Stratford, Essex on 28 July 1844. He was the eldest of nine children, having five brothers, one of whom died young, and three sisters. His father, Manley Hopkins, from whom Gerard derived his second name, was a prosperous, cultivated and versatile man. He ran a successful marine insurance business in London, and he was for some forty years Consul General for the then independent kingdom of Hawaii, a post obtained through the influence of a younger brother who was prominent in the Hawaiian government service. In addition, he had substantial literary interests, reviewing poetry for *The Times* and publishing his own poetry. As well as all this, he was interested in mathematics, publishing a book on cardinal numbers and a manual on marine insurance.

Gerard's mother, the daughter of a London doctor, was fond of music and literature, and she took an interest in her son's poetry. She was even-tempered and motherly, devoting her life to her large family. Stratford, now absorbed into east London, was a rural village in those days. The Hopkins's house was a spacious one, and they kept the retinue of servants − cook, housemaid, nursemaid − which was normal for middle-class families. The family grew rapidly, and by 1852 there were four children. Needing more space, the family moved when Gerard was eight to the North London village of Hampstead. They were rising in the world, and their house in a new development of gentlemen's residences reflected this. It was near Hampstead Heath and had a garden of several acres with splendid views over London. They were to live there for the next thirty-four years.

Manley Hopkins was a moderate High Anglican and was soon active in the affairs of the local church. Family prayers were the norm in his household. By 1860 there were eight children in the family. The second eldest was Cyril, whom Gerard never particularly liked; Lionel followed him and then came Kate, Grace, Arthur, Millicent and Everard. Arthur and Everard were to become talented commercial artists, Cyril joined his father's business and Lionel became a distinguished Chinese linguist. None of the girls married. Millicent entered an Anglican nunnery, Grace was a musician and Kate, Gerard's favourite sister, accepted the role of looking after her parents as they aged. Living with the family was Manley's unmarried sister, Anne, who was a capable artist. Her portrait of Gerard at the age of fifteen hangs in the National Portrait Gallery. It shows him with an intelligent, sensitive, delicate face.

At the age of ten, Gerard was sent to Sir Roger Cholmeley's School for Boys at Highgate, about three miles across Hampstead Heath. The school, which later became Highgate School, had an ancient foundation, but had fallen on hard times when the Reverend

John Dyne was appointed headmaster in 1838. He raised its reputation, and by the time Gerard left in 1863 it had become a highly successful minor public school. Gerard was one of fifty or so boarders, and at first he found the change to the rigours of boarding-school life difficult to bear. John Dyne believed in hard work and discipline, reinforced by the liberal use of the birch or the riding whip. Gerard received his full share of beatings and was at loggerheads with his headmaster throughout his time at the school.

Nonetheless, he was an academic high-flyer, excelling in the classical studies in which the school specialised. He collected a number of school prizes, including the Governor's gold medal for Latin verse in the last year, at the same time gaining a scholarship to Balliol College, Oxford. Because of his slight build he had no enthusiasm for games, but he played enough to avoid the dislike of his form-mates. They admired the obstinate way he stood up to the headmaster. Even his practice of reading a passage from the New Testament every night in the dormitory did not turn them against him. He hated the school but he never let it get him down. In his last year, an altercation with the Reverend Dyne led to him being deprived of the use of a private room for study. He later boasted that he 'cheeked Dyne wildly' and was beaten with the riding whip. However, he won in the end because he persuaded his father to let him become a day-boy, enabling him to study in the evenings in peace and also enjoy the walk to and from the school each day.

One illustration of his obstinacy was his bet with another boy that he could go without liquids for three weeks. He lasted until his tongue went black and a teacher was informed. It demonstrated his determination but also a certain masochism in his personality. His two favourite historical characters shared the same outlook. One was Savonarola, the fifteenth-century Italian monk who preached against the pleasures of the flesh and was eventually tortured and burnt at the stake by the enraged citizens of Florence; the other was Origen, the divine of the early Christian church who had himself castrated to eliminate sexual desire and was later imprisoned and tortured. How far Hopkins's masochistic tendencies stemmed from the beatings he had at school may only be guessed at, but as with Swinburne, there was nothing in his home life to engender it.

In 1860, when he was fifteen, Gerard won the school prize for poetry with a poem called *The Escorial*, which was the subject prescribed for the competition. The poem describes the famous sixteenth-century Spanish palace built by Philip II to celebrate a victory over the French, and is very much in the romantic vein of Keats, with loving descriptions of beautiful works of art. Keats was a great favourite of his at the time. Gerard also amused himself with satirical poems and drawings about the staff. His artistic skill is shown by his illustrations for one of the few other poems of his schooldays which have survived. This was called *A Vision of the Mermaids* and was written at Christmas 1862. It was a long poem and was embellished with pen and ink sketches of beautiful mermaids.

Gerard's only poem to be published in his lifetime appeared in a minor literary journal called *Once a Week*, in February 1863. His father had connections with the journal and probably used his influence to get it accepted. The poem was *Winter with the Gulf Stream*, and describes a mild winter's afternoon with the sun setting. Hopkins liked it enough to revise it some eight years later, but such lines as:

> *Into an azure mist, the sun*
> *Drops down engulf'd, his journey done.*

gave little promise of an extraordinarily original poet in the making.

At this distance, it seems a pity that he did not enjoy a better relationship with his father. Manley Hopkins took an interest in his son's poetry; he took him on trips to Germany, Belgium and Holland and was very proud of his academic ability. But Gerard was inclined to laugh at his father, mocking his pompous manner. He was ready to rebel against him, and this rebellion was to take an extreme form.

He left school with no regrets and went up to Balliol College, Oxford in April 1863, some seven years after Swinburne. He fell in love with Oxford immediately. It was at that time Matthew Arnold's city of dreaming spires, and many years were to pass before it became a busy industrial town. The Fellows who administered the colleges and lectured the undergraduates were still mostly celibate clergymen. Religious thought and discussion were of intense interest to Fellows and undergraduates alike. All members of the University, from under-graduates to professors, had to accept, in theory at least, the Thirty-

Nine Articles of the Anglican faith, and daily attendance at chapel was obligatory. Within the Anglican community there were three principal persuasions: the High Church or Anglo-Catholics, led at that time by Canon Pusey, Professor of Hebrew; the Low Church or Evangelicals, who were firmly Protestant; and the Broad Church party who accepted a reasonable degree of divergent opinion and attempted to reconcile Christianity with modern scientific thought. The most prominent member of the last was Benjamin Jowett, Professor of Greek, who in due course became Master of Balliol.

University religion offered more than an opportunity to worship God; it provided political excitement and intrigue as the different ecclesiastic factions vied with each other. There were unbelievers too within the University, and controversy with them was equally challenging. Gerard Hopkins, with his High Church family background, was naturally drawn initially to the Anglo-Catholics, enjoying the ritualistic form of service which they favoured.

He was studying for a Bachelor of Arts degree in Classics, which comprised Greek and Latin language and literature, philosophy and ancient history. The course lasted four years, with a major examination called Mods after two years and a final one known as Greats. He was immediately happy at Oxford. He delighted in walking and talking with fellow undergraduates and in boating on the river Cherwell, which he told his mother in a letter must be the summit of human happiness. He attended the breakfast feasts which were a feature of University life and the numerous drinking parties called 'wines' given by Fellows and undergraduates. The society was exclusively male and it resulted in close friendships between young men, which could be both possessive and passionate.

The most significant and enduring friendship Gerard made at Oxford was with Robert Bridges, who was of the same age and also a devout Anglo-Catholic. Later, Bridges was to lose his faith. He studied medicine and became a doctor in a London hospital until, in middle age, he gave it up and devoted the rest of his life to literature. He was a prolific poet, writing in a quiet classical manner, radically different from Hopkins's individualistic style. His mature work was in tune with the establishment tastes of the time and he was appointed Poet Laureate in 1913, holding the position until his death in 1930. Hopkin's friendship with Bridges was of fundamental importance to posterity, for his many letters to Bridges over the years are the source of much of what is known about his ideas on poetry. Bridges was critical of Hopkins's work and not a little puzzled by it; but nevertheless we owe it to him that most of it survived at all. He preserved Gerard's poems and then, well after his death in 1889, arranged for them to be published. If he had not done so, Hopkins's poetry would have died with him and the world would have been unaware of his genius.

Benjamin Jowett made a lasting impression on Gerard, as he had on Algernon Swinburne before him. Another University Fellow to influence him was Walter Pater, then a young don in his mid-twenties who had just started his career as a critic of art and literature. Pater was later to become a central figure in the so-called Aesthetic Movement, whose members believed that art was an end in itself. Hopkins, like Pater, believed in the importance of great art, but art for him was an expression of God's glory, and art for art's sake was not enough. Another influence on the young Hopkins was John Ruskin, who had become the leading art critic of the day. From Ruskin he learnt to look at natural beauty in a concentrated way, studying such natural objects as streams, lakes, trees, flowers and leaves intensely and minutely. He became obsessed from time to time with a particular plant or tree. On the Isle of Wight during the summer vacation of 1864 he developed, for example, a passion for ash leaves, sketching them and describing them in precise detail.

He wrote many poems whilst at Oxford, experimenting with a variety of metres and verse forms. Mostly the themes were religious ones, influenced by Dante Gabriel Rossetti and his sister, Christina. Perhaps the best known of these early poems is *Heaven-Haven*, subtitled *A Nun takes the Veil*. Short and limited in its aims, it is, with its individualistic use of words, a promise of what was to come:

> *I have desired to go*
> *Where springs not fail,*
> *To fields where flies no sharp and sided hail*
> *And a few lilies blow.*

And I have asked to be
Where no storms come,
Where the green swell is in the havens dumb,
And out of the swing of the sea.

Another well-known poem of his undergraduate days is *The Habit of Perfection*, in which he hymns the virtues of silence, fasting and the acceptance of poverty. *Palate, the hutch of tasty lust/Desire not to be rinsed with wine*, he urges us, comforting us with the thought:

The can must be so sweet, the crust
So fresh that comes in fasts divine!

His message is that in controlling the pleasures of the senses, we come nearer to God and experience a more profound happiness:

O feel-of-primrose hands, O feet
That want the yield of plushy sward,
But you shall walk the golden street
And you unhouse and house the Lord.

Hands which love to touch the petals of flowers; bare feet which glory in walking on the grass: these must be denied their pleasure for the greater joy of the golden street of heaven and the rapture of God within us replacing our limited selves. Already he was risking obscurity with hyphenated compound words which, used as adjectives, heighten the impact of the image. In another verse we see the alliterative linking of words which was to become another of his poetic stock-in-trades:

Be shellèd eyes, with double dark
And find the uncreated light:
This ruck and reel which you remark
Coils, keeps and teases simple sight.

As Ruskin recommended, he kept a notebook, in which he trained his perceptive powers by recording in exact detail what he saw in nature. He also used to play with words, grouping them together

81

round a theme and using word association to extend his list, taking pleasure in alliteration and using words which sound like what they mean: *grind, grate, crush, crash* being a typical sequence. He used to illustrate entries in his notebook with little sketches: the sequence *crook, crank, kranke, crick, cranky*, for example being accompanied by a drawing of a crank-wheel.

Gerard Hopkins was popular at Balliol, being full of fun and spontaneous gaiety. He was still small and slight with a prominent nose and chin. His manner was somewhat girlish and he was no sportsman, mixing with the religious and aesthetic rather than the sporty and hearty. In February 1865, he met a young man who made a great impression on him. This was Digby Dolben, who was a distant cousin of his friend Robert Bridges, and was good-looking and intensely religious. Gerard was attracted both by his physical beauty and his spiritual intensity; and though their meeting lasted only a few days, the impression on him was an enduring one. He wrote a number of letters to Dolben, but the youth's response was not enthusiastic and the friendship dwindled, though Gerard's yearning persisted. At that time, he was writing sonnets very like those of Shakespeare. One of them begins: *Where art thou friend, whom I shall never see?* and another asserts: *My love is lessened and must soon be past.* He was slowly and reluctantly reconciling himself to the idea that his life must be one without sexual love. He was feeling intense remorse at his sexual interest in males and excessive guilt about masturbation. A short, heartfelt poem, written at the end of 1865, expresses these feelings:

> *Trees by their yield*
> *Are known: but I –*
> *My sap is sealed,*
> *My root is dry.*
> *If life within*
> *I none can show*
> *(Except for sin),*
> *Nor fruit above,*
> *It must be so –*
> *I do not love.*

He was never to meet Dolben again. Two years later, at the age of nineteen, the young man was drowned in a swimming accident. Gerard never forgot him.

During 1866, he was reflecting on whether to become a Roman Catholic, as some of his young acquaintances had already done. As an Anglo-Catholic, he already accepted most of the doctrine and practices of the Roman Church apart from the supremacy of the Pope, and this was for him the key question. He was already half-way to believing that the Catholic Church, founded by Jesus Christ on St Peter, possessed the true apostolic succession and that the Church of England was merely a breakaway grouping. A visit to a Benedictine monastery with two of his friends in June 1866 made him more sure of this. On 17 July he recorded in his diary that it was impossible for him to remain in the Church of England. About five weeks later he wrote to the Reverend John Newman asking for an interview. Newman, a prominent Anglo-Catholic, had been converted to the Roman Church in 1840, and was famous for his book, *Apologia Pro Vita Sua*, published in 1864 in which he set out the reasons for his conversion. He had founded a Roman Catholic school, the Birmingham Oratory, and it was there on 20 September 1866 that Gerard met him. He found him friendly and sympathetic, and was told that he could be received into the Roman Catholic Church quite soon.

The big problem for Gerard was the reaction of his parents to his intention. They were deeply religious but, sharing the prejudices of many English people at the time, they would certainly be appalled, and would use every possible argument against it. Gerard may well have taken pleasure in shocking his father, but he had a real fear of the pressure his parents could bring to bear. He told his friends of his momentous decision, but left his parents till last, so that the conflict would not be long drawn-out. They received a letter from him on 13 October telling them that he had thought long and hard about his decision and that it was irreversible. Their response was shocked incredulity, and they begged him to wait at least until he had taken his degree. His reply was to urge them to pray hard so that they too could see the light. Stubbornly holding to his decision, he was received into the Roman Catholic Church by Dr Newman on Sunday, 22 October 1866.

His position at Balliol was now a difficult one. The official line of the Catholic hierarchy was that Catholics should not study at Oxford or Cambridge because of their Church of England foundations. The University authorities, for their part, did not make it easy for Catholic undergraduates, fining them occasionally for going to Mass instead of to chapel. Nevertheless, Gerard persevered with his studies and in June 1867 was awarded a first-class degree. Dr Newman offered him a job as a teacher at the Birmingham Oratory, and in September he started work there. Newman had said that he would not find the work hard, but in fact he did. Teaching wore him down. He liked the boys but got on less well with his colleagues, and he was always tired and lacking in energy. He spent the Christmas holiday with his family as he had always done, his parents showing him a kindness and tolerance which he had not expected. He had already made up his mind to become a priest, but he did not relish telling them, particularly his mother.

At Easter 1868 he left the Oratory with no regrets. His intention now was not only to join the priesthood but to enter the Jesuit Order. This was to be a further and greater shock for his parents, since the Jesuits were both disliked and feared by the ordinary middle-class Englishman. The Society of Jesus, to give the Order its full title, had been founded by Ignatius Loyola in the sixteenth century, and its association in Elizabethan times with Spanish attempts to overthrow the English monarchy had engendered in many people an almost primitive loathing which persisted well into the nineteenth century. In becoming a Jesuit, Gerard would be debarred from all hope of an academic career or indeed from any involvement in the national life.

In May, he was interviewed for admission as a novice to the Society of Jesus, and soon afterwards learnt that he had been accepted. In three months he would begin his training, which was to be arduous and long. His parents realised that further argument was useless. They helped him take a month's holiday in Switzerland with a friend, where he climbed some of the lesser peaks and wrote a detailed account of the scenery in his journal. On 7 September, he went to Roehampton – then a pretty village five miles to the west of central London – to begin his probationary period as a Jesuit.

He was to be in residence at a large mansion set in substantial grounds known as Manresa House. The name derived from the town in Spain where Ignatius Loyola had, whilst living in a cave, devised the spiritual exercises on which the religious life of the Order was based. The induction process was a severe one, It was initially one of long periods of silence, punctuated by instruction on the poverty, chastity and obedience which was to be their lot. They had to learn to submit to their superiors, and to prepare themselves for the dislike and derision they might expect from the secular world. They then moved on to the so-called Long Retreat, which consisted of 30 days of prayer and meditation on death and divine judgement and heaven and hell and the tactics of the devil. It was designed to eliminate those who did not have the courage and perseverance to continue in the Order. Gerard thrived on it: it appealed to the innate masochism he had shown during his school-days. Whilst at Oxford, he had devised self-imposed penances to control his fleshly desires, and the fasting and silences he now endured were but an extension of these.

Before going to Manresa House, he had surrendered his pleasure in poetry. Fearing that it would come between him and his new spiritual life, he had burnt all his poems and had resolved to write no more. He even for a time gave up his joy in natural beauty, keeping his eyes to the ground to deny himself 'eye pleasure'.

Following successful completion of the Long Retreat, novices were accepted into the Order and their full training commenced, continuing until the age of thirty-three, thought to be the age at which Christ was crucified. They were then ready to be ordained as priests. The training years were spent in study, teaching, prayer and contemplation. They studied principally classics, mathematics, rhetoric, philosophy and theology. During this time, they did some teaching and in due course worked in parishes as assistants to the priest.

Although Gerard had given up writing poetry, he still retained his poetic sensibility, describing in his notebook the weather, cloud formations and details of plants and trees. He also continued to record unusual words and forms of speech. During his two-year Novitiate, he wrote to friends, particularly Robert Bridges, but saw little of them or of his family.

In his thinking and writing on natural beauty, he began to use the words 'inscape' and 'instress'. As scenery becomes a landscape when committed to canvas by a painter, so a particular entity, whether it be a person, a building or a flower, has a form or design which is unique to itself and which differentiates it from all other objects. It is this which Hopkins calls its inscape. An object's inscape is not comprehended at a single glance; it only becomes fully apparent from concentrated study by the observer. Instress, in essence, is the force which preserves the object's inscape and which unites it to the observer.

At the end of his Novitiate Hopkins took the requisite vows of poverty, chastity and obedience and was sent to Stonyhurst College, a Jesuit boarding school near Blackburn, Lancashire. Here he was to commence the second stage of his training, called the Philosophate, which was to last a further three years. Equipped with a new black gown, biretta and crucifix, he was, as he wrote to his mother, 'now bound to our Lord'. St Mary's Hall, the seminary where he was to live, was in the school grounds but set apart from it. He had a room of his own which gave him a view of the Pennine fells, purple with heather. He soon fell in love with the moors, dappled with light and shade, rain-swept and often shrouded in mist. It was at Stonyhurst that his reputation for eccentricity was established. He studied natural objects – be they flowers, trees, clouds or rocks – with a peculiar concentration, absorbing, as he put it, their inscape. His colleagues were amused to see him crouching on the rain-soaked paths intently examining the pebbles now glittering in the sunshine. His notebook was full of detailed descriptions of what he observed. Periodically, he practised the penance of what he called 'eye-custody', depriving himself of what to him was an exquisite pleasure.

A problem for him was that his joy in individual phenomena perceived by the senses seemed to take him away from the infinite and absolute. It could indeed be a mortal sin. It was in the works of John Duns Scotus which he read in the seminary library that he found the resolution of his dilemma. Scotus, a medieval scholar and divine, taught that the material world was a symbol of God, and thus the love of natural beauty was in fact an act of worship. The teaching of Duns Scotus was a relief and a release to Hopkins, and he studied him joyously, free from guilt. He came to revere the works of Scotus above those of Thomas Aquinas, who was the primary influence in Jesuit theology. This absorption in Scotus added further to Hopkins's reputation for eccentricity.

His moods were volatile at this time, and they continued to be so for the rest of his life. His feelings would swing from excited happiness to deep gloom. When depressed he was preoccupied with the fear of death; it was a fear intermingled with fascination. His health gradually deteriorated. He suffered from bouts of diarrhoea and from severe attacks of piles. Just before Christmas, 1872, he was sent home and there had an operation for piles from which he made only a slow recovery.

He received an occasional letter from Robert Bridges, who had qualified as a doctor and was working in a London hospital. Whilst at Stonyhurst, Gerard wrote him a long letter in which he teased him about his reactionary political views, saying that he himself was leaning towards communism. He felt it was a dreadful thing for the labouring people in a rich country to live a hard life without dignity, knowledge, comforts or delight, and he forecast an eventual revolution. Possibly as a consequence of this letter, Bridges did not write again for three years. Hopkins did not retain these views. At heart, he accepted the prevailing class system and, whilst he pitied the poor, his hopes for them were for the next world rather than this.

In August 1873, he was abruptly ordered to return to Manresa House for a year to teach English, Greek and Latin to the less well-educated novitiates. Here he had days off to see his family and friends, and could visit museums and art galleries. This posting was intended to help him recover his health, but by the end of the year he was complaining of tiredness and depression again. Although he still believed that his vocation prohibited him from writing poetry, he continued to fill his journal with jottings which might be worked up into poems. On holiday in Devon in the summer of 1874, he wrote of a night drive when he saw the night sky thick with stars; and one may think he used these notes three years later in the composition of one of his greatest poems, *The Starlight Night*.

In August 1874, he was directed to leave Manresa House and go to St Beuno's College in North Wales to undertake the final phase of his Jesuit training, the Theologate, which was to last three to four years. The College, situated high in the hills, enjoyed magnificent views of the Snowdon range. That the great Gothic-style house was cold and draughty worried Gerard little, for all around were magnificent gardens and lovely countryside. Here he was to enjoy the happiest years of his Jesuit life and to produce some of his finest poetry.

He warmed to the local people and yearned to learn Welsh and to convert them to Catholicism. One of his delights was to visit St Winefred's Well, which was just a few miles from the College. Not only did he feel drawn to the saint whose name it bore who died defending her chastity, he loved the sylvan surroundings of the well and its limpid water, which was believed to have healing properties. Hopkins, like Swinburne, had always loved water and swimming. He bathed in the well and was ecstatic about its clarity and aquamarine colouring. The well lived in his mind and five years later he attempted a verse drama about it and its legend, which he never completed. St Winefred is slain by a lustful prince whose advances she spurns. A spring gushes forth from where her dead body lies, forming a clear pool, and her father, St Bueno, cries:

> *Water, which keeps thy name (for not in a rock written,*
> *But in pale water, frail water, wild rash and reeling water,*
> *That will not wear a print, that will not stain a pen,*
> *Thy venerable record, virgin, is recorded).*
> *Here to this holy well shall pilgrimages be,*
> *And not from purple Wales only nor from elmy England,*
> *But from beyond seas, Erin, France and Flanders, everywhere,*
> *Pilgrims, still pilgrims, more pilgrims, still more poor pilgrims.*

Early in December 1875, accounts began to appear in the newspapers of the wreck at night in a snowstorm of a German ship called *Deutschland*, on a sand-bank known as the Kentish Knock near the Thames estuary. Gerard Hopkins read these accounts and was both fascinated and horrified by them. The vessel had been bound from Bremen in Germany to New York. The suffering of the passengers and crew, some sixty of whom were drowned, was terrible. But what added further pathos for Gerard was that five of those who perished were Franciscan nuns who, exiled from Germany, were on their way to a new life in the United States. The story he read in *The Times* was particularly evocative, picturing the ship fast on the sand-bank and becoming slowly water-logged. The crew and passengers were on deck or on the roof of the wheel-house or clinging to the rigging, exposed all night to the raging storm and the bitter cold. The five nuns were described as holding hands with their leader, a tall, gaunt woman crying out continually *O Christ come quickly*, until eventually they all perished. The vessel took more than 24 hours to sink and, because of the severity of the weather, a belated attempt at rescue was only possible shortly before it foundered.

Hopkins mentioned his concern over the shipwreck to the Rector of the College, who said he wished someone could write a poem on the subject, Perhaps the Rector realised that this would inspire Hopkins, and so it did. Three years later he wrote in a letter, '*On this hint I set to work . . . I long had haunting my ear the echo of a new rhythm which now I realised on paper.*' He felt absolved from his vow to write no more poetry and settled down to his task. It was to be a long one, since he could only compose in the interval between lectures and discussions, and the chill and the flickering gaslight in his room did not help. Just how long the poem took him is not known, but it is probable that it was not completed until the summer of 1876.

He began the poem as a simple account of a tragic event, but it developed into an ode of 280 lines encompassing a dramatic religious experience of his own, reflections on the suffering of man and his relationship with God and his own hope that one day England would return to the Catholic fold. It may seem strange that a major poem of such length and originality could spring so suddenly from the mind of a man who had written no poetry for seven years. But although he had imposed upon hmself poetic silence for so long, his mind had been consumed with words and word-play, with descriptions of natural beauty, with experiments with rhymes and rhythms. His study of the Welsh language too had led him to new twists of speech, notably the compression of meaning by the omission of parts of speech such as prepositions.

It is of little use coming to the poem with preconceived ideas of regularity of metre or conventional word order. Much of it is a torrent of words, tangled and twisted, breathless and incoherent. Its form is loosely allied to the Pindaric Ode, and is written in stanzas of eight lines of widely varying length and rhythm. Hopkins called it sprung rhythm. With the customary metre of poetry, a regular number of syllables is counted in each line; but with sprung rhythm, the scanning is not done with syllables but with stresses. There can be a varying number of syllables if the stresses, which may comprise more than one syllable, are regular. As Hopkins pointed out, some nursery rhymes are composed in sprung rhythm. The lines sound rhythmically regular though the number of syllables in them may vary. For example:

> Ding dong bell,
> Pussy's in the well.
> Who put her in?
> Little Johnny thin.

The first line has three syllables, the second five, the third four and the fifth five: yet it all sounds regularly rhythmic. The modern reader will find little strange in this; but what he may find difficult at first is the grammatical construction of many of Hopkins's lines: the truncation of sentences, the reversal of the normal position of words, the use of hyphenated compound nouns which serve as powerful adjectives, the employment of unusual words, some of them little used or obsolete, the cavalier use of parts of speech, with nouns used as verbs or adjectives and adjectives becoming nouns or verbs, the joining of one word with another to make a completely new adjective or adverb. All these devices heighten the excitement of his poetry and introduce a new freshness of vision. He does not intend to be obscure: for him the meaning is crystal-clear, and it can become so to us if we read and re-read his words, and even chant them to ourselves to the rhythm he intended.

There is nothing obscure about the original first four lines of *The Wreck of the Deutschland*, which as he developed the poem, appear in stanza 12:

> On Saturday sailed from Bremen,
> American-outward-bound,
> Take settler and seamen, tell men with women,
> Two hundred souls in the round —

But the next four lines have to be searched for meaning. It is as if, the placid tenor of his religious life being overthrown, Hopkins flings himself into a maelstrom of words:

O Father, not under thy feathers nor ever as guessing
The goal was a shoal, of a fourth the doom to be drowned;
Yet did the dark side of the bay of thy blessing
Not vault them, the millions of rounds of thy mercy not reeve even
  them in?

The passengers and crew were, they thought, under the protection of a merciful God and never guessed that they were fated to be wrecked on a sandbank and a quarter of their number drowned. Yet even in this disaster, did not God's mercy surround them? he asks.

Stanza 13 continues the narrative, evoking the fury of the snowstorm and the terror of the tumultuous seas:

Into the snows she sweeps,
Hurling the haven behind,
The Deutschland, on Sunday; and so the sky keeps,
For the infinite air is unkind,
And the sea flint-flake, black-backed in the regular blow,
Sitting Eastnortheast, in cursed quarter, the wind;
Wiry and white-fiery and whirlwind-swivellèd snow
Spins to the widow-making unchilding unfathering deeps.

The next three stanzas tell of the wrecking of the ship, its slow water-logging and the climb to the rigging of some of the crew and passengers. One sailor, secured to the rigging, tries to save a woman on the deck, but loses his grip and, battered by the sea, swings helplessly on the rope round his waist.

At the end of stanza 17, the tall leader of the five Franciscan nuns is introduced:

Night roared, with the heart-break hearing a heart-broke rabble,
The woman's wailing, the crying of a child without check –
Till a lioness arose breasting the babble,
A prophetess towered in the tumult, a virginal tongue told.

In the next stanza, Hopkins suddenly breaks off the story and addresses himself. It is as if he realises that his poem is not to be just a disaster tale, but is to widen into an examination of human suffering

91

and a justification of God's part in it. He takes himself to task for enjoying the unfolding tragedy and his selfish juvenile pleasure in rendering it in verse:

> *Never-eldering revel and river of youth,*
> *What can it be, this glee? the good you have there of your own?*

In subsequent stanzas he returns to the main story, in the centre of which for him are the five nuns exiled from Germany, which makes Deutschland, the name of the stricken vessel, *double a desperate name.* Duality is an important theme in the poem. Gertrude, a Catholic saint, came from the same town as Martin Luther, the Protestant reformer, whom Hopkins regards as *beast of the waste wood.* Abel and Cain both had Eve for their mother, yet one was a murderer and the other loved of God. Jesus is the *martyr-master*, both martyr on the cross and master of the world. To men the blizzard is terrible, but to Christ the *storm-flakes were scroll-leaved flowers, lily showers.*

The nuns he sees as symbols of suffering Christ: that there were five of them symbolises His five wounds. Later on, in stanza 30, the leading nun is seen as symbolising the Virgin Mary, whose feast-day is 8 December, the day following the shipwreck. He ponders on the tall leading nun calling to Christ to come quickly. The New Testament tells of the disciples in a storm on the Sea of Galilee crying to Christ to rescue them; but the nun's cry is different: she is aching to be with Jesus because she loves Him. In stanza 26, Hopkins conjures up a picture of paradise with its *jay-blue heavens.* His words become chaotic and incoherent in the next two stanzas, as he imagines the thoughts of the nun in *wind's burly and beat of endragonèd seas.* He conceives her as looking through the pain and horror to eternal bliss, as Jesus did on the cross. As though the poet were present at the scene, he calls on God:

> *Do, deal, lord it with living and dead;*
> *Let him ride, her pride, in his triumph, despatch and have done with*
> *his doom there.*

The nun is rewarded in heaven for her suffering, but what of the non-Catholics on the ship – *comfortless unconfessed*? One's heart need not bleed for them, says Hopkins in stanza 31, for maybe the shock of the disaster will turn them back to God: for *lovely - felicitous Providence* is present even in the tempest.

The last four stanzas are a hymn to the might of the Almighty. Stanza 32 sets the tone:

> *I admire thee, master of the tides,*
> *Of the Yore-flood, of the year's fall;*
> *The recurb and the recovery of the gulf's sides,*
> *The girth of it and the wharf of it and the wall;*
> *Stanching, quenching ocean of a motionable mind;*
> *Ground of being, and granite of it: past all*
> *Grasp God, throned behind*
> *Death with a sovereignty that heeds but hides, bodes but abides;*

The *Yore-flood* is presumably the flood which Noah survived. God is master of all the tides and their endless movements. Above all, He exists beyond death and cares for man but allows him free will.

The last stanza brings the poem to its climax, with Hopkins urging the leading nun, rewarded in heaven, to intercede with God on behalf of *rare-dear Britain* to bring her back to the true Catholic faith.

But what of the poem's first eleven stanzas? In essence, they are Hopkins's reflections on the wreck of the *Deutschland* and the terrible suffering of its passengers and crew. They were written after the graphic narrative, but are placed first in the poem because they are so personal to the poet himself. His spiritual desolation has a parallel in the suffering of the five nuns: they were exiles and outcasts, as he felt himself to be, and like them he is suffering for his faith. No doubt he was meditating on this sense of rejection during the long silences of his Novitiate. He had then to reconcile the torment men seemed to undergo at the hands of a beneficient God, and this need was revived by the suffering of the good and innocent nuns.

No part of the poem is easy to comprehend at first or even second perusal. Repeated reading enables the drift of the poet's words to be absorbed, and this is particulary true of these opening stanzas. Stanza 1 expresses his submission to his Maker:

Thou mastering me
God! giver of breath and bread;
World's strand, sway of the sea;
Lord of living and dead.

In stanza 2, he evokes the awe and horror he felt as a novice priest, meditating alone on his knees upon the might of an omnipotent, infinite Being:

Thou heardst me truer than tongue confess
Thy terror, O Christ, O God;
Thou knowest the walls, altar and hour and night:
The swoon of a heart that the sweep and the hurl of thee trod
Hard down, with a horror of height:
And the midriff astrain with leaning of, laced with fire of stress.

In the third and fourth stanzas, his spiritual experience is too deep for ordinary expression. Instead we have to intuit what he is feeling from an agonised torrent of words. He reaches out to God in one flash of comprehension, fleeing, as he puts it, *with a fling of the heart to the heart of the Host.* He is sand in an hour-glass; he is water both still and falling. Falling water is like Christ's gift of mercy to humanity.

Some aspects of God are comprehensible to him in the wonders of the physical world. In stanza 5, in joyous humility he acknowledges the stars, so far away, and the starlight by which God is wafted towards the earth; he feels God's glory in thunder, recognizing Him in the dappled-with-damson sunset. God is behind all the splendour and wonders of the world, the poet tells us; but to comprehend Him even a little, He must be studied and dwelt upon in every aspect, so that His essence is real and is united with us, even if only occasionally do we understand Him.

The sixth and seventh stanzas assert that we cannot truly comprehend God from the world's beauty, nor from its terrors either. True understanding resides in Christ and His crucifixion: in His sacrifice for our sins. Unaware, whether we wish it or not, our faith as a:

> . . . . *lush-kept, plush-capped sloe*
> *Will, mouthed to flesh-burst,*
> *Gush! flush the man, the being with it, sour or sweet,*
> *Brim, in a flash, full!*

Hopkins calls to God to use storms and wreckings to turn men's hearts to him. He praises Him:

> Beyond saying sweet, past telling of tongue,
> Thou art lightning and love. . . .

He urges Him to forge His will on man with fire and anvil; or to master him with the beauty of spring; or to bestow on him a sudden, dazzling conversion as He did with St Paul, or a slow and gradual coming to faith, as with St Augustine. Before all else, God the King must be adored, he says. We mortals, though we like to forget it, are but dust:

> *Flesh falls within sight of us, we, though our flower the same,*
> *Wave with the meadow, forget that there must*
> *The sour scythe cringe, and the blear share come.*

Despite its difficulties, the poem is probably one of the greatest in the English language. It is not comprehended easily, but repays considerable study. Hopkins knew he had written something very special, but, naive as ever, he expected others to recognise this too, Inevitably, they did not. He read part of the poem to a colleague who told him that scarcely a line of it was comprehensible. Undeterred, he sent the completed poem to the Jesuit periodical, *The Month*. The editor tried to view it favourably but found it unreadable. He passed it to another reader who observed that trying to understand it had given him a headache. Hopkins had marked the stresses over some of the words to help with the scanning, but this added to the reader's confusion. The editor felt that he could not publish something that he himself could not understand, and so the poem, to Hopkins's dismay, was rejected. As with Beethoven, some of whose music was initially received with incomprehension, Hopkins was composing for future generations rather than his own.

He hoped that Robert Bridges at least would give him some encouragement when he sent the poem to his friend some two years later, but he was disappointed once more. The religious content of the work repelled Bridges; he hated any kind of self-revelation in poetry; and in any case to him the poem was largely unreadable. He replied to Gerard telling him that he would never read it again. Many years later, in 1918, when he came to prepare his friend's poems for publication, he seemed to appreciate that the poem was a great one, but nevertheless described it as a metrical experiment, which because of its difficulty stood like a dragon at the gate to Hopkins's poetry.

Since then, many people have attempted to mitigate the menace of the dragon by explaining and interpreting *The Wreck of the Deutschland*. Public taste has moved on: variations of metre are no longer a difficulty, nor is an eccentric approach to grammar and syntax. Obscurity has been acceptable from Robert Browning's time, and indeed more recently has been considered a virtue. Thus the poem is much more in tune with modern ideas of poetry. The way through its obscurity is to read and re-read it until its meaning percolates through and its breathless, seemingly incoherent language and syntax become a joy rather than a stumbling-block.

Hopkins never again wrote such a long poem, full of what he conceded were 'oddnesses'. However, after his long self-imposed poetic silence was broken, after the dam had burst in a torrent of words and images, his full genius for a brief period had full rein. During the early months of 1877, he was studying hard for an examination in theology. He also had to contend with the fierce cold, against which the heating of the College was quite inadequate. He was feeling extremely tired, but nevertheless managed to write two wonderful sonnets on consecutive days, both of them glorying in the power of God. They were the first sonnets he had written for twelve years, and he sent them to his mother for her birthday.

One of them was called *God's Grandeur*, in which he portrayed the beauty and magnificence of God's world shining through the squalor of mankind's activities:

> *The world is charged with the grandeur of God.*
> *It will flame out, like shining from shook foil;*
> *It gathers to a greatness, like the ooze of oil*

Crushed. Why do men then not now reck his rod?
Generations have trod, have trod, have trod;
And all is seared with trade; bleared, smeared with toil;
And wears a man's smudge and shares man's smell: the soil
Is bare now, nor can foot feel, being shod.

And for all this, nature is never spent;
There lives the dearest freshness deep down things;
And though the last lights off the black West went
Oh, morning, at the brown brink eastward, springs –
Because the Holy Ghost over the bent
World broods with warm breast and with ah! bright wings.

In the second sonnet, *The Starlight Night*, he was again looking at the sky to discern God's glory, though this time it was a clear starry night. It is a poem filled with ecstasy and exclamation marks – sixteen of them!

Look at the stars! look, look up at the skies!
O look at all the fire-folk sitting in the air!
The bright boroughs, the circle-citadels there!
Down in dim woods the diamond delves! the elves' -eyes!
The grey lawns cold where gold, where quickgold lies!
Wind-beat whitebeam! airy abeles set on a flare!
Flake-doves sent floating forth at a farmyard scare!
Ah well! it is all a purchase, all is a prize.

Buy then! bid then! – What? – Prayer, patience, alms, vows.
Look, look: a May-mess, like on orchard boughs!
Look! March-bloom, like on mealed-with-yellow sallows!
These are indeed the barn; withindoors house
The shocks. This piece-bright paling shuts the spouse
Christ home, Christ and his mother and all his hallows.

The poem is brilliant, effusive reaction to the starlit skies. Images tumble over each other in breathless exuberance. The whitebeam is a tree with white undersides to its leaves; albeles are white poplars; flake-doves floating at a farmyard scare are the white feathers of

97

panic-stricken fowls; prayer, patience, alms, vows are the price we pay for this splendour, which is like an orchard, snowy with spring blossom. Christ, he concludes, is enclosed within the stars, along with His virgin mother and all His saints.

Despite his weariness, Gerard continued to mine his new-found vein of poetic riches. During May 1877, he wrote four more sonnets, all of them on the theme of the transcendence of God in the loveliness of Nature. One of them, *The Windhover*, he regarded as the best thing he ever wrote. Walking in the countryside, he is enraptured by the sight of a windhover, or falcon, in flight. In describing it, he takes more than his usual liberties with syntax, but the result is breathtaking:

> *I caught this morning morning's minion, kingdom of daylight's*
>   *dauphin, dapple-dawn-drawn Falcon, in his riding*
> *Of the rolling level underneath him steady air, and striding*
> *High there, how he rung upon the rein of a wimpling wing*
> *In his ecstasy! then off, off forth on swing,*
> *As a skate's heel sweeps smooth on a bow-bend: the hurl and gliding*
> *Rebuffed the big wind. My heart in hiding*
> *Stirred for a bird, – the achieve of, the mastery of the thing!*
>
> *Brute beauty and valour and act, oh, air, pride, plume, here*
> *Buckle! AND the fire that breaks from thee then, a billion*
> *Times told lovelier, more dangerous, O my chevalier!*
>
> *No wonder of it: sheer plod makes plough down sillion*
> *Shine, and blue-black embers, ah my dear,*
> *Fall, gall themselves, and gash gold-vermilion.*

In using the word, *dauphin* in the second line of the sonnet, Hopkins is thinking of the French prince in Shakespeare's *Henry V*, who feels his mettlesome horse is like a hawk trotting the air. He maintains the horse-riding metaphor when referring to the falcon being *run upon the rein*; that is, circling round as if on a long training-rein. He longs to be like the bird with its splendid mastery of the sky; but realises he must *buckle* (or crush) his admiration for its *brute beauty and valour*, for far lovelier is the beauty of Christ, whom he calls *my chevalier*, or gallant knight. Hard, unremitting toil on the land creates the shining loveliness of the ploughed furrows, for which he uses the archaic word, *sillion*. A dying fire creates gorgeous colours in its embers: and, in the same way, Christ's crucifixion gave rise to unparalleled spiritual beauty.

Hopkins's sonnet *Spring* is simpler in that he does not transmute his joy in the natural world into something spiritual and infinite: it is sufficient to see God in the beauty of nature:

> *Nothing is so beautiful as spring –*
> *When weeds, in wheels, shoot long and lovely and lush;*
> *Thrush's eggs look little low heavens, and thrush*
> *Through the echoing timber does so rinse and wring*
> *The ear, it strikes like lightnings to hear him sing;*
> *The glassy peartree leaves and blooms, they brush*
> *The descending blue; that blue is all in a rush*
> *With richness; the racing lambs have fair their fling.*

He concludes by saying it is like the Garden of Eden, and we should enjoy it *before it cloud, Christ, lord, and sour with sinning.*

In his sonnet, *In the Valley of the Elwy*, he draws a similar moral. Thinking of some people who once were kind to him, he relates his feelings to the Welsh countryside:

> *Lovely the woods, waters, meadows, combes, vales*
> *All the air things wear that build this world of Wales.*

He reflects that all people living there are not so lovely, and asks God to remedy man's imperfections. The fourth sonnet of this brief spell of poetic inspiration was *The Sea and the Skylark*. In it, Hopkins recalls a moment near Rhyl when he hears in the moonlight the sound of the tide tumbling against the shore and, at the same time, the song of an ascending skylark:

> *Left hand, off land, I hear the lark ascend,*
> *His rash-fresh re-winded new-skeinèd score*
> *In crisps of curl off wild winch whirl, and pour*
> *And pelt music, till none's to spill nor spend.*

Here we have the lark's song pictured as a skein of silk falling from the sky, unwinding from a reel or winch as the bird lets it fall in wild glee until all is spent. As in other lines of Hopkins's poetry, there is a repressed sexual analogy, unconscious no doubt, but adding to the tension of the poetry. Hopkins often expressed his love for Christ in near-erotic terms, as indeed did Christina Rossetti, who also repressed her physical needs for higher spiritual experience. The glorious sound of sea and birdsong, says the poet, puts to shame the sordid life of *the shallow and frail town* of Rhyl.

In writing a poem called *Penmaen Pool* for the visitors' book at an inn whilst on holiday in Barmouth in North Wales, Hopkins returned to something like the simplicity of his early poems at Oxford:

> *You'll dare the Alp? You'll dart the skiff?*
> *Each sport has here its tackle and tool:*
> *Come, plant the staff by Cadair cliff;*
> *Come, swing the sculls on Penmaen Pool.*

But his exciting freedom with diction and syntax was not to be denied, and he went on to praise the local beer in the new Hopkins style:

> *And ever, if bound here hardest home,*
> *You've parlour-pastime left and (who'll*
> *Not honour it?) ale like goldy foam*
> *That frocks an oar in Penmaen Pool.*

By the beginning of March 1877, Gerard had passed his examination in theology and was looking foward to staying on at St Bueno's for a fourth year, but this was not to be. After his final exam in July, it was decided that his performance was not good enough to qualify him for the final year. This was the first academic set-back of his life, and he felt it keenly. He could still be ordained as a Jesuit priest, but the most prestigious teaching posts in the Order would be denied him. During August, as yet unaware of the decision, he was in an exalted frame of mind, and the two great poems of this period reflect this. *Pied Beauty* has probably appeared in more anthologies than any other of his works. His notebooks are full of depictions of chequered, dappled countryside; and they contain too lists of the farming tools of rural England, which he delighted in recording. In *Pied Beauty*, he celebrates all these as aspects of God's magnificence. The poem is in curtal sonnet form, comprising only eleven instead of the normal fourteen lines:

> *Glory be to God for dappled things –*
> *For skies of couple-colour as a brinded cow;*
> *For rose-moles in all stipple upon trout that swim;*
> *Fresh-firecoal chestnut-falls; finches' wings;*
> *Landscape plotted and pierced – fold, fallow, and plough;*
> *And all trades, their gear and tackle and trim.*
> *All things counter, original, spare, strange;*
> *Whatever is fickle, freckled (who knows how?)*
> *With swift, slow; sweet, sour; adazzle, dim;*
> *He fathers-forth whose beauty is past change:*
> > *Praise him.*

The other poem of his happy August period was *Hurrahing in Harvest*, which expressses an exuberant outburst of joy, which he experienced whilst walking back to St Bueno's from fishing in the river Elwy:

> *Summer ends now; now, barbarous in beauty, the stooks arise*
> *Around; up above, what wind-walks! what lovely behaviour*
> *Of silk-sack clouds! has wilder, wilful-wavier*
> *Meal-drift moulded ever and melted across skies?*
>
> *I walk, I lift up, I lift up heart, eyes,*
> *Down all that glory in the heavens to glean our Saviour;*
> *And, eyes, heart, what looks, what lips yet gave you a*
> *Rapturous love's greeting of realer, of rounder replies?*
>
> *And the azurous hung hills are his world-wielding shoulder*
> *Majestic – as a stallion stalwart, very-violet-sweet! –*
> *These things, these things were here and but the beholder*
> *Wanting; which two when they once meet,*
> *The heart rears wings bold and bolder*
> *And hurls for him, O half hurls earth for him off under his feet.*

Natural beauty, he reflects, exists to be seen and appreciated by man. And when he sees God's glory in nature, the effect is tumultuous and *half hurls earth for him off under his feet.*

After a short holiday with his family, Gerard returned briefly to St Bueno's, and on Sunday, 23 September 1877, at the age of thirty-four, he was ordained a Roman Catholic priest in the Jesuit Order. It was the culmination of nine years' training, dedication and spiritual development. By now he knew that he would be leaving St Bueno's, where he had been so happy. Before he departed he had a circumcision operation, not as a religious rite but for urgent medical reasons. He soon recovered and then was posted to Mount St Mary's College in Chesterfield, Derbyshire.

He was not very well there, suffering once more from diarrhoea; but he was well enough to write some poetry, and one of the poems from his brief stay was *The Loss of the Eurydice*. The *Eurydice* was a naval training ship which foundered off the Isle of Wight in a sudden storm on 24 March 1878, losing all but two of her crew of three hundred. As with the *Deutschland* poem, he started by writing lines which he eventually placed in the body of the poem. These concern a young, drowned sailor whom he tends to idealise, and whose death epitomises all that was lost in the terrible tragedy:

> *They say who saw one sea-corpse cold*
> *He was all of lovely manhood mould,*
> *Every inch a tar,*
> *Of the best we boast our sailors are.*
>
> *Look, foot to forelock, how all things suit! he*
> *Is strung by duty, is strained to beauty,*
> *And brown-as-dawning-skinned*
> *With brine and shine and whirling wind.*
>
> *O his nimble finger, his gnarled grip!*
> *Leagues, leagues of seamanship*
> *Slumber in these forsaken*
> *Bones, this sinew, and will not waken.*

The entire poem consists of four-lined verses like these, written in sprung-rhythm, so that each verse can be read straight through in one entity. The description of events is not as moving as in the *Deutschland* poem, and there are no stricken nuns to carry the emotional burden of the disaster, but the advent of the terrible storm arriving out of a bright sky is certainly dramatic:

> *And you were a liar, O blue March day.*
> *Bright sun lanced fire in the heavenly bay;*
> *But what black Boreas wrecked her? he*
> *Came equipped, deadly-electric,*
>
> *A beetling, baldbright cloud thorough England*
> *Riding: there did storms not mingle? and*
> *Hailropes hustle and grind their*
> *Heavengravel? wolfsnow, worlds of it, wind there?*
>
> *Now Carisbrook keep goes under in gloom:*
> *Now it overvaults Appledurcombe;*
> *Now near by Ventnor town*
> *It hurls, hurls off Boniface Down.*

Boreas, in Greek myth, is the god of the north wind; and Hopkins perhaps unwittingly reveals here his classical education, for in theory he believed that classical allusions had no place in poetry. We have to imagine a dominating, clearly-defined cloud sweeping down from the north across England, driven by great winds and throwing down hail so thick that it looks like ropes hanging from the sky, and hailstones so large that they are like gravel from the heavens. The snow which follows is like a wolf-pack enveloping all in a white swirling world of its own.

The ship's captain goes down with his ship *through the champ-white water-in-a-wallow*: an ordinary man, according to Hopkins, who, doing his duty when called upon, *doffs all, drives full for righteousness*. From evoking the horrors of the shipwreck, Hopkins goes on to relate the event to the loss, as he sees it, of England to Protestantism: it is as hard for him to understand why God tolerated that as to comprehend His purpose in permitting the Eurydice to sink. He submitted the poem to *The Month* but, like the *Deutschland* poem, it

103

was rejected. He sent it to Robert Bridges, but again received scant encouragement.

He and Bridges were beginning to correspond more frequently. Bridges may not have appreciated Gerard's poetry, but he kept the copies sent to him; if he had not done so, they would never have reached the public eye. Gerard's vocation prevented him developing close friendships in the flesh and he had to rely on letters.

He was moved to Stonyhurst College again for a few months, and it was while he was there that he wrote on impulse to a fellow-poet, Richard Dixon, who had been a master at Cholmeley's School for a short time while he had been there. That he was drawn to Dixon's poetry is surprising since it is conventional verse in the mock-medieval genre which Tennyson and Dante Gabriel Rossetti had popularised. Dixon had in his youth been a member of the Pre-Raphaelite Brotherhood, but at the time Hopkins wrote to him was a middle-aged Anglican clergyman. He commiserated with the public's neglect of Canon Dixon's verse, though there is little doubt that he was expressing too his own feelings about the lack of interest in his own work. He might say that Christ's approval was all that mattered, but deep-down he felt the rejection of his contemporaries quite strongly. He kept up a correspondence with Dixon for the rest of his life.

After a few weeks at Stonyhurst Hopkins was on the move again, this time to London to assist a parish priest. The church, in Farm Street, Mayfair, was a fashionable one with a wealthy congregation. Father Gallwey, whom Gerard had known and liked at both Manresa House and St Bueno's, was the Rector there. To Gerard's superiors the posting must have seemed an ideal one for him, but again they were to be disappointed. The unworldly, shy Jesuit did not go down well with the sophisticated congregation. He had not been a very effective school-teacher, but as a preacher he was even worse. One of the three sermons he gave there was particularly unsuited to his audience. A sermon of his at St Bueno's when he compared the Sea of Galilee to a human ear, had had his colleagues in near hysterics; but to compare the Holy Church and its seven sacraments to a cow with seven full udders, as he did at Farm Street, was to the fashionable ladies of the congregation not a joke but an exhibition of bad taste.

By September 1878 he had been moved, as assistant priest, to the

Catholic parish church of St Aloysius in Oxford. He had been happy in Oxford as an undergraduate, but now things were very different. He had no ready circle of friends and was a member of a sect which was viewed with suspicion if not outright dislike. What was more, he never took to the ebullient Father Parkinson for whom he worked. He wrote to Bridges, dejectedly, telling him that he was unlikely to write much more poetry for lack of time, and also because love was the great inspirer of poetry and he was permitted to love but Christ, and the exploitation of such love might be sacrilegious.

In this, however, he was wrong, and the ten months he spent in Oxford were poetically productive. Robert Bridges had published anonymously a pamphlet containing a sequence of sonnets, called *The Growth of Love*. Surprisingly, despite their friendship, Gerard had known nothing of Bridges' poetry, and, when he read the poems, he wrote praising them. He also told Bridges that he himself had two sonnets in preparation. One of these was *Duns Scotus's Oxford*, in which he recalls that the great theologian had once walked the Oxford streets more than three hundred years before. He laments the *base and brickish skirt* now marring the town which had once been a:

> *Towery city and branchy between towers;*
> *Cuckoo-echoing, bell-swarmèd, lark-charmèd, rook-racked,*
> *river-rounded.*

The other sonnet was in praise of the composer Henry Purcell, whose music Hopkins loved and whom he hoped was not damned because he was not a Catholic. He likens Purcell to a great storm-fowl who walks *the thunder-purple seabeach*, and then takes off, spreading its wings showing *plumèd purple-of thunder*, which *fans fresh our wits with wonder*.

While at Oxford he also wrote *Binsey Poplars*. In the course of one of his many solitary walks, he saw near Godstow that the aspens which flanked the river had been cut down. This apparently wanton destruction inspired him to express feelings as fresh and meaningful now as they were then:

My aspens dear, whose airy cages quelled,
Quelled or quenched in leaves the leaping sun,
All felled, felled, are all felled;
Of a fresh and following folded rank
Not spared, not one
That dandled a sandalled
Shadow that swam or sank
On meadow and river and wind-wandering weed-winding bank.

O if we but knew what we do
When we delve or hew —
Hack and rack the growing green!
Since country is so tender
To touch, her being so slender,
That, like this sleek and seeing ball
But prick will make no eye at all,
Where we, even where we mean
To mend her we end her,
When we hew or delve:
After-comers cannot guess the beauty been.
Ten or twelve, only ten or twelve
Strokes of havoc unselve
The sweet especial scene,
Rural scene, a rural scene,
Sweet especial rural scene.

There was an army barracks at Cowley, a suburb of Oxford, and one of the young soldiers stationed there asked Gerard if he would give him his first Communion, which he duly did. He was struck by the beauty and innocence of the lad, and expressed his feelings about him in a poem, written in July 1879, called *The Bugler's First Communion*. The reader may sense a homoerotic element in this poem, dressed though it is in Christian language. Gerard hopes that the communion wafer, the *leaf-light*, will endow the soldier with courage, truth and modesty and *breathing bloom of a chastity in mansex fine*, and he asks the soldier's guardian angel to guard him well. He expresses his joy at visiting the soldiers in the barracks and his pleasure at the influence he has over them:

106

How it does my heart good, visiting at that bleak hill,
When limber, liquid youth, that to all I teach
Yields tender as a pushed peach,
Hies headstrong to its wellbeing of a self-wise self-will!

He has faith in the eucharist, the consecrated elements of bread and wine:

Nothing else is like it, no, not all so strains
Us: fresh youth fretted in a bloomfall all portending
That sweet's sweeter ending;
Realm both Christ is heir to and there reigns.

Despite his prayers, Gerard is not over-sure that the young soldier will remain chaste; and when he sent the poem to Bridges, who questioned its good taste, he observed that he half-hoped the soldier would be killed in Afghanistan, where his regiment was going, so that he might escape the temptations of the world. Such a line of thought is not easy to accept, and one may think that, despite his prayers and penances, for Hopkins the lusts of the flesh were not easily subdued.

Later in the year he attended a wedding, and in *At the Wedding March*, he expresses the hope that the marriage bed will be graced with *lissome scions, sweet scions,* meaning heirs; and then lamenting, one may think for all the joys in life his vocation has denied him, he turns to Christ, the only person to whom he may be wedded. About that time he preached a sermon which made it clear that he envisaged Jesus with a physical body. He saw him as well-built, with beautiful features, auburn hair parted in the middle, curls round his ears and a long forked beard. His bearing, he said, was majestic and his limbs lovely and lissome. He went on to say that he looked forward to seeing the matchless beauty of the Lord's body in heaven. His religion permitted him such fantasies and he gloried in them.

Never happy in Oxford, Hopkins welcomed a move to Bedford Leigh, near Manchester, after only ten months. But this proved only a staging post on the way to Liverpool, where he was given the position of junior curate at the church of St Francis Xavier. Owing to the influx of Irish immigrants, Liverpool had a vast Catholic population, and the church's congregation was an enormous one. His short stay at Bedford Leigh had led Gerard to believe that his vocation lay in ministering to the urban poor, and initially he welcomed the Liverpool posting. He was rapidly disillusioned. He did not enhance St Francis Xavier's high reputation for compelling sermons. Once more he misjudged the needs of his listeners, treating them to flights of poetic rhetoric instead of the solid gospel-teaching to which they were used. Of urban poor there were plenty and the squalor of their lives had reached a level of degradation which Gerard had never seen or even imagined. Around the church there stretched appalling slums, and it was with the inhabitants of these that Gerard worked. He soon came to loathe the violence and drunkenness of the filthy spittle-strewn streets. He witnessed a horse show and mentally contrasted the proud and handsome beasts with the squalid besmirched appearance of those who watched them. He wrote to Bridges, in something like despair, that the drunkards went on drinking, the filthy remained filthy, and he was too fatigued to do any writing. Human nature, he added, was so inveterate that he wished he had seen the last of it.

During 1880, however, he did write two remarkable poems. One of them, *Spring and Fall*, was composed after one of his periodic visits to say Mass in a private chapel of a country house in the village of Lydiate, to the north of Liverpool. He addressed the poem to a young girl, though he had no particular child in mind. Goldengrove was a wooded estate near Lydiate where he used to stroll:

Margaret, are you grieving
Over Goldengrove unleaving?
Leaves like the things of man, you
With your fresh thoughts care for, can you?
Ah! as the heart grows older
It will come to such sights colder
By and by, nor spare a sigh
Though worlds of wanwood leafmeal lie;
And yet you will weep and know why.
Now no matter, child, the name:
Sorrow's springs are the same.
Nor mouth had, no nor mind expressed
What heart heard of, ghost guessed:
It is the blight man was born for,
It is Margaret you mourn for.

The simplicity of the poem has made it a popular anthology piece. The child laments the fall and rotting of the woodland leaves; but she will, the poet says, have more profound things to weep over as she grows older. Mankind is fated to wither and die, and it is herself for which she really mourns. Some critics, looking deeply into the poem, have suggested that Hopkins was mourning as much for himself as for *Margaret*.

His other outstanding Liverpool poem was *Felix Randal*, a sonnet about a once strong and healthy farrier whom Hopkins used to visit *as sickness broke him*. The last six lines are full of pathos:

> *This seeing the sick endears them to us, us to it endears.*
> *My tongue had taught thee comfort, touch had quenched thy tears,*
> *Thy tears that touched my heart, child, Felix, poor Felix Randal;*
>
> *How far from then forethought of, all thy more boisterous years,*
> *When thou at the random grim forge, powerful amidst peers,*
> *Didst fettle for the great grey drayhorse his bright and battering sandal!*

In August 1881, Gerard was directed to Glasgow to help with parish duties for a fortnight. He was asked to stay on until the end of September and was glad to do so. He never returned to Liverpool and dreaded ever being sent there again. Glasgow had slums quite as fearsome, but he found the people more cheerful and friendly. He had the opportunity to take a short trip to the Scottish mountains, and he enjoyed a walk along the shores of Loch Lomond. It was there that he wrote *Inversnaid*, in which he invoked the joy and beauty of the wild scenery in a spate of words and racy rhythm:

> *This darksome burn, horseback brown*
> *His rollrock highroad roaring down,*
> *In coop and in comb the fleece of his foam*
> *Flutes and low to the lake falls home.*
>
> *A wind-puff bonnet of fawn-froth*
> *Turns and twindles over the broth*
> *Of a pool so pitchblack, fell-frowning.*
> *It rounds and rounds Despair to drowning.*

Dogged with dew, dappled with dew
Are the groins of the braes that the brook treads through,
Wiry heathpacks, flitches of fern,
And the beadbonny ash that sits over the burn.

What would the world be, once bereft
Of wet and of wilderness? Let them be left,
O let them be left, wildness and wet;
Long live the weeds and the wilderness yet.

The last verse might well have been written for present-day conservationists to quote.

From Glasgow, Gerard went once more to Manresa in Roehampton for what was called his Tertianship, or third period as a novice priest. This was a ten-month period of retreat in which he was required to review his experiences so far and renew his spirit of piety. He resolved to write no poetry during this period, but he continued to advise his friends, Bridges and Dixon, on their verse. Canon Dixon offered to help him to get his poetry published, but he would have none of it. In a letter to Dixon he revealed how painful his experience of poverty and misery in Liverpool and Glasgow had been. He spoke of the degradation of the country and the hollowness of the century's civilisation, but this did not lead him to thoughts of revolution; indeed, as he grew older he became more patriotic and right-wing.

His correspondence with Bridges grew more frequent and intimate, although he never used his friend's first name, addressing him usually as *Dearest Bridges* and signing himself *Your affectionate friend, Gerard M. Hopkins*. They criticised each other's poetry severely but constructively. They were critical of each other's way of life. Bridges had no time for Catholicism, let alone Jesuitism, and always seemed to be hoping that Gerard would see the light and give it all up. Gerard, for his part, was critical of what he saw as Bridge's lack of spiritual feeling and social concern. At the age of 40, Bridges resigned from his hospital appointment and retired to a Berkshire village to devote himself to literary work. He married and developed a happy family life, and in his letters to Gerard was always kind and generous despite occasional rebuffs. Over the years he reached a greater understanding of and liking for his friend's poetry.

On 15 August 1882, Gerard completed his 14 years of training and took his final vows as a Jesuit priest. By September, he was once more at Stonyhurst College, teaching Latin, Greek and English to the older boys. He had time to write poetry now but was unable to make full use of it. In the two years he was at Stonyhurst he wrote only three poems of any merit, and all three of them were full of regrets at the passing of beauty. One of them, *Ribblesdale*, is a sonnet concerned directly with man's destruction of the countryside. We are given our *rich, round world* and heedlessly we *reave* or plunder it without *reck of world after*.

He had been working on and off for some years on his verse drama about St Winefred's Well, and whilst at Stonyhurst this time, he wrote two choruses for it, to be spoken or chanted by maidens, entitled *The Leaden Echo* and *The Golden Echo*. The work illustrates how some of his poems can be better understood if they are read aloud. The transience of the maidens' beauty is the theme of *The Leaden Echo*, and the maidens chant their despair. *The Golden Echo* is a song of reassurance: physical beauty comes from God, and humanity, being mortal, returns that beauty to Him, and He ensures its eternal existence in other forms. The choruses are an experiment in alliteration and repetition, which might have been very effective had the drama ever been staged. In *The Golden Echo*, the maidens' chant of resignation and acceptance is moving and lovely:

> *Undone, done with, soon done with, and yet dearly and dangerously*
>   *sweet*
> *Of us, the wimpled-water-dimpled, not-by-morning-matchèd face,*
> *The flower of beauty, fleece of beauty, too too apt to, ah! to fleet,*
> *Never fleets more, fastened with the tenderest truth*
> *To its own best being and its loveliness of youth: it is an*
>   *everlastingness of, O it is an all youth!*
> *Come then, your ways and airs and looks, locks, maiden gear.*
>   *gallantry, gaiety and grace,*
> *Winning ways, airs innocent, maiden manners, sweet looks, loose locks,*
>   *long locks, lovelocks, gaygear, going gallant, girlgrace-*
> *Resign them, sign them, seal them, send them, motion them with breath,*
> *And with sighs soaring, soaring sighs deliver*

111

Them; beauty-in-the ghost, deliver it, early now, long before death
Give beauty back, beauty, beauty, beauty, back to God, beauty's
self and beauty's giver.

The third poem of this otherwise poetically arid period of Hopkins's life was in praise of the Virgin Mary and written to hang on the wall of the College during the month of May. It was piously entitled *The Blessed Virgin Compared to the Air we Breathe*, and because it was likely to be read by casual passers-by, he endeavoured to comply with popular taste. Thus he did not use sprung rhythm but composed the poem in regular iambic trimeter, which comprises three metrical feet of two syllables, one short and one long. The poem is full of typical Hopkins touches. He feels girdled, he says, by *wild air, world-mothering air*, which puts him in mind of the Blessed Virgin who winds humanity round with mercy. He addresses her:

Be thou then, O thou dear
Mother, my atmosphere;
My happier world, wherein
To wend and meet no sin;
Above me, round me lie
Fronting my forward eye
With sweet and scarless sky;
Stir in my ears, speak there
Of God's love, O live air,
Of patience, penance, prayer:
World-mothering air, air wild,
Wound with thee, in thee isled,
Fold home, fast fold thy child.

Whilst complaining of weariness, he was able to take up new interests, which included piano-playing, composing music and learning Anglo-Saxon. In July 1883 he spent a few days in Hampstead with his parents and then accompanied them on a brief trip to Holland. Back at Stonyhurst College in August, he met the third poet with whom he was to conduct a lengthy correspondence over a number of years. This was the Catholic poet Coventry Patmore, who came to stay at the College for a day or two before speech-day. Gerard was given the task of looking after him, and they immediately struck up a close relationship based on their mutual interest in poetry. They subsequently wrote frequently to each other, Gerard doing so at great length, submitting his friend's poetry to detailed criticism. On the whole, Patmore did not appreciate Hopkins's poetry. He confessed to Robert Bridges that it had the effect of *veins of pure gold imbedded in masses of quartz.*

At Stonyhurst, Gerard wrote more music than he did poetry, but it was music of no great merit for, like his sketching, it was little above amateur level. Poetry was the one art in which he was incomparably gifted, though for a time he could find little inspiration. It came as a relief to him at the end of January 1884 to be offered the new post of Professor of Greek at University College, Dublin, with which went a Fellowship at the Royal University of Ireland. These were high-sounding titles, but they did not carry the status he might have hoped. The Royal University was mainly an examining body, and his duty was the arduous one of conducting and marking six examinations a year for which hundreds of students sat. As Professor of Greek at University College, which had recently been taken over by the Jesuits, his relatively lowly task was to give lessons in Latin and Greek to somewhat undisciplined students who often had little interest in their subject. He soon realised too that as an Englishman and a convert as well, he could not expect to be immediately popular with his academic colleagues.

Dublin at that time was a shabby decaying city, and he was dismayed at its greyness and poverty. He was unhappy too at the run-down state of the College, a once grand house in St Stephen's Green, and its lack of equipment and books. Always odd in his manner, his eccentricity became more pronounced. He was obsessional in his allocation of marks for the hundreds of examination scripts he marked, awarding quarter and half marks and agonising long into the night as he did so. His students found his lectures comic; and they had some reason to, if it is true that he would allow himself to be dragged along the classroom floor by his heels to illustrate how Hector was treated by Achilles during the Trojan Wars. He was soon complaining of over-work and of eye-strain, believing, despite the reassurances of his doctor, that he was going blind. He began in due course to have fears about his sanity, and he wrote painful letters to Bridges about his mental anxieties, with which his friend was not sympathetic.

His agony of mind started to affect his religious faith, and during 1885, he gave voice to his spiritual desolation in six desperate, despairing sonnets. He wrote to Bridges telling him that he would be sending him copies of these poems but he never did, and they were not discovered until after his death. In *To Seem the Stranger*, he voices his feelings of loneliness and exile, away from his family and his country and separated, he believes, from God. *Carrion Comfort* reveals how close he was to suicide, as he desperately insists that he will not feast on despair, and that he will not choose not to be. The poem concludes with a picture of himself wrestling with God in the dark. His images are shapeless and his words chaotic. The effect is made all the more poignant by his efforts to keep within the restrictions of the formal sonnet structure.

His third sonnet, *I Wake and Feel*, portrays him lying awake in the dark, feeling that this is how he will always be: like the damned in hell, forever contemplating their *sweating selves*, their pleas to God, like his letters to his lost love Dolben, always unanswered. In *No Worst, There is None*, receiving no comfort from his religious faith or anything else in life, he takes us into the tortured mind of the severely depressed, for whom only sleep or death brings respite:

> *O the mind, mind has mountains; cliffs of fall*
> *Frightful, sheer, no-man-fathomed. Hold them cheap*
> *May who ne'er hung there. Nor does long our small*
> *Durance deal with that steep or deep. Here! creep,*
> *Wretch, under a comfort serves in a whirlwind: all*
> *Life death does end and each day dies with sleep.*

The fifth poem, *Patience, Hard Thing*, is Gerard's prayer to endure the pains of living: patience which is *natural heart's ivy*. The final sonnet of this heart-rending sequence is *My Own Heart*. Here, he comforts himself with the thought that God reveals himself not at the will of the dejected sufferer but in His own time, as when on a dark day the skies between mountains brighten unexpectedly, and God's smile *lights a lovely mile*.

This group of poems has been called 'the terrible sonnets', but they portray more than simple terror. In them, Gerard is not a Jesuit, nor even a Christian: he is a symbol of petrified humanity in its darkest hour, aware only of the isolation and seeming meaninglessness of an uncomprehending world. But the sonnets do not end in final despair. They evince, if not great hope, at least, a determination to endure the dark night of the soul: that dark night, which other mystics have experienced, when God seems to have turned His face away for ever.

Hopkins's condition of emotional turmoil and spiritual despair produced great religious poetry, but his colleagues knew nothing of it. They were unaware of his suffering, nor indeed that he was a poet at all. They simply saw an eccentric little English Jesuit academic, over-conscientious and aloof. Katharine Tynan, an Irish poet and novelist, later described him as small and childish-looking, yet like a child-sage. She said he had a small, ivory-pale face and was nervous and very sensitive. Politically, he was at odds with the Irish colleagues with whom he worked. He regarded the Irish as rebellious and ungovernable. Gladstone, the Liberal Prime Minister of the time, was trying to legislate for Irish Home Rule, but Hopkins was against it. He was a staunch British patriot, seeing the British Empire as a force for freedom and civilisation. His hope was for a Holy British Empire, which would bring Catholicism to the entire world. His sonnet *The Soldier*, written about this time, sounds jingoistic to modern ears. It tends to glorify the arts of war, linking them strangely with Christ and his second coming as a soldier.

Recovering somewhat from his depression, he spent a holiday in August 1885 with Coventry Patmore in Hastings. In the spring of 1886, he stayed with Bridges at Yattendon and enjoyed meeting his friend's wife. He went to his parents very little and there was a certain estrangement from them, even from his mother. His happiest time seems to have been when he spent a fortnight's holiday in Wales with one of his younger colleagues at the College, regaining, for a short period only, some of the gaiety of his former years. His poetic output was moderately good, but he was dissatisfied with it, increasingly criticising himself for lack of achievement. He regarded his years in Ireland as wasted ones, and he complained that everything he undertook miscarried. In a sad but beautiful sonnet, *Thou Art Indeed Just Lord*, he upbraided God for letting sinners prosper, whilst he, himself, was always disappointed:

> . . . *See, banks and brakes*
> *Now leavèd how thick! laced they are again*
> *With fretty chervil, look, and fresh wind shakes*
> *Them; birds build – but not I build; no, but strain*
> *Time's eunuch, and not breed one work that wakes.*
> *Mine, O thou lord of life, send my roots rain.*

Two other major poems he wrote during his Dublin period were *Harry Ploughman* and *Tom's Garland*. Both were sonnets and both concerned working men. In *Harry Ploughman*, Gerard praises the farm labourer and his powerful physique, indicating again his appreciation of male beauty. *Tom's Garland* is more of a puzzle, and its meaning escaped both Bridges and Dixon, so that he had to explain it to them. He begins by idealising the simple working man and his hard but straightforward life, lived without care. But the curse of the time, the poet says, is that such a man does not share in the prosperity of the nation and that, if unemployed, he may become a loafer or a tramp or even a revolutionary. Hopkins considered the sonnet *pregnant and highly wrought*. Certainly it was a tract for the times.

Another poem written in Dublin has the long and obscure title of *That Nature is a Heraclitean Fire and of the Comfort of the Resurrection*. It too is a fourteen-line sonnet, and is in sprung rhythm with lines of inordinate length. Heraclitus was a philosopher of ancient Greece who held that all creation is in a state of flux and is formed from the basic principles of fire. The sonnet begins in the joyful vein of his nature poems written at St Bueno's; but really, Hopkins reflects, the beauty of the world is fluctuating and impermanent. Nothing lasts, certainly not the achievements of mankind. Consolation lies in Christ's resurrection, which is a *beacon, an eternal beam*. Since man is saved by the resurrection, the poet is like Christ: *This Jack, joke, poor potsherd, patch, matchwood, immortal diamond*.

In celebration of his brother Everard's wedding in 1888, Gerard composed a poem, never completed, entitled *Epithalamion*, or marriage song. It was written while he was supervising an examination and is full of sensual imagery which seems to well up unbidden from his unconscious. A listless stranger comes upon a group of boys bathing joyously in a river:

116

Sees the bevy of them, how the boys
With dare and with downdolphinry and bellright bodies huddling out,
Are earthworld, airworld, waterworld thorough hurled, all by turn and
    turn about.

He finds a pool for himself, sweet and fresh and overhung with trees, strips and: *froliclavish, while he looks about him, laughs, swims.* Gerard explains rather unconvincingly that the rural scene represents wedlock and the water is married love. However, one cannot help thinking the poem is really a fantasy about happy, naked boys which serves to while away a dreary afternoon's invigilating.

Gerard said in a letter to Bridges that he had become haggard-looking and wrinkled round the eyes; and the photograph taken of him in 1888, a year before he died, bears this out. Even though he was only forty-four, he said he was feeling old. His eyes were troubling him and his spirits were often low. He experienced a sense of self-loathing and he hated his academic life in Dublin, but could not look forward to anything else. Bridges blamed the Jesuit authorities for being uncaring and for over-working him, but they seemed to do what they could to give him congenial work and reasonable holidays. The fact was that he was suffering from a depressive illness which was little understood at the time.

He wrote two letters to Robert Bridges in the spring of 1889, which appear to have been so unpleasant that his friend destroyed them. And then on Easter Monday, guilty at what he had done, he addressed a sonnet to Bridges excusing his behaviour. It was the last poem he ever wrote, and in it he voices his despair at his lack of poetic inspiration:

> *Sweet fire the sire of muse, my soul needs this;*
> *I want the one rapture of an inspiration.*
> *O then if in my lagging lines you miss*
> *The roll, the rise, the carol, the creation,*
> *My winter world, that scarcely breathes that bliss*
> *Now yields you, with some sighs, our explanation.*

His winter world is middle age, and he is resigning himself to an existence without the divine spark of inspiration.

In a letter dated 29 April accompanying the sonnet, he told Bridges he was feeling ill. Two days later, he wrote to his mother, telling her he had rheumatic fever. He went to bed and called a doctor, but felt no better. On 8 May, in another letter to his mother he told her his illness was diagnosed as a sort of typhoid. His condition improved for a time, but by early June he had had a severe relapse, and his parents were sent for. He died on Saturday morning, 8 June 1889, having received the last rites of the Catholic Church. He was forty-five.

In a sonnet called *Spelt from Sibyl's Leaves*, which he had written in Dublin during a depressive phase, Gerard had dwelt darkly on God's judgement, the sorting of the sheep from the goats and the eternal damnation of the wicked in hell, where *selfwrung, selfstrung, sheathe and shelterless, thoughts against thoughts in groans grind*. But on his death-bed he suffered none of these terrible fears. Placid and contented, he was heard to repeat softly to himself: *I am so happy; I am so happy*. Unlike Christina Rossetti, his Christian faith did not falter, and he breathed his last in the certainty of a life to come.

To the British public his poetry was unknown. The Jesuit authorities were not even aware that he had been a poet. They buried him in the Jesuit part of the Catholic cemetery at Glasnevin to the north of Dublin, and his grave was unmarked. Their official publication recorded merely that he had a most subtle mind, which too quickly wore out the fragile strength of his body. Fortunately, during his lifetime, Gerard had sent to Robert Bridges most of his poems; and his friend, whilst not appreciating many of them, had preserved them with a view to possible future publication. Over the years, Bridges arranged for one or two of them to be published in anthologies. In 1917, he himself edited an anthology in which he included a few more of his poems, but they made little impression. In 1918, he found a publisher interested in issuing Hopkins's complete poetic works, and at last his poems were available to a wider public. Even then their popularity was not immediate, and it was not until the end of the 1920s that they became widely read and appreciated. In 1953, a paperback edition of Hopkins's poems, together with a selection of his letters and journal entries, was published. This has since been reprinted a number of times.

It is hard to think of Hopkins as a Victorian poet, but that is what he was. Born seven years after Victoria came to the throne and dying twelve years before she died, no-one could be more a product of the Victorian era than he. But, though he thought he was writing for his own generation, they never had the chance to appreciate his work, and it is unlikely that they would have thought much of it had they had the opportunity to read it. The educated poetry readers, reared on Tennyson, Christina and Dante Gabriel Rossetti and Swinburne, could enjoy the traditional verse of Robert Bridges, but Hopkins's contorted grammar and syntax would have been too much for them. Whether he knew it or not, he was writing for a future generation. His verbless or incomplete sentences, his passionate questions and exclamations, his extraordinary use and mis-use of adjectives and adverbs, his portmanteau nouns: all of these would have been unacceptable at the time, as would the sprung rhythm.

He was not the inspirer of the so-called Modernist school of poetry, since, by the time his poetry reached the general public, the work of T S Eliot and Ezra Pound had already been published. But his poetry could be enjoyed by readers who appreciated Eliot and Pound. Like them, he expresses obscure and painful states of mind, and he leads us into realms of feeling which could not be reached by the relatively regular metre and rhyme of much of the Victorian poetry. He pushes the English language to the extreme. We feel the tumultous storm of the *Deutschland* poem through the words he uses. His emotions come bursting through in a torrent of words, imaginative diction and exuberant rhythm. To read him is not a comforting experience, for whilst he enhances and extends our capacity for joyous emotions, he takes us also to depths of profound despair. Odd, original individualistic, he is impossible to classify as a poet. We must simply be grateful that so tortured a life brought such a new sensibility and sensitivity to English poetry.

THOMAS HARDY

When the Present has latched its postern behind my tremulous stay,
And the May month flaps its glad green leaves like wings
Delicate-filmed as new-spun silk, will the neighbours say,
'He was a man who used to notice such things'?

THOMAS HARDY

Thomas Hardy was both a major novelist and an outstanding poet, and it is difficult to say in which genre he achieved the most. But the man in the street who has seen the portrayal of Hardy's novels on the stage or in the cinema or on television could be excused for thinking that Hardy's primary genius lay in prose. It is not widely known that, whilst he spent some twenty-five years in writing novels, he was a poet all his adult life, and for his last thirty years wrote almost nothing but poetry.

His earliest known poem, *Domicilium*, was begun when he was seventeen, and he seems to have written some forty poems during his twenties. When he started writing novels in his late twenties, his poetic output largely ceased, and was not resumed until his novel-writing finished in his mid-fifties. From then on, he wrote poetry until the year of his death at the age of eighty-eight.

Hardy was essentially a lyric poet, and one thinks of lyric poets, like Shelley and Keats, as essentially youthful; but Hardy was an old poet, the vast majority of his poems – some nine hundred of them – being written during the last third of his life. He stored in his memory and in his notebooks, scenes, situations, anecdotes which in due course were to beome the subjects for his poems. He looked back over his long life and saw human beings in perspective, how buildings and scenery changed, though human nature did not. He recognized the tragedy in life, and tried to portray it as it actually is. He studied God, and tried to depict Him, without sentimentality, as he felt God really was.

What ended his novel-writing career, when he seemed in full spate, and turned him into a full-time poet writing obsessionally for more than thirty years? He tells us it was because the critics would not permit him to depict the true pain and squalor of life. What the puritans and hypocrites criticised him for rendering in prose, they would ignore or overlook if said in poetry. As he put it, if Galileo had said in verse that it was the earth rather than the sun which moved, the Vatican would have left him alone.

Hardy came from humble stock and rose in the world to mix with the greatest in the literary world, being awarded the Order of Merit and eventually being buried in Westminster Abbey. If three words could embody the subject matter of his poetry, they would be: nature, time and humanity. Nature pervades, time moves forward, humanity suffers and dies.

Hardy's father, like his father before him, began work as a self-employed stone-mason in Dorset. Within twenty years he was a master-mason employing six men. He continued to prosper, and at his death in 1892 had accumulated a considerable estate. As a young man he was something of a philanderer. He married Jemima Hand in 1839, when she was three months pregnant. She was a domestic servant, and at the time was a cook for a local clergyman. She was the daughter of a servant on her father's side, but her mother was an educated yeoman-farmer's daughter. Jemima's father died young and her mother was left a penniless widow with seven children. The children were brought up on parish relief, and Jemima went into service when she was thirteen.

Thomas Hardy's parents went to live with his father's widowed mother in a cottage in the hamlet of Higher Bockhampton, a few miles from Dorchester in Dorset. Hardy was born on 2 June 1840, and his birth nearly cost his mother her life. He appeared to be dead at first and was a very delicate infant. Mary, the next child, was born a year later, but Thomas continued to receive much of his parents' attention because he had so narrowly survived.

His parents were a handsome and attractive couple. Jemima, like her three sisters, had great vitality, and had inherited from her mother a passion for reading. She was a major influence on her son all his life. His sister Mary, too, was a life-long companion and confidante. From his father Thomas inherited a love of music. He was given an accordion on his fourh birthday, and he used to dance happily to his father's country tunes. As he grew older he learnt to play hundreds of country dances on the fiddle. Under his mother's tuition, he was able to read by the time he was three. In nearby

Puddletown, a thriving village, lived some of his mother's numerous relatives, the Hands; and he went there often as soon as he was able to walk the two-and-a-half miles on his own.

One of his mother's sisters, Maria, who had married a cabinet-maker called Sparks, lived there. She had sons and daughters and young Thomas loved visiting them. Another sister, Mary, was married to a cobbler, John Antell. She had a soft spot for Thomas, whom she had helped to nurse when he was a sickly infant. Antell, self-educated and intelligent but addicted to drink, may have been Hardy's model for Jude in his last novel, *Jude the Obscure*.

There was much poverty in rural Dorset at the time. Hardy's family home was a thatched cottage with mud walls and illumin-ated by rushlights and warmed by a single fire. The heath across which he walked to Puddletown was a frightening place after dark. The Hands and the Hardys were economically above the agricultural labourers, but the slightest slip through illness or intemperance could have reduced them to abject poverty. There were brutal aspects to rural life, and his parents would tell him frightening tales. He heard from his father of the hanging of four labourers for rick burning, and the tale terrified him. His mother told him of a girl who had committed suicide and had been buried with a stake through her body on a bleak hilltop, and this was no less frightening. Both parents had a store of legends and country anecdotes and they filled their son's mind with the rural scenes and characters which were to become part of his novels.

The first school he attended was run by a Mrs Julia Martin, who became very fond of him. It was in the nearby village of Stinsford, and was a church school founded for promoting the education of the poor. He started there in the autumn of 1884, and within his first year he was reading a translation of Virgil's *Aeneid* and Dr Johnson's *Rasselas*.

Not only was his mother educationally ambitious for her clever son, she was jealous of Mrs Martin's influence over him; so in 1850 she moved him to a larger school in Dorchester, under the aegis of a Nonconformist Society. Education at the time was provided not by the state but by religious societies which were state-aided, and his new school had a good reputation.

Thomas excelled at his lessons, his ability at reading standing him in good stead. At the age of twelve, he started Latin as an optional extra, for which his parents paid more. He was a familiar figure in the town, a quiet, studious-looking boy, always carrying a satchel full of books. After Mary, born in 1841, his parents had a son, Henry, in 1851 and a daughter, Kate, in 1856. It was a small family by local working-class standards, and they had time to devote to their children.

Thomas perservered with his fiddle-playing, performing at local weddings and dances but, at his mother's insistence, he seldom accepted money for it. She allowed him to accompany his father to dances and festivals, but she watched carefully over his moral education. He had no male friends, but at the age of fourteen he became interested in girls, falling in love with a succession of pretty faces, all of them older than him and beyond his reach. When he was fifteen he was caught making physical advances to Rebecca Sparks, the oldest of his girl cousins, and his aunt Maria forbade him from visiting the house for a time.

His parents encouraged his education in every way, and at sixteen he was learning French with the aid of a French governess at his school. Whilst he was assisting his father in renovating a large manor house, the architect for the project, John Hicks, observed his intelligence and ability and offered to take him on as an apprentice for a small fee; and a month after his sixteenth birthday he began work in Hicks's office in Dorchester. Hicks was an intelligent, well-educated man who encouraged his staff to read books. He joined in their conversations, which ranged over literary and religious topics, and generally stimulated Thomas's intellectual development.

It was when he was about seventeen that Thomas got to know the Moule family. The Reverend Henry Moule was vicar of Fordington, a suburb of Dorchester, which with the coming of the railway, was a growing town. A man of intellectual tastes, he had seven sons, all of whom distinguished themselves in the Church or as scholars. Thomas's particular friend was Horace, the fourth eldest son, who was eight years his senior. Horace went to Cambridge University and later became a classics master at a public school. At the time when Thomas met him, he had left Cambridge, having failed to gain a degree. Good-looking, highly intelligent and full of charm, he made an immense impression on Thomas, and he was to have a great influence over him for several years.

As part of his self-education, Thomas was also learning Greek, and Horace was very helpful to him in this. He was instrumental in extending his reading too. In short he was just the sort of man that Thomas wanted to become. Horace wrote poetry modelled somewhat on Wordsworth, and Thomas tended to follow him in this. His early poem, *Domicilium,* written in blank verse, was about his grandmother recalling the days when she moved as a newly-married woman to her cottage in Higher Bockhampton:

> *Our house stood quite alone, and those tall firs*
> *And beeches were not planted. Snakes and efts*
> *Swarmed in the summer days, and nightly bats*
> *Would fly about our bedrooms.*

Small and slight and seeming young for his age, Thomas looked more like a youthful curate than a normal country lad. For some years indeed, he did cherish the idea of entering the Church. Most clergy had degrees in the classics, but the Church of England was expanding and it is just possible he would have been considered for ordination. At the time he was certainly very devout, attending church both morning and evening, and writing lengthy comments in the margins of his Bible and prayer-book. He enjoyed the services, loving both the music and the words of the hymns and psalms. He naturally linked words with music, something evident in his poetry.

He was greatly influenced by John Keeble's *Christian Year,* with its poems for each Sunday and Holy Day. In later life, he became very critical of the Church of England, regarding its clergy as snobbish and self-seeking, and feeling its doctrine had been rendered ridiculous by modern science; but this was certainly not how he felt as a young man. His interest in the Bible spurred him on to study Greek. So keen was he not to waste potential study-time, he took a room in Dorchester to cut out the long walk from home to work. Horace Moule encouraged him in his study of the classics, and, despite the difference in social standing their frienship became very close.

Thomas was still determined to become an architect, and he

needed wider experience. Hicks gave him a letter of introduction to an architect friend in London, and in April 1862, he went into lodgings in Kilburn. This architect was unable to offer him a post; however he referred him to a colleague, Arthur Blomfield, and on 5 May he started work in Blomfield's drawing office.

There he found a new level of sophistication. His colleagues were public school or university men, and their conversation was racy and irreverent and they introduced him to a world for which his strict and narrow upbringing had not prepared him. He was not prepared either for the squalor and immorality of the London streets, where there were prostitutes everywhere and the poverty of the down-and-outs contrasted harshly with the affluence of the rich.

Music was Thomas's great pleasure. Blomfield organised an office choir, which Hardy readily joined. He also availed himself of the wealth of professional music which the metropolis offered, and regularly attended concerts and operatic performances. He was eager to fill the gap in his knowledge of art, and frequently visited art galleries. All the time he was reading widely, being literally obsessed with cultural self-improvement. However, he did not neglect his architectural studies. In March 1863, he won a silver medal in an essay competition of the Royal Institute of British Architects. Horace Moule was in London at this time, reading for the Bar and contributing to literary journals, and they were frequently in each other's company.

Martha Sparks, one of Thomas's many cousins, was now a lady's maid in Paddington, and he took her out occasionally, and was undoubtedly very fond of her. On his visits home at Christmas, he saw a lot of her younger sister, Tryphena, and was attracted to her too. The Sparks girls were very like his mother in appearance, and this may have been part of their fascination for him. His sister Mary had been studying at Salisbury to become a certificated teacher, and she went on to work at a school in Berkshire. They corresponded frequently and he saw as much of her as he could. Despite his wide reading, his outlook was still somewhat parochial, and although great events were stirring in the world, such as the American Civil War and the emergence of Italy as an independent state, he never mentioned them in anything he wrote.

Horace Moule gave Hardy a copy of Palgrave's newly published

Golden Treasury of Lyrical Poetry, which stimulated further his interest in poetry. He set about studying the book, as he had with art, in a methodical way. Wordsworth, Coleridge, Browning and Shelley were favourite poets of his. He was particularly taken with Shelley, annotating his copy of his poems in some detail. In 1865, Algernon Swinburne published his poem *Atalanta in Calydon*, and it filled Hardy with delight. When, in 1866, Swinburne's collected verses, *Poems and Ballads*, appeared in the bookshops, he was so entranced, that he read them, totally absorbed, as he walked along the busy London streets. Another contemporary poet who intrigued him was George Meredith, whose long poem, *Modern Love* appeared in 1862. Thomas's early sonnets indicate the influence Meredith had on him, for he sometimes followed him in adding two extra lines to the fourteen-line Shakespearean form, and like him he was clearly under the influence of Shakespeare in his early poetry.

Hardy was fascinated by words. His copy of a popular rhyming dictionary is still in existence, and he annotated it with additional words and rhymes of his own, architectural terms and Dorsetshire dialect words being among these. During this period of obsessional preoccupation with poetry, he tried his hand at all sorts of metres and a wide variety of subjects. In the office he established himself as a poetry expert, and would give short talks to his colleagues on the subject. He was strongly drawn to brevity in his early verse – in stark contrast to Tennyson and Swinburne, but not unlike some of Browning's poetry.

He could see the comic side of life, but mostly dwelt on the darker aspects. An early sonnet written in 1866 called *Hap*, or fate, tells us that he could accept the human condition if an all-powerful God were deliberately vengeful and enjoyed giving suffering; but life was not like that. Everything is governed by chance, and pain and joy are without meaning and are meted out haphazardly. Another sonnet, a sixteen-line one called *Neutral Tones*, written in 1867 is thought to record his final meeting at Findon in Sussex with a girlfriend, Eliza Nicholls, at which their relationship was ended. The poem's emotional tension is powerful though terse:

We stood by a pond that winter day,
And the sun was white, as though chidden of God,
And a few leaves lay on the starving sod;
– They had fallen from an ash, and were gray.

Your eyes on me were as eyes that rove
Over tedious riddles of years ago;
And some words played between us to and fro
On which lost the more by our love.

The smile on your mouth was the deadest thing
Alive enough to have strength to die;
And a grin of bitterness swept thereby
Like an ominous bird a-wing ...

Since then, keen lessons that love deceives,
And wrings with wrong, have shaped to me
Your face, and the God-curst sun, and a tree,
And a pond edged with grayish leaves.

It was the first of the type of poem which became so typical of Hardy. He catches with feeling a momentary episode which remains with him long afterwards. Hardy wrote other sonnets involving Eliza Nicholls, a Dorset girl in domestic service in London. Whilst he was in London, he was often lonely and depressed, and fell in love at the drop of a hat. Once he fancied himself in love with Eliza's younger sister, but she was not slow to reject him.

At the same time, he was slowly losing his religious faith. The books on science which he read seemed to show that mankind was an accidental phenomenon in a meaningless world. His physical health too was declining as his long hours of reading and the smoky atmosphere of the big city took their toll. He had spent five years in the capital and was in need of a change. Blomfield did not try to prevent him when he accepted an offer from Hicks to work again in his Dorchester office. In July 1867 he returned to Bockhampton and resumed his old routine of walking daily to Dorchester from his parents' home. He gradually recovered his health, and was pleased to see more of his sister Mary, who was now working as a teacher in the nearby village of Minterne. His cousin Tryphena was now a lively, good-looking sixteen-year-old, intent like Mary on becoming a certificated school-teacher. Thomas, susceptible as ever, began to fall in love with her, as he had done previously with her two elder sisters, Rebecca and Martha.

Whilst in London, he had submitted his poems to a number of literary journals, but without success. Back in Dorset, he persevered with his poetry, but was increasingly drawn to the idea of writing a novel. By the end of 1867, he had nearly completed the first draft of a story to be called *The Poor Man and the Lady*, based on his knowledge of rural life and his London experience. The book was finished in June 1868, and he submitted it at Horace Moule's suggestion to the publisher Alexander Macmillan. He did not accept it but was sufficiently encouraging for Hardy to try again.

In the summer of 1869, Thomas was sent to Weymouth to direct a major architectural project which involved the rebuilding of a church. It was his first undertaking in which he had a free hand, and he was happy there enjoying the summer in a crowded seaside town. He had time to work on a second novel called *Desperate Remedies*, which, as advised by Macmillan, had an involved plot and much suspense. He also wrote some poetry, and his poem *Singing Lovers* dates from his Weymouth period, though it was not published until many years later. He used to swim in the sea every morning before work and in the evening would take out a rowing boat. The poem records him rowing with *two singing lovers in the stern*, though he is without his own love. The lovers are embracing, glorying openly in their love, while he watches them and sighs. The poem ends:

> *The moon's glassed glory heaved as we lay swinging*
> *Upon the undulations. Shoreward, slow,*
> *The plash of pebbles joined the lovers' singing,*
> *But she of a bygone vow*
> *Joined in the song not now!*

So many times Hardy fell in love and so often he felt rejected! If it were Tryphena he was thinking of, there was little doubt that her career came before her love for him. She was to be sponsored as a trainee by the British and Foreign Bible Society, whose Nonconformist morality was of the strictest, and she could not afford the slightest slip. At one time he is said to have presented her with a ring, but that is probably as far as the relationship ever went.

Early in 1870 he returned to Bockhampton, where his sister Mary was at home too. His father's business was prospering, and he now had his eighteen-year-old son Henry working with him. Thomas had plenty of time to work on his novel, and in March he sent the nearly-completed manuscript to Macmillan. His employer, Hicks, who had recently died, had left certain assignments outstanding, and one of these was the restoration of the decaying parish church of St Juliot, near Boscastle on the north coast of Cornwall. The Rector had repeatedly requested a new survey, and on 7 March, Thomas set out for Cornwall. It took twelve house on several trains for him to reach the county town of Launceston, and he completed the last seventeen miles by pony and trap. He arrived at the rectory at St Juliot in the evening, having set out at 4 a.m. He found the elderly Rector in bed with gout, and only the Rector's sister-in-law there to receive him. She was a blonde, blue-eyed young woman called Emma Lavinia Gifford. Thomas Hardy had met his wife-to-be.

Emma Gifford was the youngest but one of a family of five children of an unsuccessful, heavy-drinking solicitor. At twenty-nine, she was a few months younger than Thomas. Her elder sister Helen had married the Reverend Caddell Holder, Rector of St Juliot, and Emma had been living with them for the past two years. She was energetic and vivacious, and Thomas was soon head over heels in love with her. Tired of living with her sister, she was equally ready for a romantic attachment. They had much in common. She enjoyed poetry and had aspirations to be a writer, and they both loved the countryside. The weather was sunny and warm, and the magnificent cliff scenery entranced them both. Across the downs, Emma rode her pony, her hair streaming in the wind, while Thomas watched her admiringly. Short and spare in build with a large beard, he was not immediately attractive, but she admired his intelligence, his literary background and his air of professional competence. For him, it was probably her energy and love of life which attracted him most, coupled with the fact that she came from a higher stratum of society.

He returned to Dorset on 12 March, his head fuller of thoughts of Emma than of his plans for St Juliot church. After her death many years later, he recalled those days:

> *Time touches her not*
> *But she still rides gaily*
> *In his rapt thought*
> *On that shagged and shaly*
> *Atlantic spot,*
> *And as when first eyed*
> *Draws rein and sings to the swing of the tide.*

On 8 August the same year he returned to St Juliot and stayed there for three happy weeks, enjoying the countryside with Emma. They were both very much in love, and like all lovers were oblivious to each other's faults. They sketched one another amid the beautiful scenery, embraced in the privacy of the rectory garden and passionately declared their love for each other. The Rector and his wife gave them every encouragement and opportunity, and by the end of Thomas's holiday they were engaged to be married.

His novel *Desperate Measures*, which was a mixture of detective story and Gothic horror, had been rejected by Macmillan as being too sensational and sexually explicit. But, after some alterations, the book was accepted by another publisher, William Tinsley, provided Thomas contributed £75 towards the publication costs. By March 1871 the book was in the shops and Hardy was a published author. The reception was mixed. Whilst the rural background was liked, the crime and the sexual scenes made the book unsuitable for the subscription library readership which was largely female. Hardy lost money on the venture, and he needed his architectural work to give him sufficient money on which to marry. He was bitterly sensitive about the reviewers' criticisms, but was determined to carry on writing.

Whilst most of the time he was determined to marry Emma, his thoughts still strayed towards his cousin Tryphena, and he wrote to both women. Tryphena was now in her second year at her teachers' training college, but she returned to Dorset for her brief vacations and she saw Thomas at these times. Another source of doubt and indecision was his religious beliefs. Whilst in London he had become agnostic in his outlook, but Emma's influence had restored his

133

practice of church attendance and he was still reading the Bible closely and annotating his copy. Nevertheless, he found it hard to reconcile the Christian faith in a loving God with all the suffering he saw around him. People he knew had died in pain; and then there was Tryphena's sister, Martha, whom he had once loved. She had married a butler, had been dismissed from her job and now had twins and was living in poverty, no longer the smart young woman he had once courted. She was later to emigrate to Australia and suffer worse poverty there. Hardy turned more and more towards the concept of a malign fate which dogged men and women whatever they did to prevent it. He recorded with approval in his notebook his mother's notion that in life a figure stands in front of us with its arm uplifted, ready to knock us back from any pleasant prospect.

He took lodgings again in Weymouth and, while working on building new schools in the locality, started a new novel, *Under the Greenwood Tree*. This was a relatively short book which had little plot but was full of rustic scenes. It initially found favour with Macmillan, but eventually Hardy sold the copyright to Tinsley for £30. The sum was paltry, but at least he was in print again; and better things followed, for Tinsley offered him £200 for a serial story for his monthly journal, *Tinsley's Magazine*. Hardy had already made a beginning on a new novel which he eventually called *A Pair of Blue Eyes*, and he turned this into a monthly serial, on the understanding that in due course it would be published as a book in three volumes.

The heroine of *Under the Greenwood Tree* is a school-teacher not unlike Tryphena, while the story of *A Pair of Blue Eyes* takes place in Cornwall with a heroine clearly based on Emma. Biographers have made much of this, and certainly it seems to indicate some emotional turmoil. His indecision was eventually resolved in the August of 1872. By this time, Tryphena had successfully completed her training, and commendably for one so young, had obtained the post of head-mistress of a girls' school in Plymouth. On 7 August, Thomas set off for Cornwall, travelling by boat via London and Plymouth. In all probability he saw Tryphena in Plymouth and finally ended their relationship. It seems likely that she returned his ring, perhaps thinking that a secure career was better than the possibility of marriage to one so evasive and uncertain.

From Plymouth, Thomas went first to Emma's parents who lived near Bodmin, presumably to ask her hand in marriage. They did not welcome him, and Mr Gifford is said to have referred to him subsequently as low-born churl, who presumed to marry into his family. He went on to Lanivet, near Bodmin, to stay with friends of Emma. In a poem called *Near Lanivet*, he later recorded a bizarre event in which Emma wearily leant against an old Celtic cross by the St Austell Road:

> *Her white-clothed form at this dim-lit cease of day*
> *Made her look as one crucified*
> *In my gaze at her from the midst of the dusty way,*
> *And hurriedly 'Don't' I cried.*

He tries to make light of the incident, but she wonders, if not in the body, may not someone be crucified in spirit. The poem ends forebodingly:

> *And we dragged on and on, while we seemed to see*
> *In the running of Time's far glass*
> *Her crucified, as she had wondered if she might be*
> *Some day. – Alas, alas!*

Hardy continued to send Tinsley monthly instalments of *A Pair of Blue Eyes*. Pressed for time, he did not hesitate to make use of incidents involving Emma, who was so like the novel's heroine, Elfrida. She had for example once written to him pointing out how reserved he was and had added, 'I take him as I do the Bible: find out what I can, compare one text with another, and believe the rest in a simple lump of faith.' Almost exactly the same words are used in the book by Elfrida, addressing the reserved writer, Knight, who is in love with her. Hardy's hero, Stephen Smith, is, like himself, a young architect who has a similar humble background. Both Emma and Thomas were aware of the difficulties arising from their differing backgrounds. Although she may not have met his family, she is unlikely to have had much doubt as to his working-class origins. In those days she was very loyal to him and always encouraged him in his literary aspirations.

His prospects were further enhanced when in October 1872 he

received a letter from Leslie Stephen, editor of the *Cornhill Magazine*, offering to buy the next serial novel he wrote. This was a triumph for a relatively unknown author, since the journal had a high reputation and a wide circulation. Hardy readily accepted the offer, but had to play for time, since he had not yet completed *A Pair of Blue Eyes*. This was published in three volumes in May 1873, and was the first of his novels to appear under his own name. The reviews were favourable, and with news of the likelihood of publication in New York, his literary future looked assured and he need no longer accept occasional architectural assignments.

The one person whom he found hard to please was his mother. Not only did she feel that an author's career was inferior to an architect's, she disapproved of employing local scenery and characters. Furthermore, since he was using her cottage as a base from which to write, he had to reassure her that his books were likely to be read in London only and certainly not in Dorchester.

Towards the end of September 1873, Horace Moule committed suicide by cutting his throat in his rooms in Queen's College, Cambridge, which he was using as a base whilst working for the Poor Law Inspectorate. Hardy had visited him there in June and had found him in good spirits; but the cycle of depression had caught up with him again, and alcohol had done nothing to relieve it. Thomas had been closer to Horace Moule than to any other man, and he was never able to replace his friendship. He wrote of him in a deeply-felt poem, *Standing by the Mantlepiece*, in which Moule is speaking to him. His friend touches the melting wax of a lighted candle, which is shaped like a shroud – a portent of death – and says:

> *This candle-wax is shaping to a shroud*
> *To-night. (They call it that, as you may know) –*
> *By touching it the claimant is avowed,*
> *And hence I press it with my finger – so.*

It would seem that Moule has made some advance to Hardy, perhaps a sexual one, which has been rejected, for in tones of heavy gloom Moule says:

But since all's lost, and nothing really lies
Above but shade, and shadier shade below,
Let me make clear, before one of us dies,
My mind to yours, just now embittered so.

Since you agreed, unurged and full-advised,
And let warmth grow without discouragement,
Why do you bear you now as if surprised,
When what has come was clearly consequent?

Since you have spoken, and finality
Closes around, and my last movements loom,
I say no more: the rest must wait till we
Are face to face again, yonside the tomb.

And let the candle-wax thus mould a shape
Whose meaning now, if hid before, you know,
And how by touch one present claims its drape,
And that it's I who press my finger – so.

It is clear that Horace Moule is thinking of taking his own life, and that Hardy sees himself, if not the cause of his suicide, at least as having a part in the tragedy. It is significant that Hardy witheld this poem for many years; it appeared only in his final collection, *Winter Words*, which was published posthumously. Hardy mourned his friend for the rest of his life. Moule's melancholy death may have seemed further proof of the malignity of fate for, after his new book, *Far from the Madding Crowd*, which was already partially written, Hardy wrote no more novels with a happy outcome, all his heroes coming to sad ends.

Hardy spent the Christmas of 1873 with Emma in Cornwall, and on his way home by train he was pleased to buy a copy of the *Cornhill Magazine* containing the first instalment of *Far from the Madding Crowd*. Leslie Stephen was to prove an admirable editor, advising Hardy, as each instalment was received, against his tendency to over-write dramatic scenes and shrewdly suggesting minor cuts and alterations. Hardy employed a wealth of local colour in the book, based on incidents he had heard of or had actually experienced. It was his first novel with which Emma did not assist him in fair-copying and proof-reading, and this is likely to have been because it revealed too much of his humble origins. It is unlikely that he would have told her that his mother had been brought up as a pauper child and that many of her relatives were servants.

On the other hand, he was learning things about her which had not at first been apparent. Despite her middle-class background, she was relatively poorly educated. This was brought home as he began to mix with Leslie Stephen and his literary friends. Stephen's wife was the daughter of the novelist William Thackery, and Hardy was now moving into a new world. Although he still loved Emma, he developed romantic feelings both for Mrs Stephen's sister, Annie Thackery, and for the illustrator of his new book, Miss Helen Paterson. Years later, exaggerating the situation, he told a friend that Miss Paterson was the woman he might have married, but for 'a stupid blunder of God Amighty'! In his poem *The Opportunity*, dedicated to H.P. he wrote:

> *Had we mused a little space*
> *At that critical date in the Maytime,*
> *One life had been ours, one place,*
> *Perhaps, till our long, cold claytime.*

It was poor verse and nothing but a daydream, for she was soon to marry someone else. Emma was intent on marriage in any case, and now Hardy was becoming increasingly prosperous there was no reason for further delay, even though the families on both sides disapproved. The wedding took place at St Peter's Church, Paddington on 17 September 1874, with Emma's uncle, Canon Gifford, officiating. Only six people attended the ceremony, and no member of Hardy's family was among them, not even his beloved sister Mary. He had outgrown his humble background, and perhaps his family realised it.

Thomas and Emma spent the first night of their honeymoon in Brighton, and then crossed to France and after several days in Rouen, travelled on to Paris. There they viewed the familiar tourist sights, with Emma enthusing over them in her diary and Thomas recording impressions for possible material for future books. They were back in

London by the end of September and found furnished rooms near Surbiton, some way out of town. Thomas's novel-writing rhythm was temporarily interrupted but he wrote occasional verse. The winter brought snow and he wrote two poems on the subject, both of them descriptive and slight. One of them, *Snow in the Suburbs*, observes wryly:

> *A sparrow enters the tree,*
> *Whereon immediately*
> *A snow-lump thrice his own slight size*
> *Descends on him and showers his head and eyes,*
> *And overturns him,*
> *And near inurns him,*
> *And lights on a nether twig, when its brush*
> *Starts off a volley of other lodging lumps with a rush.*
>
> *The steps are a blanched slope,*
> *Up which, with feeble hope,*
> *A black cat comes, wide-eyed and thin;*
> *And we take him in.*

Neither Thomas nor Emma recorded anything personal about their honeymoon or their five months' stay in the London suburbs.

It was while he was at Surbiton, nevertheless, that Thomas Hardy emerged as an established author. This arose from the success of *Far from the Madding Crowd*, which was published in two volumes by Smith, Elder on 23 November 1874. It received very favourable reviews, and after only two months the first edition of a thousand copies had sold out. The story was a strong one, the characters were firmly drawn and the rural setting was much to the taste of the readers. Industrialisation of the country was proceeding rapidly. Millions of people now lived in large towns and nostalgia for the simple country life was powerful, not least amongst people who would never have exchanged their paved streets, gas-lit homes and water-closets for the rigours of rustic life.

The success of *Far from the Madding Crowd* led Leslie Stephen to ask for a new serial for the *Cornhill Magazine*. Hardy's work was also in demand from other journals. He could not afford to be distracted from writing stories, but at the same time he was thinking about poetry and making notes for future poems. In March 1875, he and Emma moved back to the centre of London, renting a house in Westbourne Grove, near where he used to live. He was seeing a lot of Leslie Stephen and enjoyed their theological and philosophical discussions, which provided the intellectual stimulus which he had once had from Horace Moule.

He was establishing a reputation as a regional novelist with his stories about his fictional west-country setting, Wessex. However, his next novel was very different, being a humorous study of London life. It was called *The Hand of Ethelberta* and concerned relationships between servants and their employers, and was written from the servants' point of view. The heroine is a butler's daughter who establishes herself in middle-class society – in some ways an allegory of Hardy's own career. It was published in serial form in the *Cornhill Magazine* beginning in the summer of 1875. Hardy was engaged in writing successive instalments whilst he and Emma were living in Swanage and looking for a house in Dorset. On their way to Swanage, they stayed briefly in Bournemouth and there they had a quarrel, which he depicted in a poem, *We Sat at the Window*:

> We sat at the window looking out
> And the rain came down like silken strings
> That Swithin's day. Each gutter and spout
> Babbled unchecked in the busy way
> Of witless things:
> Nothing to read, nothing to see
> Seemed in that room for her and me
> On Swithin's day.
>
> We were irked by the scene, by our own selves; yes,
> For I did not know, nor did she infer
> How much there was to read and guess
> By her in me, and to see and crown
> By me in her.
> Wasted were two souls in their prime
> And great was the waste, that July time
> When the rain came down.

Hardy did not like Bournemouth and the weather was bad; but their mutual hostility stemmed from Hardy's mother's refusal to come to see them in Bournemouth. She had not fully accepted Emma as her daughter-in-law, and in any case she could not see why they could not visit her in Bockhampton. Hardy appeared intent on keeping Emma away from his home village, for though he was seeking a home in Dorset, he did not want it to be near Bockhampton. His sisters visited him at Swanage, but again his parents did not come. Emma was not to meet them until the end of 1876, when she and Thomas spent Christmas with them. He never allowed her to meet the rest of his family.

Towards the end of May 1876, after a fortnight in London, Thomas and Emma made another trip to the Continent, going first to Rotterdam and then on into Germany as far as Heidelberg. They then travelled to Brussels, where Thomas was intent on seeing the battlefield of Waterloo. Emma was exhausted and unwell, but he did not allow anything to interrupt their intinerary. The Napoleonic Wars had become an obsession with him: the year before, he had visited Chelsea Hospital to seek out and talk to veterans of Waterloo. He did so again on returning from his trip. Thirty years later, his overpowering interest was to result in the publication of his long epic poem, *The Dynasts*.

Lodging for a short time in Yeovil, they continued their search for a permanent home, and in July they rented a semi-detached, bay-windowed villa in Sturminster Newton in north Dorset. It occupied a fine position overlooking the river Stour. This was their first home together, and they were happier there than they were to be anywhere else. Subsequently, Thomas wrote a poem about this time, calling it *A Two-Years' Idyll*. The first verse reads:

Yes; such it was;
Just those two seasons unsought,
Sweeping like summertide wind on our ways;
Moving, as straws,
Hearts quick as ours in those days;
Going like wind, too, and rated as nought
Save as the prelude to plays
Soon to come — larger, life-fraught:
Yes; such it was.

He goes on to hint in the remaining two verses, at the *larger, life-fraught* plays which were to come. But this was for the future: the present was an idyll.

Thomas and Emma made positive efforts to meet local people and be accepted by them. Amongst their acquaintances was William Barnes, the parson-poet who lived in the area and made it well known by his dialect poetry. But Hardy did not use the local scenery as a background for his next book, *The Return of the Native*. For this he returned once more to his familiar Bockhampton. By early 1877, he had made sufficient progress with it to send a draft of the opening chapters to Leslie Stephen. Surprisingly, Stephen rejected the book for serialisation in the *Cornhill Magazine*, saying the plot was unsuitable for a family magazine. He was after a simple, pastoral tale which Hardy no longer wished to write. Eventually, he placed it with a journal called *Belgravia*, whose editor was only prepared to pay £20 per instalment, less than half the sum he had received for *The Hand of Ethelberta*. Publication in book form by Smith, Elder brought him more money, as did serialisation in America. Nevertheless, it made him think seriously about how to maximise his earnings. He aspired to be a shrewd businessman, but he was haunted by themes more powerful than his business instincts.

The tragic death of Horace Moule had confirmed Hardy's loss of faith in a loving Christian God. If God existed, he thought, He cared little for individual men and women, and might even be deliberately malevolent. All the novels Hardy wrote from this time on were to pursue this theme of a malevolent fate dogging the footsteps of the principal characters. Hardy himself became increasingly preoccupied with what he saw as the cruel fate of women. The unwanted pregnancies of young, unmarried girls, the deaths in childbirth, the drudgery of the lives of working girls: these themes haunted him. Whilst the Hardys were at Sturminster Newton, a young maid in their household ran away and in due course gave birth to a baby who died after two days. He linked the gloom of a rainy June afternoon with this domestic tragedy in his poem *Overlooking the River Stour,* and lamented in his usual terse, allusive manner his lack of sensitivity to the misery of others:

Closed were the kingcups; and the mead
Dripped in monotonous green,
Though the day's morning sheen
Had shown it golden and honeybee'd;
Closed were the kingcups; and the mead
Dripped in monotonous green.

And never I turned my head, alack,
While these things met my gaze
Through the pane's drop-drenched glaze,
To see the more behind my back ...
O never I turned, but let, alack,
These less things hold my gaze!

Some have read into this last verse Thomas's feelings about Emma: that in his striving to achieve he had neglected to observe significant events in his marriage. For all was not well. There are hints that the sexual side was unsatisfactory, and an indication that Emma could not share the intellectual interests of her husband. Possibly believing that a change of house and background would be the answer to their problems, they decided to move back to London. They took a lease of a house in Tooting in the south London suburbs, and moved in towards the end of March 1878.

Emma's hope was that, once back in London, her husband could enhance his literary standing by mixing with publishers, editors, critics and fellow authors. He certainly tried to do this by getting himself elected to London's main literary club, the Savile, and wining and dining with its members.

One of the publishers with whom he established a close relationship was Charles Kegan Paul, who had for twelve years been the vicar of a Dorset village and was now a distinguished literary gentleman. Kegan Paul invited the Hardys to his parties and extended their range of literary acquaintances. He made the mistake, although it did no damage to their friendship, of referring to Hardy as having sprung from a race of labouring men. Hardy was quick to reply that in fact his family were independent master-masons, knowing that, in the class-ridden society of the day a hint of working-class origins would be damaging to his image as a man of letters. Kegan Paul was the editor of a literary journal, the *New Quarterly Magazine*, and in it he published two of Hardy's short stories.

Hardy was always subject to fits of melancholy, and he used poetry to deal with these feelings. A short poem, written at the time, called *A January Night*, is an example:

> *The rain smites more and more,*
> *The east wind snarls and sneezes;*
> *Through the joints of the quivering door*
> *The water wheezes.*
>
> *The tip of each ivy shoot*
> *Writhes on its neighbour's face;*
> *There is some hid dread afoot*
> *That we cannot trace.*
>
> *Is it the spirit astray*
> *Of the man at the house below*
> *Whose coffin they took in today?*
> *We do not know.*

Another poem, written many years later, *Beyond the Last Lamp*, recalls an incident near Tooting Common on a similar night of darkness and rain, and it too evokes a sense of dread. The poet is walking in the rain, and as he passes *the last lone lamp*, he meets two people pacing arm-in-arm, their faces wan and downcast. They seem to him like two lovers who are no longer in love:

> *The pair seemed lovers, yet absorbed*
> *In mental scenes no longer orbed*
> *By love's young rays. Each countenance*
> *As it slowly, as it sadly*
> *Caught the lamplight's yellow glance*
> *Held in suspense a misery*
> *At things which had been or might be.*

Some hours later the same night, he passes the spot again, and the pair are still there, walking slowly and linked together. The poet reflects thirty years later:

Though thirty years of blur and blot
Have slid since I beheld that spot,
And saw in curious converse there
Moving slowly, moving sadly
That mysterious tragic pair,
Its olden look may linger on –
All but the couple; they have gone.

Whither? Who knows, indeed . . . And yet
To me, when nights are weird and wet,
Without those comrades there at tryst
Creeping slowly, creeping sadly,
That lone lane does not exist.
There they seem brooding on their pain,
And will, while such a lane remain.

Were they ghosts he saw? Or were they creatures of his own mind —
himself and Emma perhaps, recalling in sadness the days when they
had been so deeply in love?

In September 1880, Hardy travelled down to Bockhampton for a
family conference. His uncle James had died in March, and Thomas
was becoming more conscious of his family responsibilities. His
father, now in his late sixties, was suffering from severe rheumatism.
His younger sister Kate had left home to follow her sister Mary into
teaching, and Hardy felt he should live nearer his parents and take
more responsibility for them. The solution seemed to be that he
should buy some land in Dorset and build a house on it. Soon after
this decision, he fell dangerously ill and was in great pain. He was
diagnosed as suffering from an internal haemorrhage, but this was
guesswork since at that time X-rays were not available. He was
advised to stay in bed, his feet above his head, for as long as might be
necessary, and this he did, fearing for much of the time that he would
die. In the last verse of his poem *A Wasted Illness*, he wrote:

145

Where lies the end
To this foul way? I asked with weakening breath.
Whereon ahead I saw a door extend –
The door to death.

He did not pass through the door, and was not to do so for another fifty years. The illness was 'wasted' because he did not die, and he felt he would have in due course to approach death's door once more, and suffer again all the pain he had endured. Modern medical opinion inclines to the view that Hardy's illness was a stone in either the bladder or the kidney, and his long-drawn out recovery is blamed on the treatment ordered. But perhaps the restoration to full health was delayed because he did not rest properly. His strong sense of duty coupled with his determination to preserve his reputation at all costs led him to keep up the instalments of his current novel, *A Laodicean*, which was being serialised in America. The title refers to someone lukewarm or indifferent in religious matters, this being the stance of the hero of the novel, an architect. It seemed to reflect Hardy's own views at the time. His long illness and immobility gave him the opportunity to think through his ideas about the world. It was, he came to believe, an imperfect place in which the hopes of mankind could never find fulfilment, and which had been created by a God who was, if not malevolent, at least indifferent, to the suffering of his creation.

As soon as Hardy had recovered sufficiently, he and Emma continued their search for a home in Dorset. In June 1881 they took a lease of a villa with a large garden in Wimborne, and there they spent the next two years. They tried to put down roots but were not very successful. Hardy worked on his next novel, *Two on a Tower*, which was concerned with the love of a young astronomer for a wealthy older woman, their tortured emotions set against the background of the stars and the vast interstellar spaces which held no place for human feelings. He was also for a time caught up in the excitement of the production of *Far from the Madding Crowd* as a play, travelling up to Liverpool to see it staged.

Novel-writing was his bread and butter, but poetry was always in his mind. He continued to make notes for poems he would one day write, amongst these were jottings for his intended poetic masterpiece, *The Dynasts*. When *Two in a Tower* was published in England in book form in 1882, it was immediately criticised for its sexual overtones. Particularly repulsive to the more strait-laced readers was the pregnancy of the heroine, not simply because the infant is conceived out of wedlock, but because she entraps an innocent bishop into matrimony and foists her illegitimate child upon him. Again, the earthiness of Hardy's upbringing was at odds with the middle-class morality of many of his readers.

Hardy's relationship with his wife was still an unsettled one. Emma was increasingly drawn towards a fundamentalist form of Christianity which was alien to him; and the sexual aspect of their marriage grew ever more unsatisfying. They were dissatisfied with life at Wimborne. The town was small and dull, they said, and the air from the river Stour was bad for their health; but these complaints perhaps reflected the basic unhappiness of their life together. One of Thomas's poems written at this time illustrates his disillusionment with married love. It is called *He Abjures Love*, and the last verse reads:

> *I speak as one who plumbs*
> *Life's dim profound,*
> *One who at length can sound*
> *Clear views and certain.*
> *But – after love what comes?*
> *A scene that lours,*
> *A few sad vacant hours,*
> *And then, the Curtain.*

Thomas and Emma spent the April and May of 1883 in London, meeting literary lions like Robert Browning. Then at the end of June they moved to Dorchester, renting a dark rambling house called Shire-Hall Place. Hardy wanted to familiarise himself still further with the customs and traditions of rural Dorset. He realized that his true *métier* was that of a pastoral writer, with roots deep in his fictional Wessex. His future novels were to be Wessex-based, and he brought to these a maturity and assurance which established him as a major English author.

He was by now forty-three, a sparely-built, short man, with a trim beard and a taciturn manner. He mixed well in literary society and got on with the local gentry, but essentially was reserved, almost withdrawn. He was happy to spend whole days writing in his study, even missing meals so as not to interrupt his creative flow. Emma played the supportive wife of a man of letters, but she yearned for the social life which she felt to be her due. Her energy was increasingly confined to her tongue, her garrulousness becoming a byword.

Thomas by this time had found some land on which to build a house and create the permanency which his life had so far lacked. He devoted a lot of time and energy to designing the building and seeings its development through to completion. The site of the house, which he was to call Max Gate, after a nearby toll-gate, was just outside Dorchester in an isolated and elevated position. We know from his poem, *Looking Across*, written in 1915, that he could see northward across the valley to Stinsford church, because he dwells gloomily on the fact that Emma, his parents and his sister Mary are buried in the churchyard there, and that is where he too wishes to be buried.

The house, now close to a busy dual-carriageway, is owned by the National Trust and is open to visitors. It is not a country mansion but a solid red-brick villa, in keeping with his wish to be respected as a successful professional man rather than a member of the country gentry. He engaged his father and his brother Henry to undertake the building work, and with only a few workmen employed, the house took some twenty months to complete. An important feature of the house was Hardy's study, which at that time was on the first floor at the back, giving him privacy and freedom from interruption. He had the large garden – about one-and-half acres – planted thickly with trees, against the wind and inquisitive visitors. The house had no bathroom, but, whilst his second wife was to complain strongly about this, it was not out of line with current standards. At least there was a flush toilet, serviced by water pumped by hand each day to a tank in the roof. Servants were cheap – they employed four – so this chore did not fall upon the Hardys.

Thomas was a non-smoker, drank little alcohol and ate abstemiously. It is true that in a simple verse called *Great Things*, he hymns the pleasure of cider, but this did not mean that he drank much of it:

Sweet cyder is a great thing,
A great thing to me,
Spinning down to Weymouth town
By Ridgway thirstily.

He went on to describe dancing and love-making as great things too; but, at this time, it is unlikely that he was taking joy in these either.

By the close of June 1885, Thomas and Emma had occupied Max Gate. While developing the garden and surrounding himself with trees, Thomas settled down to a regime of concentrated writing. He had just completed his novel. *The Mayor of Casterbridge*, which is set in a Dorset background, its fictional town owing much to early Victorian Dorchester. The tragic hero, whose rise and fall is the subject of the story, plays out the Hardyesque concept of a good man pursued by a malign fate. He moved on, with little break, to write *The Woodlanders*. This has a similar pastoral setting, but the story is closer to his own domestic life, with the heroine unable to appreciate the qualities of her more lowly-born lover. This was, as with the other novels, serialised first, and then published in book form, in March 1887.

Immediately after it appeared in the bookshops, the Hardys set off for a holiday in Italy. They saw the usual sights in Florence, Rome, Pisa, Venice and Milan, and were home by the end of April, to find that *The Woodlanders* had been favourably reviewed and was on its way to becoming as popular as *Far from the Madding Crowd*. Hardy was offered the handsome advance of a thousand guineas for the serial rights of his next novel, and he soon started work on it. It was *Tess of the d'Urbervilles*, and was to take him more than four years to complete.

He was delayed by concentrating during the winter of 1887-88 on more short stories, for which magazine editors were constantly asking him. Two new stories, together with four that he had previously written, were published under the title of *Wessex Tales*. Included in the book was a map of Wessex, a fictional place comprising Dorset westwards to Cornwall. The map showed real towns like Portsmouth as well as invented names such as Casterbridge. By now, Hardy was being paid royalties instead of just a lump sum, and was steadily adding to his wealth.

149

All this time, he had been working out the plot and characters of Tess, and had made sufficient progress to be able to send his would-be publishers, Tillotson & Son, at least half the manuscript. He had been determined this time to write a story about life as it really was, with no allowances for the prudish susceptibilities of the middle-class ladies who were said to comprise the bulk of his readership. But Tillotsons questioned at once the moral aspects of the book, and when Hardy declined to make any alterations, they refused to publish it. Hardy rejected the thousand guineas advance and sought another publisher, only to discover that others had similar objections. Signs of disenchantment with novel-writing showed themselves when he wrote to a friend saying that he sometimes felt it was better to fail in poetry than succeed in prose. During 1889 and 1890 poetry was always in his mind.

On a train journey to London in March 1890, he wrote the first few lines of his poem, *Thoughts of Phena*, about his cousin Tryphena Sparks, once loved, long since married and long since lost:

> *Not a line of her writing have I,*
> *Not a thread of her hair,*
> *No mark of her late time as dame in her dwelling, whereby*
> *I may picture her there;*
> *And in vain do I urge my insight*
> *To conceive my lost prize*
> *At her close, whom I knew when her dreams were*
>   *upbrimming with light,*
> *And with laughter her eyes.*
>
> *What scenes spread around her last days,*
> *Sad, shining, or dim?*
> *Did her gifts and compassions enray and enarch her sweet ways*
> *With an aureate nimb?*
> *Or did life-light decline from her years,*
> *And mischances control*
> *Her full day-star; unease, or regret, or forebodings, or fears*
> *Disennoble her soul?*

Thus I do but the phantom retain
Of the maiden of yore
As my relic; yet haply the best of her — fined in my brain
It may be the more
That no line of her writing have I,
Nor a thread of her hair,
No mark of her late time as dame in her dwelling, whereby
I may picture her there.

It was a curious coincidence that Hardy began his poem a few days before Tryphena died, not knowing anything about her circumstances and having only a nostalgic memory of her. He completed the poem later. He tended to dwell a great deal on missed chances and what might have been, and upon the many girls he once thought he was in love with.

Hardy concentrated each winter on his writing, and he and Emma were socially isolated at these times. They remedied this by regularly spending the late spring and early summer in London, staying either in an hotel or rented apartments. His reputation now was such that he was much in demand from hostesses seeking literary lions. He and Emma visited museums and art galleries and attended theatres and concerts. She enjoyed this social whirl and so did he; but he was always looking to extend his experience and knowledge of the world.

Early in 1890, he completed six short stories, entitled *A Group of Noble Dames*, which had been commissioned by the editor of a journal called *The Graphic*. But once again his work was criticised as verging too closely on the immoral. He agreed to substantial revisions, but felt angry and humiliated. He was anxious too about the fate of *Tess of the d'Urbervilles* at the hands of *The Graphic's* editor, who had contracted to serialise it. He was forced, for the purpose of the serial, to substitute a mock marriage for the seduction or rape of Tess which appears in the book. Fortunately, his publishers in America demanded no such amendment; but it made him dream of the freedom from pettiness which poetry-writing would give him.

Hardy maintained his close ties with his parents, and since Bockhampton was only an hour's walk from Max Gate, he frequently visited them on Sundays. His close affinity with his mother did not please his wife, but she could do nothing about it. She wanted to involve herself in her husband's work, but intellectually was out of her depth. Her inconsequential chatter and dowdy appearance were sometimes an embarrassment to him when in London, where she contrasted painfully with the many attractive, intelligent women eager to make his acquaintance at the parties they attended. Sometimes he left Emma behind in their hotel, and she resented this.

In November 1891, *Tess of the d'Urbervilles* appeared in book form, with the sub-title *A Pure Woman*. It is a story of an innocent young woman betrayed by men and eventually hanged for murdering one of them. Whilst it shocked some of its early readers, it eventually came to be recognized as his greatest novel. He was to endure many criticisms of it, however, which hurt him deeply.

There are some photographs of him at this time, and some perceptive criticisms too, and they bear witness to his shortness of stature and slight physique. He had a small beard and moustache, greying hair and keen, observant eyes. Early in 1892, he shaved off his beard, giving a pronounced change in his appearance which some acquaintances attributed to an increase in self-confidence, engendered by his growing prosperity. By then he had been elected to the Athenaeum, one of the most exclusive of gentlemen's clubs, in recognition of distinguished merit in the literary field. He had surely arrived.

But whatever his renown, he maintained his links with his family. When his father died in July 1892, he became even closer to his mother, and the animosity between her and Emma grew ever more pronounced. Emma's dislike of Jemima was extended to Thomas's sisters, Mary and Kate; and although they had been friendly enough in the past, she now discouraged them from visiting Max Gate. Thomas did not show his feelings but he revealed thoughts about a failing marriage in his next novel, *The Well-Beloved,* in which an ageing but still romantic sculptor rails at his fate in being bound by marriage to a now old and shrivelled woman.

Faithful in body to Emma, Thomas had a roving eye and mind. He thought often of the women he had been attracted to in the past, however slight their contact, and he was always looking for someone with whom he could fall in love. He found such a woman in Mrs Florence Henniker, whom he met when visiting Dublin in May 1893. Married to a senior army officer, she was a woman of

152

intelligence and culture. Thomas wrote letters to her, and he squired her around London when opportunity offered, giving her lessons in architecture. She enjoyed his company but was unwilling for the relationship to go further. After many months the friendship cooled, and he wrote a number of poems regretting this. One of them, called *At an Inn*, tells of a visit he and Mrs Henniker made to Winchester Cathedral. At an inn, they are treated as if they are lovers:

> *And we were left alone*
> *As Love's own pair;*
> *Yet never the love-light shone*
> *Between us there!*
> *But that which chilled the breath*
> *Of afternoon,*
> *And palsied unto death*
> *The pane-fly's tune.*

It may be surmised that *that which chilled the breath of afternoon* was some kind of a rejection by Florence – perhaps of a kiss he offered.

In his poem *In Death Divided*, Hardy imagines himself and Florence Henniker both dead, but buried in graves miles apart, and observes with morbid satisfaction:

> *No shade of pinnacle or tree or tower,*
> *While earth endures,*
> *Will fall on my mound and within the hour*
> *Steal on to yours;*
> *One robin never haunt our two green covertures.*
>
> *And in the monotonous moils of strained, hard-run*
> *Humanity,*
> *The eternal tie which binds us twain in one*
> *No eye will see*
> *Stretching across the miles that sever you from me.*

Later, with the relationship still cooling, Florence failed to meet him at the British Museum as arranged, and he used the incident in *A Broken Appointment* for forlorn recrimination:

You did not come,
And marching Time drew on, and wore me numb –
Yet less for loss of your dear presence there
Than that I thus found lacking in your make
That high compassion which can overbear
Reluctance for pure lovingkindness' sake
Grieve I, when as the hope-hour stroked its sum,
You did not come.

You love not me,
And love alone can lend you loyalty:
– I know and knew it. But, unto the store
Of human deeds divine in all but name,
Was it not worth a little hour or more
To add yet this: once you, a woman, came
To soothe a time-worn man, even though it be
You love not me?

From the end of 1893, Hardy worked on what was to be his last novel, *Jude the Obscure*. It was initially called *The Simpletons* and then became *Hearts Insurgent*, under which name it was serialised in the United States, beginning in December 1894. The hero, *Jude*, fated to struggle against his lowly origins, never achieves the education and position in society to which he aspires. Nor does he find satisfaction in his love for the heroine, Sue. Their unmarried relationship ends in desperate tragedy when their two young children are murdered by the child of his earlier unhappy marriage. Sue leaves him and he dies alone in drunken misery.

The full version of the novel was published in book form in England in November 1895, and was ferociously attacked by the critics as shameful and obscene. Hardly anyone had a good word for it. Even those who could accept the immorality of the story found it hard to stomach the unrelieved gloom. One prominent person, however, did praise the book, his fellow-poet Swinburne, who found in it *beauty, terror and truth*. Hardy had expressed at last his true feelings about society's hypocritical attitude to sexual love, and his opinion of marriage which bound and confined the free spirit. He had also revealed the stultifying effect of the class system on the educational aspirations of the lower orders. All this was too much for the middle-class Victorian public. His work, they said, was decadent and immoral, and a bishop burnt his book and boasted of doing so.

Mrs Patrick Campbell, the famous actress, who was anxious to appear as Tess in the stage version of *Tess of the d'Urbervilles*, wrote a letter to Hardy congratulating him on his novel, though even she did not like the coarseness of some of the language. But nearer home, indeed within his own house, the hurt to female sensibilities was profound. Emma had known of and put up with Thomas's friendship with Florence Henniker, but what she could not accept in her husband's book was its contempt for the institution of marriage. Not only did it challenge her deeply-held Christian beliefs, it seemed to strike at the very heart of their relationship, which she still cherished. She began, so far as she could, to develop a life independent of his, and gradually became his critic rather than his supporter.

Within limits he welcomed this, and he began a new romantic friendship with a Mrs Agnes Groves, an intelligent woman in her thirties who, like Florence Henniker, had literary aspirations. He met her at her father's country house in Wiltshire when he danced with her at an open-air ball. Many years later, on Agnes's death, he recalled the event in *Concerning Agnes*:

> *I could not, though I should wish, have over again*
> *That old romance,*
> *And sit apart in the shade as we sat then*
> *After the dance*
> *The while I held her hand, and, to the booms*
> *Of the contrabassos, feet still pulsed from the distant rooms.*

Following the disapproving reception of *Jude*, Hardy turned with even greater longing towards the idea of ceasing to write novels and concentrating totally upon poetry. He had always been subject to changes of mood, and in the late 1890s his mind was increasingly filled with melancholy. In *Wessex Heights*, written in 1896, he expressed his feelings of isolation and alienation:

There are some heights in Wessex, shaped as if by a kindly hand
For thinking, dreaming, dying on, and at crises when I stand,
Say, on Ingpen Beacon eastward, or on Wylls-Neck westwardly,
I seem where I was before my birth, and after death may be.

In the lowlands I have no comrade, not even the lone man's friend –
Her who suffereth long and is kind; accepts what he is too weak to mend:
Down there they are dubious and askance; there nobody thinks as I,
But mind-chains do not clank where one's next neighbour is the sky.

In the towns I am tracked by phantoms having weird detective ways –
Shadows of beings who fellowed with myself of earlier days:
They hang about at places, and they say harsh, heavy things –
Men with a wintry sneer, and women with tart disparagings.

As for one rare fair woman, I am now but a thought of hers,
I enter her mind and another thought succeeds me that she prefers;
Yet my love for her in its fulness she herself even did not know;
Well, time cures hearts of tenderness, and now I can let her go.

So I am found on Ingpen Beacon, or on Wylls-Neck to the west,
Or else on homely Bulbarrow, or little Pilsdon Crest,
Where men have never cared to haunt, nor women have walked with me,
And ghosts then keep their distance; and I know some liberty.

Another poem of this period, *In Tenebris*, plumbs even deeper the
wells of regret and despair. The poem is in three parts, each headed
by a melancholy quotation from the Psalms. The first part is written
tersely, its few words accentuating the desperation. The last of its six
verses reads:

Black is night's cope;
But death will not appal
One who, past doubtings all,
Waits in unhope.

The second section has splendid rhythms and rhymes, like something
from Swinburne in format, if not in content. It contrasts men who

are happy with those, like himself, who are not:

> *When the clouds' swol'n bosoms echo back the shouts of the many and*
> *strong*
> *That things are all as they best may be, save a few to be right ere long,*
> *And my eyes have not the vision in them to discern what to these is so*
> *clear,*
> *The blot seems straightway in me alone; one better he were not here.*

> *Their dawns bring lusty joys, it seems; their evenings all that is sweet;*
> *Our times are blessed times they cry: life shapes it as is most meet,*
> *And nothing is much the matter; there are many smiles to a tear;*
> *Then what is the matter is I, I say. Why should such an one be here?*

In the final part, Hardy reflects that there were times in the past when he might have died happy:

> *Say, on the noon when the half-sunny hours told that April was nigh,*
> *And I upgathered and cast forth the snow from the crocus-border,*
> *Fashioned and furbished the soil into a summer-seeming order,*
> *Glowing in gladsome faith that I quickened the year thereby.*

> *Or on that loneliest of eves when afar and benighted we stood,*
> *She who upheld me and I, in the midmost of Egdon together,*
> *Confident I in her watching and ward through the blackening heather,*
> *Deeming her matchless in might and with measureless scope endued.*

But this was before he had learnt *that the world was a welter of futile doing.*

If Hardy's melancholy was triggered by criticism of *Jude the Obscure*, there was more to come when *The Well-Beloved*, serialised in America in 1892, appeared in book form in 1897. Despite some not unfavourable reviews, a comment which galled him was one expressing dismay and disgust at the depressing spectacle of genius in decline. Hoping that he would be able to render in verse ideas and emotions which the public could not accept in prose, Hardy wrote no more novels and turned finally and irrevocably to poetry.

He continued to spend part of the year in London, and Emma and he enjoyed frequent visits to the Continent. They both took up the new craze for cycling, which, with no cars on the roads, was still in its idyllic phase. Emma was increasingly opinionated and assertive, and his method of dealing with her was to maintain an impassive silence. He did not have access to her diary nor did he read her letters, so he was not fully aware of the extent of her discontent.

At the close of 1898, he published his first book of collected poems, *Wessex Poems and Other Verses*, illustrated by his own sketches. During the years he had been writing fiction, he had been filling his notebooks with material for poems he hoped one day to write. Ironic or poignant situations between people were mixed with descriptions of rural scenes. Most of the poems in the collection had been written in the 1890s and were based on these notes, and even the few which had been written earlier were substantially revised. He chose a wide variety of poems, as if to display himself in all his moods. The stanza forms were varied, but in all the poems the metre and rhyme were regular; there was no free verse or sprung rhythm and no obscurity. He said what he had to say and was brief and to the point. Whilst there was some comic verse, the general impression was one of sadness and pessimism. His poem *Neutral Tones* was included in the collection, and its bleak note of regret was typical of this. Another poem, *I look Into My Glass* articulates his view of the cruelty of time:

> *I look into my glass,*
> *And view my wasting skin,*
> *And say, 'Would God it came to pass*
> *My heart had shrunk as thin!'*
>
> *For then I, undistrest*
> *By hearts grown cold to me,*
> *Could lonely wait my endless rest*
> *With equanimity.*
>
> *But Time, to make me grieve,*
> *Part steals, lets part abide;*
> *And shakes this fragile frame at eve*
> *With throbbings of noontide.*

For the remaining thirty years of his life, Hardy was to pour out poetry, and this theme of the passing of time leading to unhappiness would be a constant one. Critics did not know what to make of *Wessex Poems*. The musical rhythms of Tennyson and Swinburne were largely absent, and for many, these were the essence of poetry. Hardy's verses seemed clumsy and even uncouth, and the persistent pessimism was hard to take. Furthermore, he was a great novelist and many people did not want to view him as a poet. One critic even felt he should burn his poems, lest they diminish his fame when he was dead. Emma was very unhappy about the book. The poems which recalled his former loves, such as *Thoughts of Phena* and *Neutral Tones*, were deeply hurtful and she particulary resented *The Ivy-Wife*, which she felt portrayed her as destroying her husband:

> *In new affection next I strove*
> *To coll an ash I saw,*
> *And he in trust received my love;*
> *Till with my soft green claw*
> *I cramped and bound him as I wove ...*
> *Such was my love: ha-ha!*
>
> *By this I gained his strength and height*
> *Without his rivalry.*
> *But in my triumph I lost sight*
> *Of after-haps. Soon he,*
> *Being bark-bound, flagged, snapped, fell outright*
> *And in his fall felled me!*

Emma had come to feel that she was all but equal to Thomas in literary ability. She believed that without her advice and encouragement, he would not have been so successful, and she felt angry at his ingratitude. She also strongly resented the help he had given to Florence Henniker and Agnes Groves in their literary endeavours. A further bone of contention was religion. Her Christian faith had begun to verge on the fanatical, while his agnosticism had become increasingly cynical and despairing. By now their minds had no common ground. Whilst he tried to maintain a façade of domestic harmony, she made no attempt in her letters to her friends to hide her seething discontent. Both of them pursued a policy of what she called 'maximum separateness'. Whilst he found this tolerable because it enabled him to work undisturbed, for her it was a ground for further resentment.

In November 1901, Hardy's second collection of poems was published, *Poems of the Past and the Present*. In the Preface he said it comprised a series of feelings and fantasies written down in widely differing moods and circumstances and at various dates. The collection of 99 poems begins with some verses about the Boer War, all emphasising the pity and futility of it. Then, after a number of poems about his various European journeys, there is a series reflecting his views on life and on God. These philosophical poems are probably amongst his best work. They have a constant theme which is cumulative in its effect, leaving a feeling of pessimism, cynicism and despair.

The Mother Mourns warrants careful reading. It is the plaint of Mother Nature who, in creating mankind, has unwittingly conceived a creature who has outgrown her and has become her critic rather than her admirer:

> *'Give me', he has said, 'but the matter*
> *And means, the gods lot her,*
> *My brain could evolve a creation*
> *More seemly, more sane'.*

In *I said to Love*, the poet is world-weary again:

> *I said to Love,*
> *'Thou art not young, thou are not fair,*
> *No elfin darts, no cherub air,*
> *Nor swan, nor dove*
> *Are thine; but features pitiless,*
> *And iron daggers of distress',*
> *I said to Love.*

> *'Depart then Love! . . .*
> *— Man's race shall perish, threatenest thou,*
> *Without thy kindling coupling — vow?*
> *The age to come the man of now*

Know nothing of? –
We fear not such a threat from thee;
We are too old in apathy!
Mankind shall cease – So let it be',
I said to Love.

In the poem *God-Forgotten*, the poet visits God, and reminds Him of the suffering on earth; but God has forgotten that He ever created the place, and then says that in any case it surely cannot still exist:

'Some tiny sphere I built long back
(Mid millions of such shapes of mine)
So named . . . It perished surely – not a wrack
Remaining, or a sign?'

And He continues:

'And it is strange – though sad enough –
Earth's race should think that one whose call
Frames, daily, shining spheres of flawless stuff
Must heed their tainted ball! . . .

God orders his angels to put an end to earth's miseries, and the poet awaits their arrival.

In another poem, *By the Earth's Corpse*, Hardy imagines God contemplating the world on which everything is extinct, and exclaiming:

'That I made Earth, and life, and man,
It still repenteth me!'

However, in *The Darkling Thrush*, he does allow himself a spark of hope. He is surveying a wintry scene at twilight, in a mood of depression, when:

At once a voice arose among
The bleak twigs overhead
In a full-hearted evensong
Of joy illimited;

161

An aged thrush, frail, gaunt and small,
In blast-beruffled plume,
Has chosen thus to fling his soul
Upon the growing gloom.

So little cause for carolings
Of such ecstatic sound
Was written on terrestial things
Afar or nigh around,
That I could think there trembled through
His happy good-night air
Some blessed Hope, whereof he knew
And I was unaware.

These melancholy poems mingled strangely with verses recalling the
lost women whom Hardy felt he once had loved, even if he had not
as much as kissed them. Such a one was Lizbie Browne, the daughter
of a Bockhampton gamekeeper:

Dear Lizbie Browne
Where are you now?
In sun, in rain?—
Or is your brow
Past joy, past pain
Dear Lizbie Browne?

Sweet Lizbie Browne
How you could smile,
How you could sing!—
How archly wile
In glance-giving,
Sweet Lizbie Browne!

Dear Lizbie Browne,
I should have thought.
'Girls ripen fast'
And coaxed and caught
You ere you passed,
Dear Lizbie Browne.

162

But, Lizbie Browne,
I let you slip;
Shaped not a sign;
Touched never your lip
With lip of mine,
Lost Lizbie Browne!

It was no wonder that when Emma read such poems, which she had never seen before, she was sad and angry, and described them as moans and fancies written to please others. She began to speak of Thomas in derogatory terms to close friends of hers, describing him in one letter as ill-grown and undersized and referring to his relatives as peasants. Whatever his feelings, however, he never spoke ill of her. Because there were no children, it was rumoured that he was impotent, but this seems unlikely, given the sexually passionate imagination which *Tess of the d'Urbervilles* and other novels revealed.

Since the mid-1870s, Hardy had been planning a major poetic work on the Napoleonic Wars, and towards the end of the century it began to take shape, with the title of *The Dynasts*. It was to be a poetic drama in three volumes, and the first part reached the bookshops in January 1904. Intended to be read rather than staged, it was written in prose-like verse, with mythic entities such as *Shade of the Earth* and *Spirit of the Years* commenting on and interpreting the action. The second and third volumes were published in 1906 and 1908 respectively. The critics received the work favourably. It marked Hardy out as more than a great novelist, establishing him as a major man of letters, perhaps the greatest writer of his day. Whilst writing *The Dynasts*, he continued with his short poems, which seemed separate from and unaffected by his epic poem.

Towards the end of her life, Hardy's mother was deaf and bedridden, but he remained close to her emotionally and he visited her frequently. Despite the company of the great and famous with whom he increasingly mixed, he always acknowledged her as the most powerful influence on his life, and it was through her that he kept close to his roots in rural Dorset. Her death in April 1904 brought home to him that the Hardy line was coming to an end. His brother and two sisters had never married, and he himself was childless. More and more, he valued the past, looking back on it as an idyllic time gone forever.

By early January 1906, Hardy had made the acquaintance of Florence Dugdale, who in due course was to become his second wife. She was twenty-seven at the time and was working as a teacher. She had literary aspirations and greatly admired Hardy's books. She contrived to call on him while on a visit to Weymouth, and then sent him some flowers for his birthday. Their friendship blossomed. Her youth and admiration for his work was flattering to him, and he was soon finding little tasks for her to do for him at the British Museum Reading Room, which was easy for her to reach since she lived in north London.

Florence was a quiet, studious young woman, contrasting favourably, from Hardy's viewpoint, with his voluble, assertive wife. By the spring of 1907, he was occasionally visiting London museums and galleries with her. He presented her with signed copies of two of his books, and he started to help her with her literary work. She was writing stories for children at the time and he did his best to get them published. He was still seeing Agnes Groves when he was in London and he kept in touch with Florence Henniker; but increasingly his thoughts were of Florence Dugdale.

He regretted that initially he could not bring Florence to Max Gate; and their frequent meetings and partings upset him. His short poem *The Difference* summed up his feelings:

> *Sinking down by the gate I discern the thin moon,*
> *And a blackbird tries over old airs in the pine,*
> *But the moon is a sorry one, sad the bird's tune,*
> *For this spot is unknown to that Heartmate of mine.*
>
> *Did my Heartmate but haunt here at times such as now,*
> *The song would be joyous and cheerful the moon;*
> *But she will see never this gate, path or bough,*
> *Nor I find a joy in the scene or the tune.*

During this period he was preparing another collection of poetry. The book was called *Time's Laughingstocks*, and was published in December 1909. For the first time, his poetry was enthusiastically received, the first 2,000 copies selling out quickly. The book comprised 94 poems, written over a period of fifty years, with a quarter of them composed fairly recently. There were a number of ballads which were well-crafted stories. Generally, the poems were rhythmic and neatly rhymed, most of them appealing to the heart rather than the head. The metre varied widely, and the prevailing mood was one of gentle irony around the theme of the passing of time. In *God's Education* the poet addresses the Almighty as he watches the fading of his loved one's beauty:

> *I asked: 'Why do you serve her so?*
> *Do you, for some glad day,*
> *Hoard these her sweets?' He said, 'O no,*
> *They charm not me: I bid Time throw*
> *Them carelessly away.'*
>
> *Said I: 'We call that cruelty –*
> *We, your poor mortal kind.'*
> *He mused. 'The thought is new to me.*
> *Forsooth, though I men's master be*
> *Theirs is the teaching mind!'*

In 1909 came the death of Algernon Swinburne, whose poetry Hardy had so much admired ever since he had read his *Poems and Ballads* some forty years before. He placed himself beside Swinburne as a writer whose work was condemned by the hypocritical public for its sexual realism. He loved Swinburne's poetry for the magical, musical rhythms, which he himself so rarely produced. In the spring of the following year he went with Florence Dugdale to Bonchurch on the Isle of Wight to stand in respectful silence beside Swinburne's grave. looking with displeasure at the cross placed over the tomb of so notorious an atheist. To mark the occasion he wrote a lovely poem with a lilting rhythm of which Swinburne would have approved. It was called *A Singer Asleep*:

> *In this fair niche above the unslumbering sea,*
> *That sentrys up and down all night, all day,*
> *From cove to promontory, from ness to bay,*
> *The Fates have fitly bidden that he should be*
> *Pillowed eternally.*

O that fair morning of a summer day
When down a terraced street whose pavements lay
Glassing the sunshine into my bent eyes,
I walked and read with a quick glad surprise
New words in classic guise, –

The passionate pages of his earlier years,
Fraught with hot sighs, sad laughters, kisses, tears;
Fresh-fluted notes, yet from a minstrel who
Blew them not naively, but as one who knew
Full well why thus he blew.

So here, beneath the waking constellations,
Where the waves peal their everlasting strains,
And their dull subterrene reverberations
Shake him when storms make mountains of their plains –
Him once their peer in sad improvisations,
And deft as wind to cleave their frothy manes –
I leave him, while the daylight gleam declines
Upon the capes and chines.

In due course, Florence met Emma, and the two women struck up a friendship. Emma had no idea of the strength of her husband's feelings for Florence. She simply saw her as an amiable young woman who was useful in typing Thomas's work and some of her own too. For her part, Florence was resigned to being Thomas's 'heartmate' but never his wife. She hated the fierce quarrels that sometimes flared up between the Hardys, and tried to keep out of them. She worshipped Thomas but wished Emma no harm and expected her to outlive her husband.

In June 1910, Hardy was awarded the Order of Merit, a distinction which he valued above the knighthood which, to Emma's chagrin, he had declined two years before. He prized just as much the Freedom of the Borough of Dorchester, which he received four months later. Emma complained that Thomas got all the glory and that there was nothing for her. She was becoming increasingly eccentric, and Thomas's response was to withdraw emotionally from her even more. Florence Dugdale came to like them both and found their arguments extremely painful, doing her best not to be at Max Gate when they were both there.

Time, Hardy's great enemy, was dealing harshly with his appearance. In September 1912, a very old friend of his described him as looking, 'small, white and dried-up, his hair mostly gone, and his moustache faded from its original yellowish-red and thinned out so that it looked like the whiskers of a worn-out squirrel!' He was still alert and active, however, though Emma no longer was. She began to suffer from angina pains and also from gallstones, for which she refused to have an operation. In mid-November 1912 she experienced pains in her stomach and back. The pains got worse and more frequent, and on 27 November 1912 at 8 o'clock in the morning, she was found dying in her bed by her maid. The cause of her death was given as compacted gallstones and heart failure. She was seventy-two. Hardy arranged for her burial at Stinsford, near Bockhampton in a plot in the churchyard reserved for himself, alongside other members of the Hardy family.

Now that she was dead, his feelings towards her changed almost at once. Frustrated exasperation with her turned to regret at her passing and remorse for not treating her better. He installed his sister Kate as his housekeeper, packing Florence off to London after a few days in which she helped him with his correspondence. During the remainder of the year and the early months of 1913, he was engrossed in writing poetry, and all his poems were about Emma. The earliest of these expressed self-reproach for neglecting her; then, after a melancholy visit to St Juliot in March, came a series recalling the early happy days of their courtship and regretting its passing. His misery was made worse by his reading for the first time the diaries kept by Emma over the past twenty years in which she grew increasingly critical of him.

Florence Dugdale was pained and bewildered by Thomas's obsessive preoccupation with his dead wife. She nevertheless joined him at Max Gate in the spring of 1913, and worked for him as his secretary. She had for a time to put up with the presence of Lilian Gifford, Emma's niece, but within a year Lilian had been got rid of, and Florence was installed as sole mistress of the house.

Hardy's spirits gradually rose and for a time he became a relatively cheerful and affectionate companion. After a brief engagement, he and Florence were married on 10 February 1914 at Enfield Parish Church in north London. Only the closest relatives were present. To a friend, Hardy subsequently wrote that they had married in the hope that the union of two rather melancholy temperaments might result in cheerfulness. Florence was only thirty-five, but she was resigned to the role of secretary and housekeeper and, in due course, nurse. But she did not marry for financial security: she had a genuine affection for Thomas and a deep admiration for his literary achievements.

Hardy's next collection, published in November 1914, was entitled *Satires of Circumstance*. Most of the poems had been recently written, and amongst them was a group headed *Poems of 1912-13*, which included a number of his verses of remorse and regret. One, called *The Going*, laments the suddenness of Emma's passing, without any goodbye. It concludes:

> *Well, well! All's past amend,*
> *Unchangeable. It must go.*
> *I seem but a dead man held on end*
> *To sink down soon . . . O you could not know*
> *That such swift fleeing*
> *No soul forseeing –*
> *Not even I – would undo me so!*

In *Lament* he remembers Emma in happier days:

> *How she would have loved*
> *A party today! –*
> *Bright-hatted and gloved,*
> *With table and tray*
> *And chairs on the lawn*
> *Her smile would have shone*
> *With welcomings . . . But*
> *She is shut, she is shut*
> *From friendship's spell*
> *In the jailing shell*
> *Of her tiny cell.*

And she would have sought
With a child's eager glance
The shy snowdrops brought
By the new year's advance,
And peered in the rime
Of Candlemas-time
For crocuses . . . chanced
It that she were not tranced
From sights she loved best;
Wholly possessed
By an infinite rest!

In *Beeny Cliff* he recalls the sight of the cliff near St Juliot and cries:

O the opal and the sapphire of that wandering western sea,
And the woman riding high above with bright hair flapping free –
The woman whom I loved so, and who loyally loved me.

The pale mews plained below us, and the waves seemed far away
In a nether sky, engrossed in saying their ceaseless babbling say,
As we laughed light-heartedly aloft on that clear-sunned March day.

A little cloud then cloaked us, and there flew an irised rain,
And the Atlantic dyed its levels with a dull misfeatured stain,
And then the sun burst out again, and purples prinked the main.

– Still in all its chasmal beauty bulks old Beeny to the sky,
And shall she and I not go there once again now March is nigh,
And the sweet things said in that March say anew there by and by?

What if still in chasmal beauty looms that wild weird western shore.
The woman now is – elsewhere – whom the ambling pony bore,
And nor knows nor cares for Beeny, and will laugh there never-more.

The series of poems headed *Satires of Circumstance*, from which the collection took its name, originally appeared early in the book, but in subsequent editions was placed at the end. They are harsh little verses, depicting situations in which human beings often seem at their worst.

Later on, he regretted including them at all, feeling they were too brutal; but nevertheless they were vignettes of life as he saw it.

The First World War broke out in August 1914, and Hardy was soon plunged into despondency again. The terrible slaughter confirmed his pessimistic view of mankind and seemed to bear out his conviction that a benign and loving God could not exist. Florence not only had to put up with his gloom but also with his insistence that nothing whatever in Max Gate should be changed. His flow of poems of regret and remorse seemed the last straw. In a letter to a friend she wondered if she were really the right wife for him when he wrote such unhappy poems.

Although Hardy was not caught up in the patriotic fervour of the time, he wrote a number of poems supporting the struggle against evil. The young men were flocking to the colours, and his poem *Men who March Away* expresses an understanding of their cause:

> *In our heart of hearts believing*
> *Victory crowns the just,*
> *And that braggarts must*
> *Surely bite the dust,*
> *Press we to the field ungrieving,*
> *In our heart of hearts believing*
> *Victory crowns the just.*
>
> *Hence the faith and fire within us*
> *Men who march away*
> *Ere the barn-cocks say*
> *Night is going gray,*
> *Leaving all that here can win us;*
> *Hence the faith and fire within us*
> *Men who march away.*

Hardy's intense concentration on his poetry prevented him from brooding too much upon the war. He gathered many of his poems of this period together in another collection, *Moments of Vision*, published in 1917. His war poems were grouped under the subheading of *Poems of War and Patriotism*. Other poems, recalling his courtship and the early years of his marriage to Emma, added to

170

Florence's feelings of resentment and jealousy. But she was somewhat mollified when he embarked on his autobiography, which he intended should be published on his death as if it were written by her as his official biographer. She used to type his words from his manuscript as though they were her own. She published this biography under her own name shortly after her husband's death in 1928, and the elaborate deceit was not revealed until some years later. Hardy was a very private person, and to him it seemed totally right to record only what he wanted to be known about himself. Florence, of course, was happy to comply with his wishes.

In November 1915, Thomas lost his beloved sister Mary. He arranged for her to be buried beside his parents and Emma, and he took the same care over her gravestone as he had over theirs. He became more and more absorbed with the Hardy family, past and present; so much so that Florence began to feel left out, much as Emma had done. Honours were showered on him. In 1920, Oxford University made him an honorary Doctor of Literature. In the June of that year, on his eightieth birthday, a number of prominent writers, including John Galsworthy, journeyed to Max Gate to present him with the formal congratulations of the Incorporated Society of Authors. He mixed on easy terms with all the cultural lions of the day, and with leading politicians and prominent members of the aristocracy too, retaining a simplicity and naturalness which his many visitors admired. For Florence things were less happy. She was melancholy by temperament, and the thick screen of trees now surrounding Max Gate added to the gloom of the house and to her outlook. She suffered from a persistent sore throat; and keeping house and acting as secretary to a Grand Old Man of literature was increasingly a burden to her.

Without her ministrations, however, he could never have remained as poetically active as he did. Every morning would find him in his study, where he always wrote something, however little. Waiting for inspiration, he said, was useless. By lunch-time he would be tired, but come tea-time he was refreshed again and ready to talk to the visitors who arrived almost daily, amongst them the poets John Masefield, Robert Graves, Walter de la Mare and Siegfried Sassoon, who were members of what came to be known as the Georgian School, and towards whom he felt quite paternal, or even grand-paternal. To his visitors he was a genial, kindly old man. One of them said he was like a country doctor, with humour in his mouth and tragedy in his eyes.

Amongst the locals, however, he had a reputation for meanness, and Dorchester gossip had it that he was irreligious and immoral. He had a very substantial income by now, but old habits of parsimony remained with him; care over money had become second nature. He was generous enough, however, to his poor and often distant relatives, for this was part of his peasant upbringing.

In May 1922, yet another of his collections of poetry was offered to the public. The book was *Late Lyrics and Earlier*, and was accompanied by what he styled as an apology, in which he asserted his right to be gloomy if he wished. In fact, the volume included more cheerful poems than the last collection. It was a tribute to his poetic fertility at the age of eighty-two that at least half the poems were recent. The first one in the book, *Weathers*, is almost defiantly joyful:

> *This is the weather the cuckoo likes,*
> *And so do I;*
> *When showers betumble the chestnut spikes,*
> *And nestlings fly:*
> *And the little brown nightingale bills his best,*
> *And they sit outside at 'The Travellers' Rest',*
> *And maids come forth sprig-muslin drest,*
> *And citizens dream of the south and west,*
> *And so do I.*

There was a mixture of styles in the book: a *mélange* of the grave and glad. Racy songs rubbed shoulders with wry memories of women long since lost. Time touches his subjects and they wither and die. Men remember and regret. Some poems are suffused with sadness, but none with black despair. Hardy's admirers loved the collection and it was well received by the critics.

Even in his eighties he was susceptible to the charms of young women, and he found his dream girl of the moment in a young amateur actress called Gertrude Bugler. She was a member of a local drama society calling itself The Hardy Players. The Players produced an annual Hardy play, and he first noticed Gertrude when, in 1920, she acted in an dramatised version of *The Return of the Native*. Her fresh young beauty reminded him of *Tess of the d'Urbervilles* as she had been portrayed on the professional stage. and he told her that he hoped that she would one day appear in this role. In November 1924, she did play the part of Tess with the local group, and there was much gossip about the attention Hardy paid her. Subsequently, sponsored by Hardy, she was offered the part in a London production of the play. By this time, Florence was beside herself with worry about her husband's infatuation, and she called at Gertrude Bugler's house to beg her to withdraw, saying that Hardy's health would suffer if he went to London to see her perform. In the end, Gertrude did back out and Hardy accepted the situation; but Florence was growing increasingly depressed and dissatisfied with her life.

Hardy too was often depressed, but his poetry kept him going. In November 1925, at the age of eighty-five, he published yet another collection which he called *Human Shows*. As before, the book was a mixture of poems from the past and more recently written pieces. He varied style and metre, as ever, but made no move toward the Modernist school of free verse. He was a Victorian poet, it seemed, stranded in the twentieth century.

There were 152 poems in the collection. Fewer than half were, as he put it, poems of tragedy, sorrow and grimness; but he was still criticised for his melancholy. It is true there were two rather bleak philosophical poems, in one of which God explains that to Him everything that has ever been still exists, though we see them as dead and past; in the other God asserts that He never intended that death, so important to human beings, should have any meaning. In contrast to these were sixteen love songs and eleven deliberately humourous pieces. Nevertheless, the old sadness kept coming through. Once more, he laments Emma's death, and describes time as the melancholy passing of the years: lovers mismarry; a young woman, whose lover has recently died, enjoys herself at a dance and then remorsefully vows never to dance or sing again; he voices the feelings of a woman recently dead and buried; he views the portrait of a woman about to be hanged; a young soldier at his wife's death-bed falls alseep; another young soldier says farewell to his wife and his mother; he sees schoolgirls playing on the lawn who disappear at the sound of a bell, and he reflects that this is the lot of us all; he watches a hearse go by on a rainy day; and he records an epitaph on a pessimist:

173

I'm Smith of Stoke, aged sixty-odd,
I've lived without a dame
From youth-time on; and would to God
My dad had done the same.

In June 1926, Hardy marked his eighty-sixth birthday with a philosophic, world-weary poem, called *He Never Expected Much*:

Well, World, you have kept faith with me,
Kept faith with me;
Upon the whole you have proved to be
Much as you said you were.
Since as a child I used to lie
Upon the leaze and watch the sky,
Never, I own, expected I
That life would all be fair.

'I do not promise overmuch
Child; overmuch;
Just neutral-tinted haps and such',
You said to minds like mine.
Wise warning for your credit's sake!
Which I for one failed not to take,
And hence could stem such strain and ache
As each year might assign.

December 1926 saw the death of Florence's much loved and very delinquent dog, Wessex. She and Thomas mourned him and he was interred in their pets' cemetery in the garden. Both had a great love for animals. Thomas was still writing verse but destroying quite a lot of it as soon as it was written. He watched carefully over the re-printing of his novels and his poetry, and over the dramatisations of the novels which were appearing frequently. He still enjoyed the company of his tea-time visitors. The Prince of Wales had been one of them, much to the anxiety of Florence, who demanded extra servants to do the catering. Bernard Shaw had called and so too had H G Wells, accompanied by Rebecca West. T E Lawrence came more than once and gave Florence a ride on his motorcycle. Virginia

Woolf, after a visit, recorded her impression of Hardy as a puffy-cheeked, cheerful old man, confident about all he had done. She saw Florence as having the sad, lacklustre eyes of a childless woman; and no doubt Florence's melancholy came through to all her visitors, hard as she tried to please them.

Hardy was now selecting and revising poems for his next collection of verse, to be published, he hoped, on his ninetieth birthday. He gathered together poems which reflected all stages of his life, from his childhood in Bockhampton onwards. The collection was to be called *Winter Words*; but he was never to see it in print. He was ill and bed-ridden over the Christmas of 1927, living on beef-tea. He was nursed by Florence and her sister Eva. He rallied a little towards the end of December, and early in January asked for some bacon to be grilled for him over an open fire as his mother used to do. The recovery was short-lived, however, for his body was worn out and his strength gone. His mind began to wander, and on 11 January 1928 at nine o'clock in the evening, while Eva was taking his pulse, he died. He was eighty-eight.

Sir James Barrie, the playwright, who had been visiting him and had stayed on in Dorchester, began at once to lobby the Prime Minister, Stanley Baldwin, to secure a burial in Westminster Abbey. Hardy's heart was removed and was later interred in Stinsford churchyard, where his first wife and his parents and grandparents lay. His body was cremated and his ashes buried in Westminster Abbey on Monday 16 January. The Abbey was thronged with the great and the famous, among them the Prime Minister and the literary giants of the time; Rudyard Kipling was a pall-bearer. After the service, large crowds, despite the pouring rain, filed by the open grave in Poets' Corner. One feels that Hardy would have enjoyed the gloom, and would have taken a wry pleasure in the dignatories of the Church intoning religious sentiments in which he did not believe. At Stinsford, the interment of his heart took place at the same time, but in bright sunshine, with the birds singing.

Florence, who came to feel that the Abbey ceremony had been a mistake, was now a rich woman. She devoted the nine years remaining to her to watching over her dead husband's literary interests and defending his reputation. The first volume of *The Early Life of Thomas Hardy*, secretly written by Hardy but published under her name, appeared in the same year as his death. The second volume took another two years to produce, because she had to write the concluding portion herself from documents he had left. This monumental deception deceived the public for some time, but the garrulousness of old age proved Hardy's undoing. Late in his life, he had carelessly revealed the true authorship to a visiting American writer; but the secret was kept until 1943, five years after Florence's death.

The revelation led to immense speculation as to what Hardy had to hide. His relationships with young women up to his meeting with Emma – aged twenty-nine – were omitted from his memoirs; so too were any details of his humble origins. No doubt these matters meant more to him than they do to us today; but they are of great importance nevertheless, as the portrayal of the rural peasantry and his understanding of young women, shown by the memorable heroines of his novels, are essential factors in his literary success.

Perhaps the hardest thing to comprehend in his many-sided genius is the intense emotion which lay behind his dry exterior. He had a passion for women and both sympathized and empathized with them, yet he did not make either of his wives happy. His feelings dwelt in the past: he valued the love of the dead, rather than the living. In his poem *Afterwards* he projected his mind into the future and pondered on what people would think of him after his death. His hopes were modest, for he asked only to be remembered for appreciating the beauty of nature:

> *When the Present has latched its postern behind my tremulous stay,*
> *And the May month flaps its glad green leaves like wings,*
> *Delicate-filmed as new-spun silk, will the neighbours say,*
> *'He was a man who used to notice such things'?*
>
> *If it be in the dusk when, like an eyelid's soundless blink,*
> *The dewfall-hawk comes crossing the shades to alight*
> *Upon the wind-warped upland thorn, a gazer may think,*
> *'To him this must have been a familiar sight.'*
>
> *If I pass during some nocturnal blackness, mothy and warm,*
> *When the hedgehog travels furtively over the lawn,*

One may say, 'He strove that such innocent creatures should
      come to no harm,
But he could do little for them; and now he is gone.'

If, when hearing that I have been stilled at last, they stand at the door,
Watching the full-starred heavens that winter sees,
Will this thought rise on those who will meet my face no more,
'He was one who had an eye for such mysteries'?

And will any say when my bell of quittance is heard in the gloom,
And a crossing breeze cuts a pause in its outrollings,
Till they rose again, as they were a new bell's boom,
'He hears it not now, but used to notice such things'?

This is lovely poetry; but we remember Hardy for more than this. We recall that his noticing eye took in the trivial ironies and tragedies of human existence: the old shepherd waiting vainly in the rain to be hired at the annual hiring fair; the raindrops on the window watched by a couple consumed by anger with each other; the sad, self-absorbed lovers walking slowly in the rain; the market-girl, eager to sell her honey and apples and garden herbs, but standing unnoticed. We recall his ballads, his narrative poems, his dramatic vignettes of the human situation, his aching yearnings for the dead and the past. He wrote more than a thousand poems before he resolved to write no more, in his last poem saying:

Why load men's minds with more to bear
That bear already ails to spare?
From now alway
Till my last day
What I discern I will not say.

We remember him for all he did discern and all he did say – so memorably.

RUDYARD KIPLING

For me this land, that sea, these airs, those folk and fields suffice
What purple Southern pomp can match our changeful Northern skies,
Black with December snows unshed, or pearled with August haze –
The clanging arch of steel-grey March, or June's long-lighted days?

RUDYARD KIPLING

Joseph Rudyard Kipling was a literary phenomenon. Not only was he a master of fictional prose, particularly the short story, he was also a poet of outstanding talent. Other writers, such as Thomas Hardy, excelled in both prose and poetry, but largely kept them separate. Kipling combined both literary forms, believing that they were complementary, one being incomplete without the other. No writer, before or since, has achieved his astonishing facility in this respect. His earliest short stories were prefaced by an appropriate verse; and later in his literary career, he would frequently bracket a story with a poem at each end. In his novels, each chapter would be headed by a poem. Most of these poems he wrote himself, but occasionally he would use another poet's work if it seemed particularly apposite.

His prose seldom appeared without a poem; but many of his poems stood on their own. He was a prolific poet, more so even than Hardy. He wrote verse from his boyhood onwards. When he wished to express something important, he would usually put it in verse. It was said that when he grew older he tended to think in rhyme and rhythm. Although he achieved lasting fame with his short stories, he probably valued his poetry more; and, at the time he wrote it, it made him immensely popular. This was partly because he composed in a form which the ordinary person could readily understand. By and large, he employed common words in general use; his command of rhyme and rhythm was masterly, and he avoided the classicisms and archaisms comprehensible only to the intellectual and academic.

Whilst his fiction maintained its popularity throughout his life, Kipling's poetry in later years suffered some decline in esteem. This was partly due to his political views falling out of fashion, for he was very much a political poet. But another reason was that the literary world moved on. He was out of step with the intelligentsia all his life, and was at daggers drawn with the Aesthetic Movement of the late nineteenth century. But when the poets of the Modernist school like Eliot and Pound came to the fore in the 20s and 30s, his poetic reputation plummeted.

His was the poetry of the plain man, whilst the Modernists tended to be subtle, allusive, pessimistic and somewhat obscure. He came to be seen as the author of 'jingo-jingles', voicing outdated platitudes. Collections of his poetry continued to enjoy a very wide circulation, but it was not until the early 40s of this century that the literary establishment began to appreciate and accept him again.

Kipling was born in Bombay on the west coast of India on 30 December 1865. His first Christian name, Joseph, was never used. His second, often shortened to Ruddy or Rud, commemorated his parents' first meeting at a picnic at Lake Rudyard (now Rudyard Reservoir), near Leek in Staffordshire. The Kiplings were a Yorkshire family, and his father, John Lockwood Kipling, was a writer and scholar as well as an artist, sculptor and architect. He became his son's most valued critic, and Rudyard inherited his capable craftsman's hands. His mother, born Alice Macdonald, had Scottish, Irish and Welsh blood. She came from a talented middle-class family. Three of her younger sisters married respectively the painter Edward Burne-Jones, of the Pre-Raphaelite Brotherhood; the less well-known painter, Edward Poynter; and a wealthy ironmaster, Alfred Baldwin. (One of the offspring of this last match was the future prime minister, Stanley Baldwin.)

Lockwood and Alice were married in London on 18 March 1865. Almost immediately after the wedding they set sail for Bombay, where Lockwood was to take up the post of Professor of Architectural Sculpture in the city's new School of Art. The India of those days comprised not only present-day India, Pakistan and Bangladesh, but also the lower half of Burma; upper Burma was annexed a year later. A good third of the country consisted of the so-called Native States under princes who retained local powers; but in practice the British governed the whole sub-continent.

In his autobiography, *Something of Myself*, Kipling gave his first memory of Bombay as, *daybreak, light and colour and golden and purple fruits at the level of my shoulder*. This was his recollection of early morning walks to the Bombay fruit-market with his *ayah* or nanny. He not only had an *ayah*, but also at his beck and call was his father's Hindu bearer and other domestic servants. And, such was the respect accorded to first sons, particularly British ones, he must have acquired an inflated idea of his own importance. His mother brought him back to England when he was two years old, so that she could be at home for the birth of her second child, Alice, who came to be known as Trix. Amongst his mother's family he became noted for his temper tantrums when he was crossed in any way. The advent of his sister was undoubtedly good for him. He did not resent her; indeed, he was devoted to her, remaining so for the rest of his life.

Ruddy and Trix returned to Bombay with their mother and stayed there for the next three years. Mixing as he did every day with the native servants – by this time he had a bearer of his own – Ruddy rapidly learnt the version of Hindi which they spoke, and grew more fluent in it than he was in English. He became familiar with the real India in a way that his parents never did. The sights, sounds and smells of Bombay fascinated him. He had a powerful memory from an early age, and he readily absorbed the native culture, so alien to his own. It was a very happy time, and more than twenty years later he was to recall it in his poem, *The Song of the Wise Children*:

> We shall go back to the boltless doors
> To the life unaltered our childhood knew –
> To the naked feet on the cool, dark floors,
> And the high-ceiled rooms that the Trade blows through:
>
> To the trumpet-flowers and the moon beyond,
> And the tree-toad's chorus drowning all –
> And the lisp of the split banana-frond
> That talked us to sleep when we were small.

But it could not last, for the custom of the expatriate British was to send their children back to the home country as soon as they were old enough to go to school. Taking advantage of a rare long leave, Lockwood and Alice returned their children to England when Ruddy was five and Trix was three, placing them with foster parents in Southsea and then returning to India.

Even at at the age of seventy Rudyard could still recall the

183

journey on the paddle-wheel steamer, the train across the desert – there was no Suez Canal in those days – and the arrival at the cold, dark little house he was to live in for the next six years. It was called Lorne Lodge, but Rudyard knew it as the House of Desolation. It was ruled with a rod of iron by a Mrs Holloway, who was both a Christian moralist and a disciplinarian – a frightening combination to a small boy who had known only freedom and indulgence. Her husband, Captain Holloway, was a kindly but ineffectual retired Merchant Navy officer, and after his death Aunt Rosa, as she liked to be called, could discipline her small charge entirely as she wished. This she did with frequent beatings and confinement, when she deemed it necessary, to a small, damp cellar.

How such liberal, kindly parents could choose such a home for their children is puzzling. However, Trix's recollections of life with the Holloways were not so dire, and perhaps Rudyard exaggerated, but it certainly left him with bitter memories. One of Aunt Rosa's punishments was to make him read the Bible on Sundays, but this misfired, because he enjoyed it, and it left him with an extensive knowledge of the Old and New Testaments. When she discovered that reading was one of his greatest pleasures, however, the outcome was much less happy, because her punitive attempts to deprive him of books led him to read under the bed clothes in such appalling light that his eyes were permanently damaged.

There were some happy times, and these were when he was allowed to take holidays with his Aunt Georgie, who was married to the artist Edward Burne-Jones. Here he played with his cousins and his aunt and uncle and their friends, who included the poet and painter, William Morris. In later life he described the house as a paradise. So much in love with it was he that eventually when he had a house of his own in Sussex, he acquired the bellpull which he used to tug so gleefully on his arrival there many years before.

His mother removed him from the Holloway household in March 1877, when he was eleven years old. She had returned from India because she had heard of his unhappiness and his growing short-sightedness. She arranged for him to be fitted with thick-lensed spectacles before taking him and his sister to stay on a farm in Epping Forest for the summer. Though quite near London, this was a lovely rural area in those days, and the children enjoyed themselves playing in the fields. Rudyard did a lot of reading, including Dickens, Bunyan and Fielding. In the autumn they stayed for a time in London, and Ruddy and Trix visited the museums, in particular the Victoria and Albert Museum, where Rudyard was fascinated by the ancient scientific instruments. He was also greatly absorbed by a manuscript of a Charles Dickens novel.

It was now time to find Rudyard a boarding school. The fees at the well-known public schools were too high, and his parents settled on a newly-established school at Westward Ho! on the north coast of Devon. It was called the United Services College, and it was intended largely for boys whose fathers were serving overseas. The headmaster, Cormwell Price, was a cultured man friendly with Burne-Jones, William Morris and others of the Pre-Raphaelite set. He was acquainted with the Kipling parents, and Rudyard knew him as Uncle Crom; but this did not save him from the brutality of the boarding schools of the day. He was bullied by the older boys and was caned unsparingly by the staff, particularly the chaplain. He wrote to his mother complaining, but she took little notice, even condemning him to stay on at school during the Easter holidays while she went off to Italy to meet his father on his way back on leave from India.

He had to stick it out on his own, and perhaps this helped to turn him into the confident, self-possessed young man he became. He formed a close friendship with two other boys, with whom in due course he shared a study. In 1899 he published a book of short stories called *Stalky & Co.*, which gave a fanciful semi-biographical picture of life at a boarding school. In the book, Kipling's nickname is Beetle, the plump, bookish, short-sighted member of the triumverate, the other two being Stalky and M'Turk. He fitted the Beetle description, except that in real life his nickname was Gigger, which referred to the gig-lamps – slang for spectacles – that he had to wear. He grew a moustache while still at school and tended to look mature for his age.

Rudyard and his two friends acquired a reputation as the school intellectuals. Rudyard became the principal contributor to the school magazine and eventually its editor. He was secretary of the literary society and regularly composed verses for the annual school concert.

185

His headmaster grew to like and respect him and encouraged his literary endeavours. There was an emphasis in the school on hard work, and a liking for work of all kinds remained with Rudyard all his life. As well as English and mathematics and the classics, he studied French, in which he became quite fluent. The Latin poet Horace particularly interested him, and he admired his poetry all his life.

The United Services College aimed principally to prepare boys for the Army; but his poor eyesight debarred Rudyard from this career. Pupils were not prepared for Oxford or Cambridge, and thus further formal education was ruled out too. This had its advantages, as it spared him the excessive preoccupation with the classics of more highly educated men like Swinburne and Hopkins. Thus his acute mind was allowed to roam more freely. He read the modern poets widely, even swimming his side-stroke in the sea to the rhythm of Swinburne's *Atalanta in Calydon*. He also dipped enthusiastically into French, Russian and American literature. Religion was not forced upon him, and he grew up with no strong Christian faith but a deep knowledge of the Bible. Such faith as he had as a young man was in the value of literature and art, acquired from his parents and their cultured relatives and friends. From his school he learnt to be proud of his country and its Empire.

During the school holidays, Rudyard used to visit his sister Trix, who was still living with Mrs Holloway in Southsea. On one of these visits, when he was nearly fifteen, he met a girl of about the same age who was boarding there. Her name was Florence Garrard and he fell deeply in love with her. Within a year he was pressing her to become engaged, but she demurred. He met her by chance some seven years later when he had been to India and returned, but in the end the relationship petered out.

He went to India at the behest of his father in September 1882. He was not quite seventeen, but looked rather older, with his burgeoning moustache. Lockwood Kipling had recognized his son's literary abilities for some time, and he obtained a job for him on an English-language newspaper in Lahore in the Punjab, now in Pakistan, where he himself was the Curator of the city's museum and Principal of the Mayo College of Art. Rudyard joined his parents in their gracious bungalow, and soon felt quite at home again in their adopted country.

The paper was the *Civil and Military Gazette*. His title was Assistant Editor, but over the five years he was there, he undertook most of the tasks associated with writing, making up and distributing a newspaper. He readily accepted the responsibilities placed on his young shoulders, and in less than a year he was travelling on his own to the local villages and towns, reporting on everything that was newsworthy, from village fêtes to intercommunal skirmishes. By 1886, under a new editor, he was writing weekly stories for the paper, filling blank gaps with these stories and with verses too, writing them exactly to the length required. The verse column-fillers were wry and witty, and proved so popular that a collection of them was published in book form under the title *Departmental Ditties*. The ditties were hardly great poetry, but they described the pleasures and pains of life for the British in India in such an amusing way that they became all the rage.

He arranged for the first edition to be printed on the presses of his own newspaper and paid for it himself. Light-heartedly, the collection was paper-covered and looked like an official government envelope, tied with red tape. Its full title was *Departmental Ditties and Other Verses*, there being eleven departmental ditties and fifteen other verses. Subsequent editions were issued by an established publisher, the fourth being published in London in 1890 in hard covers and including additional verses.

Kipling admired the dedication to duty of his subjects – administrators, clerks, engineers, lawyers, soldiers and the like – but he made fun of them and no-one knew quite where he stood. He widened his range of acquaintances when he joined a masonic lodge, for there he met Indian clerks and administrators too. He also frequented the messes of the British Army stationed in Lahore, talking and drinking with both officers and other ranks.

He suffered, as did many others, from the extreme temperature of the hot season from April to October. His parents and his sister would retreat to the hill-station at Simla and he would be left alone in their bungalow, tied to Lahore by his work. He had suffered from insomnia since boyhood, and the heat made it worse. At night he would move his bed from room to room seeking relief and would often sleep on the roof. He took to wandering the city streets at night, returning at dawn. He learnt a lot about real Indian life from this, He often felt lonely and depressed, and looked forward to his annual months leave in Simla, where it was cool and he had time to talk to his family, which he loved doing.

After five years in Lahore, at the age of twenty-three, he was sent south to Allahabad, a largely Hindu town in central India, to work for a sister paper called the *Pioneer*. This was a more substantial periodical than the *Gazette* and had a countrywide circulation. Amongst other duties he edited a weekly supplement, and this gave him more scope for including his stories and extending their length. His first book of fiction, called *Plain Tales from the Hills*, was published in 1888 and comprised some forty of his stories. They proved immensely popular amongst English speakers in India, and further stories from the *Pioneer* were collected and published as paperbacks as soon as there were enough to make a volume. In due course, *Plain Tales* appeared in British bookshops and achieved a steady sale.

Kipling travelled around central India, even going as far as Calcutta on the east coast. Everywhere he talked to people, his command of Hindi enabling him to communicate with Indians as easily as with his own race. He was fascinated by other people's work experience and the way things were done. He mixed particuarly with the middle ranks of the Anglo-Indians – that is, the British who had made their lives in India and ruled and administered it. He travelled extensively on the railways they had constructed amongst so much else. But he also had a liking for and an understanding of the common soldiers.

Increasingly, much as he loved India, he recognized that his literary future lay in London. In March 1889, with the blessing of his parents, he sailed from Calcutta for England, travelling via China and the United States of America. He returned to India again for only a brief visit, but he was to write about it for much of his life. India had made an impression on him which was long-lasting, indeed indelible. The heat, the dust, the monsoon rains, the teeming humanity thronging the streets, the smells, the beggars, the beauty of dawn and sunset, the squalor, the babble of voices, the festivals, the mosques, the temples, the towers of silence, the slow movement of cows in the streets: these images and memories lived with him for the rest of his life. Some of his best work, both in prose and poetry, reflected the India he knew.

A born traveller, it was characteristic of him not to return to England the shortest way. He stopped in Burma, Singapore, Hong Kong and then Canton. He made a longer stay in Japan and then sailed on to San Francisco, where he struggled to come to terms with the contrasting violence and friendliness he met there. He visited Vancouver, returned to the United States, and then sailed for England across the Atlantic, arriving in October 1889.

Kipling was far more widely travelled than the other poets we have discussed; and more mature for his age. But being wise beyond his years meant that his ideas were soon set in a pattern which was not to alter much over his life. He was a patriot, and in modern eyes has been considered to be a racist. He believed strongly that the English-speaking white race had something unique to offer to the world: the capacity to govern fairly in accordance with the law, without seeking personal advantage. Men of other races might be superior in other spheres, but government, law-giving and law-enforcement were uniquely and appropriately exercised by the white race to the benefit of all. This was the 'white man's burden', a concept widely mocked today, but one which to Kipling was very real.

The men who shouldered this burden on behalf of their compatriots for the good of others were in his view a special breed. They were honest, disciplined, restrained, conscientious and did not seek undue reward or praise. They did their duty even though the heavens might fall. The British had introduced into India something that country had never enjoyed: a civil service whose members were appointed largely on merit, and which prided themselves on being incorruptible. Its members were respected by all races, and it was they, in Kipling's eyes, who bore the white man's burden. In 1899, he expressed this concept in verses addressed to the United States, when that country assumed the government of the Philippine Islands following its successful war with Spain:

> Take up the White Man's burden –
> Send forth the best ye breed –
> Go bind your sons to exile
> To serve your captives' need;
> To wait in heavy harness
> On fluttered folk and wild –

189

Your new-caught, sullen peoples,
Half devil and half child.

Take up the White Man's burden –
In patience to abide,
To veil the threat of terror
And check the show of pride;
By open speech and simple,
An hundred times made plain,
To seek another's profit,
And work another's gain.

Take up the White Man's burden –
The savage wars of peace –
Fill full the mouth of Famine
And bid the sickness cease;
And when your goal is nearest
The end for others sought,
Watch Sloth and heathen Folly
Bring all your hope to nought.

Much of this is outdated to the modern reader; nonetheless it expresses Kipling's views at the time. The India he knew had suffered famine, drought and sporadic wars for centuries, and he saw the recently formed Indian Civil Service as bringing order out of chaos and instilling a sense of duty and concern for others which had not existed before. He may have thought that the British were good at governing, but he was not foolish enough to believe that they excelled in everything. He had an immense love and respect for the Indians amongst whom he worked, and in some of his stories and verses he portrays them as braver and wiser than his compatriots. In *The Ballad of East and West*, one of his most quoted lines runs: *Oh, East is East and West is West, and never the twain shall meet.* But he goes on to assert that on God's Day of Judgment all men will be equal in His eyes:

But there is neither East nor West, Border, nor Breed nor Birth,
When two strong men stand face to face, though they come from
the ends of the earth!

The ballad tells of a native bandit leader and a British colonel's son, equal in bravery and honour. The ballad is not concerned with women or weak men, but the egalitarian message is there: people of all races and all classes are equal in God's eyes. Kipling respected different religions too. A brief poem heading a chapter in his novel *Kim*, illustrates his attitude:

> *My brother kneels (so saith Kabir),*
> *To stone and brass in heathen-wise,*
> *But in my brother's voice I hear*
> *My own unanswered agonies.*
> *His God is as his fates assign —*
> *His prayer is all the world's — and mine.*

All religions to him were pathways to God. His portrayal of the aged sadhu, who is Kim's guide and teacher, is a masterly evocation of a Buddhist holy man with his unworldly faith of trust and love. It is important to recognize Kipling's wide sympathy and understanding, since the suggestion that he was merely a racist imperialist may come between the reader and an appreciation of his poetry.

Rudyard Kipling arrived in London in October 1889 and found lodgings over a sausage shop in Villiers Street, between the Strand and Embankment. Not quite 24, he was already known to the reading public. He was accepted into the Savile Club, as Thomas Hardy had been, and gradually made literary contacts. Like Hardy, he was initially lonely and sporadically depressed. Moreover, he was ill at ease with the prevailing literary ambience. Art for art's sake rang false, and the background of decadence and world-weariness was anathema to him. The literary intelligentsia was inclined to dismiss him as a colonial philistine, and he found it hard to meet kindred spirits.

His writing was his major solace. He wrote prolifically and speedily. *The Times* had given a favourable review of *Plain Tales from the Hills*, which had been published in England the year before he arrived in London, and the stories had become popular. Two further collections of Indian stories, *Soldiers Three* and *Wee Willie Winkie*, added to his reputation. Queen Victoria had become Empress of India in 1877, and this had created a demand for books about the sub-continent of which the public were eager to know more. In 1891 he showed his mastery of the short story by publishing a collection written in London called *Life's Handicap*, some of which had already appeared in various journals. At about the same time he published, initially in America, a novel called *The Light that Failed*. Its account of an unhappy love affair probably owed something to his abortive relationship with Florence Garrard, The hero, an artist, slowly goes blind, reflecting perhaps Kipling's youthful fear of blindness. The next year saw the publication in London of a collection of his poems, entitled *Barrack-Room Ballads and other Verses*, some of which had already appeared in journals. These poems were something quite new to the literary world.

The collection comprised 21 ballads about soldiers and a further 21 'other verses'. The soldiers in the ballads were not the idealised knights of Tennyson, nor his absurdly brave Light Brigade charging directly into the Russian guns; they were real soldiers of the working class. The ballads were written in a London cockney dialect, with every possible 'h' dropped, and in the rhythm of the music hall songs so popular at the time. They are best read aloud or sung, and many have been set to music. Though derided by the critics at the time, they were immediately very successful, and are now part of the folk-verse of the nation, appreciated and understood as much by the unlettered as the erudite.

Opposite Kipling's rooms in Villiers Street was a music hall called Gatti's. He was a frequent visitor there, accompanied by an elderly barmaid he had become friendly with. Vulgar and raucous as the atmosphere was, it gave him a social milieu in which he felt at home, as he drank and sang along with the rest. He was fascinated by the songs he heard, and many of the *Barrack-Room Ballads* are modelled on them. He was at ease with the mass culture of the time. His aim in writing about the common soldier – Tommy Atkins as he was known to the man in the street – was to give him a better image and better treatment. In his Prelude to the ballads Kipling wrote:

> *O there'll surely come a day*
> *When they'll give you all your pay,*
> *And treat you as a Christian ought to do;*
> *So, until that day comes around,*
> *Heaven keep you safe and sound.*
> *And, Thomas, here's my best respects to you!*

192

The ballads were characteristically rhythmic, and had a wide variety of form and metre. There was a lot of feeling in them, though Kipling seldom revealed his own emotions. Feeling comes through to the reader in pathos and pity for the rough and youthful soldiers with their parades and guard duties, the fear and heat and sickness they endure, the drink that brings them oblivion and the death that dogs their footsteps. Our Empire, even our civilisation, seemed to depend at times on these uncouth, ill-paid youngsters of the British slums. Kipling asks his readers not to despise them and not to forget them. In *The Young British Soldier*, we hear the old soldier's advice:

> *First mind you steer clear o' the grog sellers' huts,*
> *For they sell you Fixed Bay'nets that rots out your guts –*
> *And drink that 'ud eat the live steel from your butts –*
> *An' it's bad for the young British soldier . . .*
> *Bad, bad, bad, for the soldier . . .*
>
> *When the cholera comes – as it will past a doubt –*
> *Keep out of the wet and don't go on the shout,*
> *For the sickness gets in as the liquor dies out,*
> *An' it crumples the young British soldier.*
> *Crum, crum, crumples the soldier . . .*
>
> *But the worst o' your foes is the sun over 'ead:*
> *You must wear your 'elmet for all that is said:*
> *If 'e finds you uncovered 'e'll knock you down dead,*
> *An' you'll die like a fool of a soldier.*
> *Fool, fool, fool of a soldier.*
>
> *When first under fire, an' you're wishful to duck*
> *Don't look nor take 'eed of the man that is struck.*
> *Be thankful you're livin', and trust to your luck*
> *And march to your front like a soldier.*
> *Front, front, front like a soldier . . .*
>
> *If your officer's dead and the sergeants look white,*
> *Remember it's ruin to run from a fight:*
> *So take open order, lie down, and sit tight,*
> *And wait for supports like a soldier.*
> *Wait, wait, wait like a soldier . . .*

When you're wounded and left on Afghanistan's plains,
And the women come out to cut up what remains,
Jest roll to your rifle and blow out your brains
An' go to your Gawd like a soldier.
Go, go, go like a soldier,
Go, go, go like a soldier,
Go, go, go like a soldier,
So-oldier of the Queen!

Occasionally the ballads have the poignancy of true poetry. *Danny Deever* is one such poem. The troops are paraded to witness a comrade being hanged for murder:

'*What are the bugles blowin' for?' said Files-on-Parade.*
'*To turn you out, to turn you out' the Colour-Sergeant said.*
'*What makes you look so white, so white?' said Files-on-Parade.*
'*I'm dreadin' what I've got to watch,' the Colour-Sergeant said.*
For they're hangin' Danny Deever, you can hear the Dead March play,
The Regiment's in 'ollow square – they're hangin' him today;
They've taken of his buttons off an' cut his stripes away,
An' they're hangin' Danny Deever in the mornin'.

'*What's that so black agin the sun?' said Files-on-Parade.*
'*It's Danny fightin' 'ard for life,' the Colour-Sergeant said.*
'*What's that that whimpers over 'ead?' said Files-on-Parade.*
'*It's Danny's soul that's passin' now,' the Colour-Sergeant said.*
For they're done with Danny Deever, you can 'ear the quickstep play,
The Regiment's in column, an' they're marchin' us away;
Ho! the young recruits are shakin', an' they'll want their beer today,
After hangin' Danny Deever in the mornin'!'

The catchy rhythms of the ballads are readily set to music, and, in due course, music halls and military messes and even Victorian drawing-rooms were ringing to the sounds of Kipling's verses. Popular with the Artillery was *Screw-Guns*. These were the little guns which could be dismantled and carried on mules over the mountains. The chorus runs:

194

For you all love the screw-guns – the screw-guns they all love you!
So when we call round with a few guns, o' course you will know
  what to do-hoo! hoo!
Jest send in your Chief an' surrender – it's worse if you fights or
  you runs:
You can go where you please, you can shin up the trees, but you
  don't get away from the guns!

There is an element of mocking boastfulness in this ballad, which is
distasteful to some readers. Even more unpleasant is the cruelty and
violence attributed to the British soldier in *Loot*. But we must
remember that Kipling was portraying soldiers as he saw them, not as
plaster saints.

The Widow at Windsor evokes a similar picture of self-satisfied pride
in the might of the British Empire. The Widow of which the soldier
speaks is Queen Victoria, and he describes himself as one of *Missis
Victorier's sons*. But the pride which he feels is mixed with mockery
and irony, and not a little self-pity:

'Ave you 'eard o' the Widow at Windsor
With a hairy gold crown on 'er head?
She 'as ships on the foam – she 'as millions at 'ome,
An' she pays us poor beggars in red.
  (Ow, poor beggars in red!)
There's 'er nick on the cavalry 'orses,
There's 'er mark on the medical stores –
An' 'er troopers you'll find with a fair wind be'ind
That takes us to various wars.
  (Poor beggars! – barbarious wars!)
Then 'ere's to the Widow at Windsor,
An' 'ere's to the stores an' the guns,
The men an' the 'orses what makes up the forces
O' Missis Victorier's sons.
  (Poor beggars! Victorier's sons!)

We 'ave 'eard o' the Widow at Windsor,
It's safest to leave 'er alone:
For 'er sentries we stand by the sea an' the land

195

Wherever the bugles are blown.
(Poor beggars! – an' don't we get blown!)
Take 'old o' the Wings o' the Mornin',
An' flop round the earth till you're dead;
But you won't get away from the tune that they play
To the bloomin' old rag over 'ead!)
(Poor beggars it's 'ot over 'ead!)
Then 'ere's to the sons o' the Widow,
Wherever, 'owever they roam.
'Ere's all they desire, an' if they require
A speedy return to their 'ome.
(Poor beggars! – they'll never see 'ome!)

A powerful baritone could knock them in the aisles, as the saying was, by rendering *Mandalay*, in which a British soldier back in England nostalgically recalls his Burmese girlfriend:

By the old Moulmein Pagoda, lookin' lazy at the sea,
There's a Burma girl a-settin', and I know she thinks o' me;
For the wind is in the palm-trees, and the temple-bells they say:
'Come you back, you British soldier; come you back to Mandalay!'
Come you back to Mandalay,
Where the old Flotilla lay:
Can't you 'ear their paddles chunkin' from Rangoon to Mandalay?
On the road to Mandalay
Where the flyin'-fishes play
An' the dawn comes up like thunder outer China 'crost the Bay!

The poem goes on to wallow in nostalgia for the East:

'If you've 'eard the East a-callin', you won't never 'eed naught else.'
No! you won't 'eed nothin' else
But them spicy, garlic smells,
An' the sunshine an' the palm-trees an' the tinkly temple-bells;

And it concludes:

Ship me somewheres east of Suez, where the best is like the worst,
Where there aren't no Ten Commandments an' a man can raise a thirst;
For the temple-bells are callin' an' it's there that I would be –
By the old Moulmein Pagoda, lookin' lazy at the sea.

Read in cold print it seems absurdly sentimental, but sung in the music hall, with a pint of beer in one's hand, it struck powerfully at the hearts of simple men and women.

Early on in his stay in London, Rudyard met Wolcott Balestier, a young American publisher. They became great friends and collaborated in writing a novel called *The Naulahka*, which is Hindi for necklace. At the end of 1890, he met Balestier's sister Caroline, who in due course became his wife. Carrie was three years older than Rudyard and was a short, plump, energetic and capable young woman. Kipling's mother did not take to her and neither did his father, both considering her too domineering.

The courtship was interrupted because Rudyard fell victim to an influenza epidemic which left him weak and weary. To aid his recovery he went on a world cruise. Independent as ever, he travelled on his own, calling at South Africa, New Zealand, Australia and Sri Lanka, then still known as Ceylon. From there he made the long train journey northward to Lahore to stay with his parents. Whilst in Lahore he received a telegram telling him that Wolcott Balestier had died of typhoid on a visit to Germany. He booked a passage immediately for England to be with Carrie in her grief, and on 18 January 1892, he and Carrie were married. His affection for Wolcott was so strong that he added a dedicatory poem to his *Barrack Room Ballads*, in which he placed him with the world's heroes as he enters heaven:

> *Borne on the breath that men call Death, my brother's spirit came.*
> *He scarce had need to doff his pride or slough the dross of Earth –*
> *E'en as he trod that day to God so walked he from his birth,*
> *In simpleness and gentleness and honour and clean mirth.*

It was true that Carrie was inclined to be domineering, but in many ways Rudyard enjoyed this. He was happy for her to deal with his correspondence and to be concerned with his business affairs: it meant he could concentrate on his writing. A disadvantage was that, as her influence developed, she controlled his visitors in later years to such an extent that he became something of a recluse. But all this was far in the future. For the present they were very much in love, and within a month of their wedding set off for the United States

197

to visit Carrie's family in Vermont. They decided to settle there in due course; but first wished to continue their travels, going on to the west coast of America and thence to Japan.

In Yokohama, he was stunned to learn that the bank in which he had deposited nearly all his money had suspended payment, and all he and Carrie had left was a little cash, their travel tickets and the clothes in their trunks. They swiftly retreated via Canada to his wife's family estate at Brattleboro, and there rented from Carrie's brother a small, almost derelict dwelling called Bliss Cottage. For this they paid the equivalent in dollars of £2 a month. They lived in the cottage for a year, and it was there, on 29 December 1892 that their first child, Josephine, was born.

Then, once financially more secure, they had a house built to their own design. They both involved themselves in the construction work, and Rudyard particularly enjoyed this. He said it gave him a life-long taste for timber, stone and concrete. They called their house Naulakha, in memory of Wolcott. They lived in it for four years, and there, in February 1896, Carrie gave birth to their second child, Elsie.

It was a lonely existence, for the house was outside the town and very isolated, and they made few local friends. Nevertheless, they felt sufficiently settled for Rudyard to contemplate becoming a naturalised American. It was partly a family dispute which prevented it. Carrie's brother Beatty quarrelled with her over the ownership of the family estate. Beatty was bankrupt and was drinking heavily and he resented the Kiplings' comparative prosperity. He made threats against Rudyard and was arrested, but before the case came up for trial, the Kiplings had departed for England. Rudyard was not too sorry to go in any case, because relationships between Britain and America had so deteriorated by then that they were almost at war over the disputed border between Venezuela and British Guyana.

Whilst in Vermont, apart from holiday trips to England and Bermuda, Rudyard had devoted himself to his writing. He had a great love of children, and was never happier than when he was reading his stories to them. He wrote two books for them, *The Jungle Book* and *The Second Jungle Book*, published in 1894 and 1895 respectively, both of which have been immensely popular ever since. He gave imaginative names to the animals in the jungle and, incidently, provided Baden Powell with characters, such as Mowgli, Baloo, Bagheera and Shere Khan, for the folklore of his wolf cubs and boy scouts.

Kipling also wrote more ballads, which were published in 1896 in his third collection of verses, *The Seven Seas*. As with his previous volume of poetry, its contents were in two parts; but this time the *Other Verses* came first and his *Barrack-Room Ballads*, less numerous, were relegated to the rear. There was a new note in the *Other Verses*: an enlarged consciousness of Britain's imperial destiny. The opening poems are serious and hymn-like. The dedicatory verse is addressed to Bombay, the city of his birth; in it he thanks God that he was born in a great city, part of a mighty empire. In *A Song of the English*, he is again grateful to God for his English heritage:

> *Fair is our lot − O goodly is our heritage!*
> *(Humble ye, my people, and be fearful in your mirth!)*
> *For the lord our God Most High*
> *He hath made the deep as dry,*
> *He hath smote for us a pathway to the ends of all the Earth!*

He goes on to address his countryman as if he were an ancient biblical prophet:

> *Hold ye the Faith − the Faith our Fathers sealed us;*
> *Whoring not with visions − overwise and overstale.*
> *Except ye pay the Lord*
> *Single heart and single sword,*
> *Of your children in their bondage He shall ask them treble-tale!*

> *Keep ye the Law − be swift in all obedience −*
> *Clear the land of evil, drive the road and bridge the ford.*
> *Make ye sure to each his own*
> *That he reap where he hath sown;*
> *By the peace among Our peoples let men know we serve the lord!*

This opening poem prefaces seven interconnected 'songs', which are concerned with adventure, manliness, love of the sea and the development of the Empire. The longest poem is *The Song of the Cities*, which comprises brief statements by fifteen large cities of the British Empire, hailing England and calling her mother. In *England's Answer*, the 'mother country' responds by setting out the attributes of her character which have made her great and which unite her 'sons':

> *Wards of the Outer March, Lords of the Lower Seas,*
> *Ay, talk to your grey mother that bore you on her knees! —*
> *That ye may talk together, brother to brother's face —*
> *Thus for the good of your peoples — thus for the Pride of the Race.*
> *Also we will make promise. So long as The Blood endures,*
> *I shall know that your good is mine; ye shall feel that my strength*
> *is yours:*
> *In the day of Armageddon, at the last great fight of all,*
> *That Our House stand together and the pillars do not fall.*

This was England's imperial destiny as Kipling was beginning to understand it. The present-day reader may dislike the sentiments and point out how India, Pakistan, Ceylon, Canada, Australia, New Zealand and South Africa are independent countries now. Whilst others may say that they are still bound together in the British Commonwealth, it is fact that Britain no longer has its Empire, and Kipling's dream of a mighty imperial power has passed into oblivion.

Nevertheless, at that time he seemed to be speaking for the nation. In 1897, a year after his return to England, the country celebrated Queen Victoria's Diamond Jubilee, and imperialism played a leading part in events. Trade and empire were closely bound together in the mind of the politicians. Joseph Chamberlain, Secretary of State for the Colonies, presided over a Colonial Conference in London, attended by the premiers of eleven colonies which spanned the seven seas. Joint imperial defence and commercial development through preferential trade were high on the agenda, and Britain assumed the duty of maintaining an enormous Navy to protect her possessions. Kipling recognized the vital importance of the Navy. As he had once hymned the virtues of the Army, he now turned to the sea and Britain's ships, both naval and mercantile.

The Seven Seas included two lengthy dramatic monologues spoken by men of the sea, *McAndrew's Hymn* and *The 'Mary Gloster'*.

Here he was breaking new ground, following Robert Browning in the genre, but writing in common speech and revealing the lives and minds of working men with the sea in their blood and honest toil in their hearts.

McAndrew is the archetypal Scottish ship's engineer, who worships machinery and steam and has spent his life in their service:

> *From coupler-flange to spindle-guide, I see Thy hand, O God –*
> *Predestination in the stride o' yon connectin'-rod.*

He soliloquises as he stands on deck at night in the company of a sleepless passenger:

> *My engines, after ninety days o' race an' rack an' strain*
> *Through all the seas of all Thy world, slam-bangin' home again.*

He recalls the voyages he has made and the storms he has endured. He derides the first-class passengers who romanticise about the days of sail, and cries:

> *I'm sick of all their quirks an' turns – the loves an' doves they dream –*
> *Lord, send a man like Robbie Burns to sing the Song o' Steam!*

He listens with satisfaction to his engines:

> *They're all awa'! True beat, full power, the clangin' chorus goes*
> *Clear to the tunnel where they sit, my purrin' dynamoes.*
> *Interdependence absolute, forseen, ordained, decreed*
> *To work, Ye'll note, at ony tilt an' every rate o' speed.*
> *Fra' skylight-lift to furnace bars, backed, bolted, braced an' stayed,*
> *An' singin' like the Mornin' Stars for joy that they are made.*

The 'Mary Gloster' begins with a shipping magnate lying on his death-bed talking to his son Dickie, who, according to his father, has lived on the family's money and all his life has *muddled with books and art*:

> *'Never seen death yet, Dickie? Well, now is your time to learn,*
> *And you'll wish you held my record before it comes to your turn.*
> *Not counting the Line and the Foundry, the Yards and the village too,*

201

I've made myself a million; but I'm damned if I made you.
Master at two-and-twenty, and married at twenty-three –
Ten thousand men on the pay-roll, and forty freighters at sea!
Fifty years between 'em, and every year of it fight,
And now I'm Sir Anthony Gloster, dying, a baronite.

He speaks of his early beginnings, of his wife who advised and encouraged him and who went to sea with him on the sailing clippers and eventually died at sea. Spurred by her spirit, he went on to build steam-ships and grew ever more prosperous. He gave his son an expensive education, but lived to regret it:

Harrer an' Trinity College! I ought to ha' sent you to sea –
But I stood you an education, an' what have you done for me?

His dying wish is to be buried at sea – at the same spot in the Macassar Straits in the East Indies where his wife's body lies; and he wants to be carried there in the *Mary Gloster*, the ship in which his wife died and which bears her name. He asks for the ship to be scuttled there with his corpse inside, and he imagines the scene:

Down by the head an' sinkin', her fires are drawn and cold,
An' the water's splashin' hollow on the skin of the empty hold –
Churning an' choking and chuckling, quiet and scummy and dark –
Full to her lower hatches and risin' steady. Hark!
That was the after-bulkhead... She's flooded from stem to stern . . .
'Never seen death yet, Dickie?.. Well, now is your time to learn!'

Sir Anthony's contempt for books and pictures did not of course represent Kipling's own views, for he was a considerable artist, as was his father too, and had friends and relatives in the art world. But he had no time for the outlook of the current Aesthetic Movement, and one suspects that he could not resist a gibe at their expense.

The poem *The Long Trail* is a splendid evocation of the love of the sea and the wanderlust which were part of Kipling's nature:

You have heard the beat of the off-shore wind,
And the thresh of the deep-sea rain;

You have heard the song — how long? how long?
Pull out on the trail again!
It's North you may run to the rime-ringed sun
Or South to the blind Horn's hate;
Or East all the way into Mississippi Bay,
Or West to the Golden Gate —
Where the blindest bluffs hold good, dear lass,
And the wildest tales are true,
And the men bulk big on the old trail, our own trail, the out trail,
And life runs large on the Long Trail — the trail that is always new!

The days are sick and cold, and the skies are grey and old,
And the twice-breathed airs blow damp;
And I'd sell my tired soul for the bucking beam-sea roll
Of a black Bilbao tramp,
With her load-line over her hatch, dear lass
And a drunken Dago crew,
And her nose held down on the old trail, our own trail, the out trail
From Cadiz south on the Long Trail — the trail that is always new.

After the publication of *The Seven Seas*, Kipling was adopted by the Royal Navy as its unofficial representative, much as he had previously been by the Army. In 1897, he was asked to take part in manoeuvres by the Channel Fleet. In June of that year he was invited to Spithead to see the Jubilee Naval Review, and the sight of so much power gathered together enthralled him. He wrote to a friend afterwards that there was nothing like it under heaven — it was beyond words, beyond any description.

Rudyard and Carrie with their two daughters arrived back in England in September 1896. After renting a house in Torquay for a short time, they settled in Rottingdean, near Brighton, and Rudyard's long love affair with Sussex began. He was already a well-known writer, and he rapidly became a public figure, not only in England, but in America and Canada, indeed wherever the English language was spoken. His literary output was accessible to all classes. He was aggressively the plain man, and he wrote both prose and poetry that the general public could understand and appreciate. He was patriotic too, at a time when love of country reflected the prevailing view. He began to contribute verses to *The Times* on issues of moment to the nation, for which he did not ask a fee; and although he was not the Poet Laureate, he began to behave as if he were. At the time of the Diamond Jubilee, *The Times* published his poem *Recessional*, which put into the noblest of words the sentiments appropriate to the people of a mighty empire. A recessional is a hymn sung as the clergy and choir withdraw at the end of a church service, and the poem is a magnificent hymn for an imperial power, reflecting as it does both pride and humility:

> *God of our fathers, known of old,*
> *Lord of our far-flung battle-line,*
> *Beneath whose awful Hand we hold*
> *Dominion over palm and pine –*
> *Lord God of Hosts, be with us yet,*
> *Lest we forget – lest we forget!*
>
> *The tumult and the shouting dies;*
> *The Captains and the Kings depart:*
> *Still stands Thine ancient sacrifice,*
> *An humble and a contrite heart.*
> *Lord God of Hosts, be with us yet,*
> *Lest we forget – lest we forget!*
>
> *Far-called our navies melt away;*
> *On dune and headland sinks the fire:*
> *Lo, all our pomp of yesterday*
> *Is one with Nineveh and Tyre!*
> *Judge of the Nations, spare us yet,*
> *Lest we forget – lest we forget!*
>
> *If, drunk with sight of power, we loose*
> *Wild tongues that have not Thee in awe,*
> *Such boastings as the Gentiles use,*
> *Or lesser breeds without the Law –*
> *Lord God of Hosts, be with us yet,*
> *Lest we forget – lest we forget!*

For heathen heart that puts her trust
In reeking tube and iron shard,
All valiant dust that builds on dust,
And guarding, calls not Thee to guard,
For frantic boast and foolish word –
Thy mercy on Thy People, Lord!

The poem is full of Old Testament allusions. Its message is that God has made a special contract with the British people, and whilst they keep His Law, they will prosper; but if they put their faith in naked power, their empire will dissolve and become a ruin of the past like Nineveh and Tyre. The *lesser breeds without the Law* in the penultimate verse are those nations who do not accept the God-given sense of duty and restraint, uniquely possessed by the British. It sounds racist and arrogant too, when Kipling supposed himself to be urging humility; but, again it was in tune with the popular feelings of the time.

As well as writing poetry, Kipling was turning out stories at a tremendous rate. He wrote a novel called *Captains Courageous*, which went down particularly well in America, being about their fishermen and the hard and simple lives they led. He produced another collection of short stories called *The Day's Work*, and also wrote *Stalky & Co.*, which, as we have noted, was semi-autobiographical in a fanciful way. Boys' boarding school stories were popular at the time, and *Stalky & Co.* was a cut above most of them. Stalky, M'Turk and Beetle are three resourceful lads and they usually get the better of their enemies, which include teachers as well as boys. Younger readers loved it and still do, for the book has never gone out of print.

Kipling's *Just So Stories* were published in 1902. They delighted small children, and many of their elders too, and have done so ever since. He illustrated the book himself, displaying a considerable artistic talent, inherited no doubt from his father, who illustrated *Kim*, his novel about India which appeared in the bookshops at about the same time. *Kim* has not much of a plot, but it represents a splendid evocation of India as Rudyard knew it. Kimball O'Hara, the hero of the story, is the little abandoned orphan son of an Irish sergeant, wandering as a vagabond around Lahore. He encounters an elderly Tibetan holy man and they travel together for a time, until

205

Kim is adopted by his father's former regiment and is sent to school. He continues his wandering during the school holidays and, when he is old enough, becomes a secret agent for the British government. Kipling poured into the book all his love for and knowledge of India's varied peoples, and it is undoubtedly the finest book he wrote.

At Rottingdean in the summer of 1897, the Kiplings had their third child, a boy they christened John. The following January, the whole family sailed to South Africa. It was an escape from the English winter, but also an opportunity for Rudyard to see the country again. He was a world-famous writer by now and the prophet of empire. It was therefore natural that he should be introduced to Sir Alfred Milner, the British High Commissioner, and meet Cecil Rhodes, founder of Rhodesia. He went sightseeing in the Transvaal and the Orange Free State, which were then independent Boer republics. Rhodes generously provided him with a house on his estate in Cape Town, which he later used for winter holidays.

In the winter of 1898-99, the Kipling family sailed to the United States to see Carrie's mother and to settle some business with Rudyard's American publishers. This trip was to prove disastrous. On their arrival in New York, they all caught heavy colds. Rudyard's condition turned to pneumonia, and his life was in the balance for several days, with anxious crowds waiting outside his hotel. In due course he recovered, but six-year-old Josephine did not, and she died just as he was beginning to improve. Josephine meant everything to him, and losing her set back his recovery. His convalescence took several months and the family did not get back to England until the June of 1899.

In the October of that year, the war in South Africa, known to us as the Boer War, broke out. The Boers, or Afrikaners, were of Dutch origin, and constituted the dominant white grouping in South Africa. They wanted self-government in a united South Africa, but the British were resolved on retaining their ultimate power in the colony. Kipling was deeply involved emotionally. During his travels in the area he had witnessed the repression of British nationals where the Boers held sway. It reinforced his belief in the governing mission of the British nation. He felt that freedom, justice and progress could only prevail if South Africa remained within the British Empire. Although there was a liberal, pro-Boer element in Britain, the dominant sentiment was imperialistic, and Kipling expressed this powerfully in prose and verse.

The Times published a poem of his, *The Old Issue*, which likened the Boers to England's old monarchs, against whose tyranny our ancestors had fought. It was a crude and inaccurate piece of propaganda, but more and better was to follow. Asked to support a fund for the dependants of soldiers serving in South Africa, he produced some verses called *The Absent-Minded Beggar*, which seized the imagination of the nation. It was an opportunity he relished. He was writing on behalf of the ordinary soldiers, who, not thinking of themselves, were fighting for their country, It seemed only fair that the British public should help their dependent families who would otherwise suffer. Sir Arthur Sullivan set the verses to music, and they were sung and recited all over the country. With royalties and performing rights, more than a quarter of a million pounds – a very large sum in those days – was raised towards the fund for soldiers' families. Two verses give the flavour of it:

When you've shouted 'Rule Britannia', when you've sung
    'God save the Queen',
When you've finished killing Kruger with your mouth,
Will you kindly drop a shilling in my little tambourine
For a gentleman in khaki ordered South?
He's an absent-minded beggar, and his weaknesses are great –
But we and Paul must take him as we find him –
He's out on active service, wiping something off a slate –
And he's left a lot of little things behind him!
Duke's son – cook's son – son of a hundred kings –
(Fifty thousand horse and foot going to Table Bay!)
Each of 'em doing his country's work
(And who's to look after their things?)
Pass the hat for your credit's sake, and pay-pay-pay!

There are families by thousands, far too proud to beg or speak,
And they'll put their sticks and bedding up the spout.
And they'll live on 'arf o'nothing, paid 'em punctual once a week,
'Cause the man who earns the wage is ordered out.
He's an absent-minded beggar, but he heard his country call,

And his reg'ment didn't need to send to find him!
He chucked his job and joined it – so the job before us all
Is to help the home that Tommy's left behind him!
Duke's job – cook's job – gardner, baronet, groom,
Mews or palace or paper-shop, there's someone gone away!
Each of 'em doing his country's work
(And who's to look after the room?)
Pass the hat for your credit's sake, and pay-pay-pay!

The 'Paul' referred to in line six of the first verse is Paul Kruger, the
Boer's political leader, who was something of a hate-figure in
Britain. The phrase in the second line, *killing Kruger with your mouth*,
became a synonym for those who talked big but did nothing. The
British Army was unprepared and heavily out-numbered at the start
of hostilities: hence the need to ship *fifty thousand horse and foot* to
Table Bay. (The exact number was 47,000, but of course that would
not scan!) The war lasted 32 months, and for eight months of this
time Kipling was in South Africa. He wrote for an army newspaper,
sent despatches home, visited the wounded and was consulted by
army and political leaders on morale and related matters. Initially, he
was full of patriotic zeal, but he became more critical as the army met
with set-backs and its leaders proved less than competent. The
combatant soldiers suffered greatly, and Kipling's heart was with
them, as shown by his hymn to the infantry, *Boots*, which has been
widely sung on stage and in military messes ever since:

We're foot-slog-slog-slog-sloggin' over Africa –
Foot-foot-foot-foot-sloggin' over Africa –
(Boots-boots-boots-boots-movin' up and down again!);
There's no discharge in the war!

Seven-six-eleven-five-nine-an' twenty mile today –
Four-eleven-seventeen-thirty-two the day before –
(Boots-boots-boots-boots-movin' up and down again);
There's no discharge in the war!

And so it goes on: the song of the infantryman as he marches day after
day in the heat. He cannot get his discharge from the army while the
war lasts; only injury or death can release him. The boots of the

marching column are driving him mad:

> *We- can- stick- out- 'unger, thirst an' weariness,*
> *But- not- not-not- not- the chronic sight of 'em—*
> *Boots- boots- boots- boots- movin' up an' down again,*
> *An' there's no discharge in the war!*

The guerilla tactics of the Boers prolonged the war, but eventually they capitulated, and a peace treaty was signed in May 1902. Kipling felt little animosity towards the Boer soldier. He wrote a poem, *Piet*, in which a British soldier expresses a grudging respect for his erstwhile foe. The penultimate verse sums it up:

> *From Plewman's to Marabasted,*
> *From Ookiep to De Aar,*
> *Me an' my trusty friend 'ave 'ad,*
> *As you might say, a war;*
> *But seein' what both parties done*
> *Before 'e owned defeat,*
> *I ain't more proud of 'avin won*
> *Than I am pleased with Piet.*
> *Ah, there, Piet! – picked up be'ind the drive!*
> *The wonder wasn't 'ow 'e fought, but 'ow 'e kep' alive,*
> *With nothin' in 'is belly, on 'is back, or to 'is feet –*
> *I've known a lot o' men behave a dam' sight worse than Piet.*

He also put in the mouth of a discharged soldier, in *Chant-Pagan*, a longing for the veldt again and a revulsion at the littleness of England:

> *Me that lay down an' got up*
> *Three years with sky for my roof –*
> *That 'ave ridden my 'unger an' thirst*
> *Six thousand raw miles on the hoof,*
> *With the Vaal and the Orange for cup.*
>
> *I will arise an' get 'ence –*
> *I will trek South and make sure*
> *If it's only my fancy or not*

That the sunshine of England is pale,
And the breezes of England are stale,
An' there's somethin' gone small with the lot.

Kipling seemed to have no such regrets. In 1902, he purchased an old country house called Bateman's in the little village of Burwash, Sussex, and lived there contentedly for the next 34 years. He continued to visit South Africa every year until 1908, when the Boers were accorded equal political rights and a Union of South Africa was established under the British Crown. He also travelled widely elsewhere, visiting France frequently and going to Egypt and Canada, among other places.

The Five Nations, the fourth of Kipling's volumes of poetry, was published in September 1903. In it he brought together most of the poems he had written about South Africa before, during and after the Boer War. Amongst these was *The Lesson,* which he wrote as the war was ending. Whilst comical in style, it aimed at confronting his fellow countrymen with the mistakes they had made:

Let us admit it fairly, as a business people should,
We have had no end of a lesson: it will do us no end of good.

The lesson in his opinion was that our army had initially been out of date, relying on foot soldiers in a terrain where horses were needed. Generally, we had relied on *the obese, unchallenged old things that stifle and overlie us.* He went on to make a more serious charge in *The Reformers* and in *The Islanders,* both of which appeared in *The Times,* and did not make him popular with the governing classes. His criticism was that the land-owners had been content for working people to fight their battle, whilst unprepared themselves to make any sort of sacrifice, even refusing access to their lands for military training. The charge, expressed in *The Islanders,* was a severe one:

Sons of the sheltered city – unmade, unhandled, unmeet –
Ye pushed them raw to the battle as ye picked them raw from the street.

Ye stopped your ears to the warning – ye would neither look nor heed –
Ye set your leisure before their toil and your lusts above their need.

> *Because of your witless learning and your beasts of warren and chase,*
> *Ye grudged your sons to their service and your fields for their*
> * camping-place.*

He turned the knife in the wound when he went on to allege further
selfishness when the war was over:

> *Then ye returned to your trinkets: then ye contented your souls*
> *With the flannelled fools at the wicket or the muddied oafs at the*
> * goals.*

He wanted a battle-hardened Britain, with conscription as the
Continental countries had, and a resolve to make and keep a mighty
empire; he feared that neither the people nor their rulers had the
stomach for this. He felt that the final settlement with the Boers was
too generous and spelt the end of his dream of South Africa as a
central constituent of the Empire – one of his *Five Nations*, along with
Canada, Australia, New Zealand and Britain.

Recessional and *The White Man's Burden* were included in the *Five
Nations* volume, printed in book-form for the first time; but there
was a sense in the country that Kipling no longer articulated the
central beliefs of the people as he had once done. A new Liberal
government came into power in 1906 which was quite out of
sympathy with his ideas. He believed that a major war was brewing
against Germany, and he turned out to be right in this. However, at
the time his ideas were dismissed as imperialist war-mongering.

He expressed his contempt for the country's leaders in verse of
which *The Old Men* is typical:

> *This is our lot if we live so long and labour unto the end –*
> *That we outlive the impatient years and the much too patient friend:*
> *And because we have breath in our mouth and think we have thoughts*
> * in our head,*
> *We shall assume that we are alive, whereas we are really dead.*

Kipling was not thinking of himself in this poem, but of the older
men who were leading the country and were unaware of the
changes all around them. He admonished them again in *The Dykes*
for neglecting England's defences:

211

Time and again were we warned of the dykes, time and again we delayed:
Now, it may fall, we have slain our sons, as our fathers we have betrayed.

The dedicatory poem of the volume, *Before a Midnight Breaks in Storm*, shows him in his most prophetic mood, foretelling a terrible disaster to come. In times of danger, the country had always relied on the protection of the sea but, with astonishing prescience, Kipling warned of *wingèd men* who would transform warfare and against whom the nation must prepare.

Kipling might fear the future, but he was happy in the present. In Bateman's both he and Carrie felt they had found their real home at last; and his poem *Sussex*, which he included in the *Five Nations* volume, celebrated this:

> *God gave all men all earth to love,*
> *But, since our hearts are small,*
> *Ordained for each one spot should prove*
> *Belovèd over all;*
> *That, as He watched Creation's birth,*
> *So we, in godlike mood,*
> *May of our love create our earth*
> *And see that it is good.*
>
> *So one shall Baltic pines content,*
> *As one some Surrey glade,*
> *Or one the palm-grove's droned lament*
> *Before Levuka's Trade.*
> *Each to his choice, and I rejoice*
> *The lot has fallen to me*
> *In a fair ground – in a fair ground –*
> *Yea, Sussex by the sea!*

Whilst he persevered with his political verse, he began again to write stories and poetry for children. He wrote not only to amuse, but to inform. He wanted them to know about England and its history and to take pride in their country. In 1906 he published *Puck of Pook's Hill*. It was a potted history of England, told by a succession of historical characters conjured up from the past for the benefit of two children by a friendly sprite called *Puck*. The book was immediately popular with both children and adults. Accompanying the stories were illustrative verses. *Puck's Song* expresses a love of England and its history:

> *See you the ferny ride that steals*
> *Into the oak-woods far?*
> *O that was whence they hewed the keels*
> *That rolled to Trafalgar.*
>
> *And mark you where the ivy clings*
> *To Bayham's mouldering walls?*
> *O there we cast the stout railings*
> *That stand around St Paul's.*
>
> *And see you, after rain, the trace*
> *Of mound and ditch and wall?*
> *O that was a Legion's camping-place,*
> *When Caesar sailed from Gaul.*
>
> *And see you the marks that show and fade,*
> *Like shadows on the Downs?*
> *O they are the lines the Flint Men made,*
> *To guard their wondrous towns.*
>
> *Trackway and Camp and City lost,*
> *Salt Marsh where now is corn —*
> *Old Wars, old Peace, old Arts that cease,*
> *And so was England born!*

In *Rewards and Fairies*, published four years later in 1910, there were more children's stories introduced by *Puck*, and more accompanying verses. Again, Sussex is the focus of Kipling's affection. In *The Run of the Downs*, he tells us:

> *The Downs are sheep, the Weald is corn,*
> *You be glad you are Sussex born!*

Of course Kipling was not Sussex born, but he wrote as though he

213

wished he had been. Though he was an inveterate traveller, he longed for English roots, and Sussex was his adopted homeland. He always claimed that what he wrote was verse, but on many occasions, for example, in *Danny Deever*, he exceeded his intentions, and produced true poetry. This was also true in *The Way Through the Woods* in *Rewards and Fairies*. The rhythm is a subtle one and a strange sense of mystery pervades:

> They shut the road through the woods
> Seventy years ago.
> Weather and rain have undone it again,
> And now you would never know
> There was once a road through the woods
> Before they planted the trees.
> It is underneath the coppice and heath
> And the thin anemones.
> Only the keeper sees
> That where the ring-dove broods,
> And the badgers roll at ease,
> There was once a road through the woods.
>
> Yet, if you enter the woods
> Of a summer evening late,
> When the night-air cools on the trout-ringed pools
> Where the otter whistles his mate,
> (They fear not men in the woods,
> Because they see so few),
> You will hear the beat of a horse's feet,
> And the swish of a skirt in the dew,
> Steadily cantering through
> The misty solitudes,
> As though they perfectly knew
> The old lost road through the woods. . . .
> But there is no road through the woods.

Rewards and Fairies also contained the well-known poem *If –*, which has been much recited to schoolboys on speechdays. The last verse runs:

214

If you can talk with crowds and keep your virtue,
Or walk with Kings – nor lose the common touch,
If neither foes nor loving friends can hurt you,
If all men count with you, but none too much;
If you can fill the unforgiving minute
With sixty seconds' worth of distance run,
Yours is the Earth and everything that's in it,
And – which is more – you'll be a Man, my son!

It seems to sum up much of Kipling's philosophy of life: retain the common touch whilst mixing with the great; respect other people but do not get too close; and work hard and be busy all the time. A relatively small, myopic person, he had a strong wish to be a Man – with a capital M – and he felt it could be done through hard work.

Love of work – his own and other people's – shines through both his prose and poetry. In his poem about the camel's hump in his *Just So Stories* for children, he light-heartedly, but nevertheless genuinely, prescribed physical activity as a cure for depression – which he himself suffered from:

The Camel's hump is an ugly lump
Which well you may see at the Zoo;
But uglier yet is the hump we get
From having too little to do.

The cure for this ill is not to sit still,
Or frowst with a book by the fire;
But to take a large hoe and a shovel also,
And dig till you gently perspire.

His poem *The Sons of Martha* also glorifies the work ethic. Martha in the New Testament story is angry with her sister Mary, who sits listening to Jesus while she is doing all the housework. Martha is rebuked by Jesus for her outburst, but Kipling takes her part. It is, he says, the Sons of Martha who do the world's work:

It is their care in all the ages to take the buffet and cushion the shock.
It is their care that the gear engages; it is their care that the switches lock.

*It is their care that the wheels run truly; it is their care to embark and
   entrain,*
Tally, transport, and deliver duly the Sons of Mary by land and main.

*They do not preach that their God will rouse them a little before the
   nuts work loose.*
*They do not teach that His Pity allows them to drop their job when
   they dam'-well choose.*
*As in the thronged and the lighted ways, so in the dark and the desert
   they stand,*
*Wary and watchful all their days that their brethren's days may be long
   in the land.*

*Raise ye the stone or cleave the wood to make some path more fair or
   flat —*
Lo, it is black already with blood some Son of Martha spilled for that!
Not as a ladder from earth to Heaven, not as a witness to any creed,
But simple service simply given to his own kind in their common need.

Kipling's own family was growing up, and after *Rewards and Fairies*,
he wrote no more children's stories. However, he continued with his
children's poems, contributing verse to an introductory history for
schools, which continued his efforts towards helping young people
appreciate their country's past and its development into a great
imperial power. He worked hard on his estate, enjoying the
company of the local craftsmen he employed. He cycled a lot, once
even travelling to Dorchester in Dorset to pedal in the company of
Thomas Hardy. He was an early motorist, acquiring a steam car in
1900 and moving on to the earliest Lanchester in 1902, about the
time he and Carrie moved into Bateman's.

Whilst he was still writing for children, he published two
collections of short stories called *Traffics and Discoveries* and *Actions
and Reactions*. He was by now a past-master in the short story genre.
He always claimed that his literary work was aided by what he called
his Personal Dæmon. He said it was with him particularly in the
Jungle Books, Kim and both *Puck* books. When this spirit was in
charge he did not try to think consciously, but just drifted, waited
and obeyed, and was amazed at what resulted. He was a consummate

craftsman, so perhaps he could put himself on auto-pilot. But there is more to Kipling than meets the eye, and maybe he was sometimes in touch with forces not easily explained. He felt he had a gift for prophecy, and quite often he was proved right when no-one at the time thought as he did.

He persevered in his role as unofficial Poet Laureate, commenting on issues of importance in verse which appeared in the national press. He foresaw the military rise of Germany and the coming of the Great War of 1914-18. He did not view it in a frenzy of patriotism. The Germans for him were the barbarians at the gates of civilisation and Great Britain had the simple but inescapable duty of repelling them. He had done his best to warn the country, in poems like *Before a Midnight Breaks in Storm* and *The Dykes*, and he felt his warnings had been justified.

In September 1914, just after war had been declared, his poem *For All We Have and Are*, appeared in *The Times*. It was a sonorous, regretful statement of the country's duty as he saw it:

For all we have and are,
For all our children's fate,
Stand up and take the war.
The Hun is at the gate!
Our world has passed away,
In wantonness o'erthrown.
There is nothing left to-day
But steel and fire and stone!
Though all we knew depart,
The old Commandments stand: —
'In courage keep your heart,
In strength lift up your hand.'

Once more we hear the word
That sickened earth of old:
'No law except the Sword
Unsheathed and uncontrolled.'
Once more it knits mankind,
Once more the nations go
To meet and break and bind
A crazed and driven foe.

Comfort, content, delight,
The ages' slow-bought gain,
They shrivelled in a night.
Only ourselves remain
To face the naked days
In silent fortitude,
Through perils and dismays
Renewed and re-renewed.
Though all we made depart,
The old Commandments stand: –
'In patience keep your heart,
In strength lift up your hand.'

No easy hope or lies
Shall bring us to our goal,
But iron sacrifice
Of body, will, and soul.
There is but one task for all –
One life for each to give.
What stands if Freedom fall?
What dies if England live?

Rudyard Kipling was forty-eight when the Great War broke out. He could not expect a combatant role, and he was distanced by age from the young soldiers to whom he had felt so close in earlier days. The Government expected him to play a major part in the propaganda war, but he was reluctant to abandon his independent position, which enabled him to criticise the lack of preparation for the war and the mistakes of the High Command. In August 1915 he was asked by the Admiralty to help in publicising the work of the Royal Navy. This was a task he welcomed. He wrote articles on the subject, accompanying them with appropriate verses. The British had the sea in their blood, and in *A Song in Storm* he asserted that the sea was the friend of our island race:

Be well assured that on our side
The abiding oceans fight,
Though headlong wind and heaping tide
Make us their sport tonight.

No matter though our decks be swept
And mast and timber crack –
We can make good all loss except
The loss of turning back.

In *Mine Sweepers* he extolled the gallantry of the little ships protecting the nation's sea-ways. There are three verses, covering morning, afternoon and evening. The first verse brilliantly evokes the choppy seas which make mine-sweeping hard:

Dawn off the Foreland – the young flood making
Jumbled and short and steep –
Black in the hollows and bright where it's breaking –
Awkward water to sweep.
'Mines reported in the fairway,
Warn all traffic and detain.
Sent up Unity, Claribel, Assyrian, Stormcock and Golden Gain.'

Noon off the Foreland – the first ebb making
Lumpy and strong in the bight.
Boom after boom, and the golf-hut shaking
And the jackdaws wild with fright!
'Mines located in the fairway,
Boats now working up the chain,
Sweepers – Unity, Claribel, Assyrian, Stormcock and Golden Gain.'

Dusk off the Foreland – the last light going
And the traffic crowding through,
And five damned trawlers with their syreens blowing
Heading the whole review!
'Sweep completed in the fairway.
No more mines remain.
Sent back Unity, Claribel, Assyrian, Stormcock and Golden Gain'.

The poem was intended to typify the Navy, with a day of courageous action being powerfully portrayed.

As a well-known public figure, Rudyard, aided by Carrie, was active in fund-raising for the Belgian refugees who flooded into the country to escape the German army. He made visits to wounded soldiers in military hospitals, and he visited troops in France, being taken to the front-line so that he could talk about it at first hand in the morale-boosting public speeches he was often asked to make.

In August 1915, he and Carrie received the official telegram dreaded by wives and parents. It told them that their eighteen-year-old son John, a lieutenant in the Irish Guards, was missing in France at the Battle of Loos. They knew in their hearts that he was dead, but it was two years before his death was established. Their grief was extreme, and they spent much time over the years seeking without success for his grave. Only very recently has it been learnt that a wrong map-reference had been given for the place where he had fallen, and John Kipling's last resting place has now been identified. It bore the epitaph accorded to all unknown soldiers: 'Known only to God'. Rudyard himself had devised these words at the behest of the Imperial War Graves Commission, of which he was a member. Without knowing it, he had penned his own son's epitaph.

While describing the naval Battle of Jutland in the autumn of 1916, he wrote his bleak little poem, *My Boy Jack*:

'Have you news of my boy Jack?'
'Not this tide.'
'When d'you think that he'll come back?'
'Not with this wind blowing and this tide.'

'Has anyone else had word of him?'
'Not this tide.
For what is sunk will hardly swim,
Not with this blowing and this tide.'

'Oh, dear, what comfort can I find!'
'None this tide,
Nor any tide,
Except he did not shame his kind —
Not even with that wind blowing, and that tide!'

'Then hold your head up all the more,
This tide,
And every tide;

Because he was the son you bore,
And gave to that wind blowing and that tide!'

Kipling's sense of desolation over the loss of his young son was given further expression in his poem *The Children*, which appeared in his volume of wartime stories *A Diversity of Creatures*, published in 1917. It is a cry of misery from the parents of sons who have been killed in the war. Who, they ask, shall return us our children? He imagines the mutilated dead bodies on the Western Front amidst the shell-holes and barbed-wire:

That flesh we had nursed from the first in all cleanness was given
To corruption unveiled and assailed by the malice of Heaven –
By the heart-shaking jests of Decay where it lolled on the wires –
To be blanched or gay-painted by fumes – to be cindered by fires –
To be senselessly tossed and retossed in stale mutilation
From crater to crater. For this we shall take expiation.
But who shall return us our children?

There is no answer to this question and no sort of comfort.

In *Gethsemane*, he likens a soldier's death in Picardy to the agony of Christ in the garden near Jerusalem, when He pleads with God to spare Him death by crucifixion:

The Garden called Gethsemane
In Picardy it was,
And there the people came to see
The English soldiers pass.
We used to pass – we used to pass
Or halt as it might be,
And ship our masks in case of gas
Beyond Gethsemane.

The garden called Gethsemane,
It held a pretty lass,
But all the time she talked to me
I prayed my cup might pass.
The officer sat on the chair,
The men lay on the grass,

221

And all the time we halted there,
I prayed my cup might pass.

It didn't pass — it didn't pass —
It didn't pass from me.
I drank it when we met the gas
Beyond Gethsemane!

There was no escape for Jesus, the poet suggests, nor for the soldier.

Gethsemane was included in Kipling's fifth and last collection of poems, *The Years Between*, published in 1919. This volume also contained his *Epitaphs of the War*, which are brief, severely compressed statements of individual responses to death. Here the dead usually comment on their own deaths and speak directly to the reader. The deaths tend to be unromantic, unpatriotic, casual and unexpected. For example, an only son says:

I have slain none except my Mother. She
(Blessing her slayer) died of grief for me.

A soldier newly arrived at the front and killed by a sniper, observes:

On the first hour of my first day
In front the trench I fell.
(Children in boxes at a play
Stand up to watch it well.)

The soldier executed for cowardice cries:

I could not look on Death, which being known,
Men led me to him, blindfold and alone.

A mutilated female corpse drifts in from the sea:

Headless, lacking foot and hand,
Horrible I come to land.
I beseech all women's sons
Know I was a mother once.

A grieving father wryly speaks — as perhaps Kipling himself had done:

My son was killed while laughing at some jest. I would I knew
What it was, and it might serve me in a time when jests are few.

Kipling's understanding and sympathy reflected the views of younger people as the First World War drew to a close. The historic divisions of culture and class were being questioned. Although he was seen as a traditionalist, Kipling could write:

We were together since the War began.
He was my servant – and the better man.

And he shared sufficient of the current end-of-war cynicism to have one of the authors of his epitaphs declare:

If any question why we died,
Tell them, because our fathers lied.

Rudyard Kipling suffered from stomach pains from 1915 onwards – perhaps triggered by the loss of his son. They were diagnosed as gastritis, and nothing much was done for him. It was not until 1923 that it was recognized that he had duodenal ulcers, for which it was too late to operate. Illness and pain were an increasingly recurring theme in his later short stories. In his late sixties he actually wrote a *Hymn to Physical Pain*, in which he saw virtue in it, in that it had the power to obliterate remorse and grief and other emotional agonies. Always protective, Carrie took over the running of the farm which was part of their estate.

Illness had little effect on Rudyard's devotion to hard work. He wrote copiously, and when he was not writing, occupied himself with work with his hands, producing, for example, facsimilies of scrolls and old documents, which he made as realistic as possible. He was now a creature of habit, writing at the same desk in his study at Bateman's and always using the same pen and black ink. Bateman's is now owned by the National Trust and is open to the public, and his study may be seen as it was in his lifetime.

We know something of his idiosyncrasies from his unfinished autobiography, *Something of Myself*, which was published shortly after his death. The self-portrait corrects the distorted image of the insensitive, aggressive imperialist which the public tended to have of him. He lived increasingly in his imagination and in the past. The style of the book is oblique, even opaque on first reading, leaving out as much as it puts in. His daughters are not even mentioned, though he loved them dearly and was heart-broken at the death of Josephine. He dwells on symbols and themes: for example, 'the house of desolation', which was his foster home at Southsea; the good house which eventually became his 'very own house' at Burwash. He writes about wisdom, friendship, pain, suffering, death; but sex and love are strangely absent. It is as if these are too personal to be dwelt upon. He idolised his mother and we hear much about her in his autobiography, but nothing of his wife. He appreciated the qualities of women but was not sentimental about them. *The female of the species is more deadly than the male*, he tells us in his poem, *The Female of the Species*: a creature of instinct, she lives by different laws. Hers is a universal sisterhood, he says in *The Ladies*;

> *For the Colonel's Lady an' Judy O'Grady*
> *Are sisters under their skins!*

He loved his sister Trixie all his life. He appreciated and depended upon Carrie. That critics should speculate on the quality of their relationship he would have sternly deprecated. In *The Appeal* he made this clear:

> *And for the little, little span*
> *The dead are borne in mind,*
> *Seek not to question other than*
> *The books I leave behind.*

When he did write about love, it usually concerned the love between dog and man. There were many of these poems, the animal portrayed giving companionship, devotion and loyalty. One verse from his poem *Four-Feet* epitomises the spirit of all of them:

> *Day after day, the whole day through –*
> *Wherever my road inclined –*
> *Four-Feet said, 'I am coming with you!'*
> *And trotted along behind.*

224

He still continued his public poems, meant for the whole nation as he saw it, and a new poem of this kind was always a literary event. In October 1919 he published *The Gods of the Copybook Headings*, placing it in the *Sunday Pictorial*, a popular tabloid, instead of the usual *Morning Post*. The poem admonishes mankind for following trendy ideas instead of sticking to the time-honoured rules for good living which the schoolchild of the day was expected to absorb while learning to write — such as 'Stick to the Devil you Know' or 'The Wages of Sin is Death'. The poem had a racy rhythm and became very popular. The last two verses give the flavour of it:

As it will be in the future, it was in the birth of Man —
There are only four things certain since Social Progress began: —
That the Dog returns to his Vomit and the Sow returns to her Mire
And the burnt Fool's bandaged finger goes wabbling back to the Fires.

And after this is accomplished, the brave new world begins
When all men are paid for existing and no man must pay for his sins,
As surely as Water will wet us, as surely as Fire will burn,
The Gods of the Copybook Headings with terror and slaughter return!

Kipling continued to travel a lot after the war. As a member of the Imperial War Graves Commission, he shared the task of reporting on the burial grounds of fallen soldiers of the Empire. His duties took him frequently to France, where he searched constantly for the last resting place of his son. In 1922, on one of these missions, he was presented to King George V, and they became friends. He saw the monarch as someone like him who cared deeply about the Empire and its future. He distrusted politicians in this regard, even tending to suspect the patriotism of his cousin Stanley Baldwin, who was Prime Minister for some of the 1920s and 1930s. Other travels took him to North Africa, Brazil and the West Indies.

During the first two decades of the twentieth century, Kipling was the country's most esteemed and widely-read poet. He had been awarded the Nobel Prize for Literature in 1907, and since then university after university had lined up to present him with an honorary degree. His verses were popular abroad too, particularly in Russia, America and France. But in Britain after the First World

War, his reputation began to decline. Sickened by warfare and un-appreciative of imperial conquest, his public began to desert him. The Empire became an object of derision rather than pride, and the divine right of the British to rule 'the lesser races' became a subject of disdain and mockery. Kipling's name came to be associated with the extremes of jingoist patriotism. Socialism and brotherly love were the popular doctrines of the young and idealistic, and Kipling provided a ready scapegoat for them.

A new Modernist school of poetry had developed, which did not subscribe to simple rhythm, regular metre and clear meaning. The work of T S Eliot and Ezra Pound was evocative and allusive, its rhythms subtle, its significance sometimes obscure. Kipling's verse, it was felt, could not possibly be poetry. The critics who had praised him dropped him, claiming they had never liked him. Younger poets detested him from the start. The liberal intelligentsia was in the ascendency, and for them his versifying was morally insensitive and aesthetically disgusting, though they could not deny that his verse still sold well and gave pleasure to many people.

Rudyard's daughter Elsie married in 1924, and his great friend, the author Rider Haggard, who shared Kipling's attitudes towards the Empire, died in 1925. He kept up his correspondence with literary acquaintances, but made no new friends, and his life tended to be somewhat lonely. Elsie and her husband were childless, so that he had no grandchildren, which he would have dearly loved.

Greatly valuing education, he interested himself in the work of universities. He had one great political cause left to pursue: to warn the nation of the dangers of German resurgence. He had opposed the harsh terms of the Treaty of Versailles, feeling that it would give Germany grounds for renewed belligerence. In May 1932 a poem of his, written in the solemn style of *The Recessional*, appeared in the *Morning Post*. It was called *The Storm Cone*:

> *This is the midnight – let no star*
> *Delude us – dawn is very far.*
> *This is the tempest long foretold –*
> *Slow to make head but sure to hold.*

Stand by! The lull twixt blast and blast
Signals the storm is near, not past;
And worse than present jeopardy
May our forlorn to-morrow be.

The storm cone raised aloft warned of the coming of a terrible storm which would threaten the ship of state. If the danger was left somewhat vague, subsequent speeches and letters to the press made it clear that he was warning of the rise of Hitler, and urging the rearming of Britain.

This was his last political campaign, and he did not live to see the war which he foretold. At the end of December 1935, he suffered a severe stomach haemorrhage and, in great pain, was admitted to the Middlesex Hospital. His stay there was a short one, and on the 18 January 1936, he breathed his last. His widow Carrie recorded in her diary: *Rud died at 12 a.m. Our wedding day.* They had been married for 45 years. He was just seventy.

Kipling was cremated and his ashes were placed in Poets' Corner, Westminster Abbey, on 23 January. Amongst the mourners were the Prime Minister Stanley Baldwin, and an array of admirals, field-marshals, politicians, ambassadors and representatives of countries world-wide. If the nation's sorrow was muted at the time it was largely because King George V was dying and much attention was focussed on him. That not one literary celebrity attended the ceremony graphically illustrates how far Kipling's literary reputation had fallen.

But it was not long before the literary world began to remember him again. In 1941, T S Eliot, no less, contributed a preface to a selection of Kipling's poems, writing not to mock but to praise. He asserted that Kipling's verses were as valuable and important as his short stories, and he pointed to his unique achievement in combining the two. He commented on his consummate gift with words and rhythm, and conceded that occasionally his verse reached the intensity of poetry. He settled in the end for describing him as a superlative craftsman and a writer of great verse. Writing a year later, George Orwell invented the category of *good-bad poet*, and placed Kipling squarely in it. By this he said he meant someone who records in memorable form some emotion which nearly every human being

227

can share. If it is accepted that Kipling could do that, then surely he was a poet, even a great one.

Kipling had never read a word of Gerard Manley Hopkins when in 1902 he published in *Kim* his poem *The Sea and the Hills*; yet he could write about the sea with a similar flood and flow of words:

> Who hath desired the Sea? — the sight of salt water unbounded —
> The heave and the halt and the hurl and the crash of the comber
> wind-hounded —
> The sleek-barrelled swell before storm — grey foamless, enormous
> and growing —
> Stark calm on the lap of the Line — or the crazy-eyed hurricane
> blowing?
>
> Who hath desired the Sea — the immense and contemptuous surges?
> The shudder, the stumble, the swerve ere the star-stabbing bowsprit
> emerges?
> The orderly clouds of the Trades; the ridged soaring sapphire
> thereunder —
> Unheralded cliff-haunting flaws and the head-sail's low-volleying
> thunder?

He could compose the long, musical rhythms of Swinburne; he could also enter the mind of others far different from himself in his dramatic monologues in the manner of Browning. For example, in *The Roman Centurion's Song*. The Centurion is ordered back to Rome after a lifetime of service in Britain, and does not want to go:

> For me this land, that sea, these airs, those folks and fields suffice.
> What purple Southern pomp can match our changeful Northern skies,
> Black with December snows unshed or pearled with August haze —
> The clanging arch of steel-grey March, or June's long-lighted days?
>
> You'll take the old Aurelian Road through shore-descending pines
> Where, blue as any peacock's neck, the Tyrrhene Ocean shines.
> You'll go where laurel crowns are won, but — will you e're forget
> The scent of hawthorn in the sun, or bracken in the wet?

228

Legate, I come to you in tears – My cohort ordered home!
I've served in Britain forty years. What should I do in Rome?
Here is my heart, my soul, my mind – the only life I know.
I cannot leave it all behind. Command me not to go!

Or again there is the tearful lament of the Danish women, sung to the harp as their Viking menfolk leave them for battle and conquest across the seas:

What is a woman that you forsake her,
And the hearth-fire and the home-acre,
To go with the old grey Widow-maker?

Yet, when the signs of summer thicken,
And the ice breaks, and the birch-buds quicken,
Yearly you turn from our side, and sicken –

Sicken again for the shouts and the slaughters.
You steal away to the lapping waters,
And look at your ship in her winter-quarters.

You forget our mirth, and talk at the tables,
The kine in the shed and the horse in the stables –
To pitch her sides and go over her cables.

Then you drive out where the storm-clouds swallow,
And the sound of your oar-blades, falling hollow,
Is all we have left through the months that follow.

Then there are his sonorous, hymn-like poems, uplifting the heart of the nation and warning it of perils to come, even foretelling the collapse of its Empire:

Far-called, our navies melt away;
On dune and headland sinks the fire:
Lo, all our pomp of yesterday
Is one with Nineveh and Tyre!

He did not reveal his feelings easily, but he could write lyric poetry straight from the heart, as we have seen, for example, in *My Boy Jack* and *The Children*.

Kipling was furthermore a superlative phrase-maker, and most of us, at some time, have used such lines as: *What should they know of England who only England know?* or *He travels the fastest who travels alone.* Apart from Shakespeare, he probably wrote more quotable phrases than any other poet in the language. *Flannelled fools and muddied oafs* and *lesser breeds without the law* trip readily off the tongue; and, when he is in his grand mode, so do such lines as: *The tumult and the shouting dies; The captains and the kings depart,* and *Far-called our navies melt away.*

When Kipling is aiming for the common touch, he describes the British soldier's native girlfriend as: *a-smokin' of a whackin' white cheroot, an' wastin' Christian kisses on an 'eathen idol's foot.* When he is in his world-wide traveller's mood, he is commanding: *Ship me east of Suez, where the best is like the worst;* or he is memorably observing:

> *It's north you may run to the rime-ringed sun,*
> *Or south to the blind Horn's hate.*

Or is he dreaming of *Great steamers white and gold* which *go rolling down to Rio . . .*

A faithless woman he condemns as *a rag a bone and a hank of hair,* and, where a man is involved, *the colonel's lady and Judy O'Grady are sisters under their skins!* When he urges us *to fill the unforgiving minute with sixty seconds' worth of distance run,* the advice he gives us is in unforgettable terms. He calls his fellow-citizens *poor little street-bred people,* but in war-time endows them with a splendid nobility, telling them:

> *There is but one task for all –*
> *For each one life to give,*
> *What stands if Freedom fall?*
> *What dies if England live?*

A gifted phrase-maker and prolific versifier Kipling undoubtedly was; but he should not be remembered just for this. In his greater moments he was an inspired poet, with tremendous powers. His unique contribution to English literature will never be surpassed.

GLOSSARY OF LITERARY
AND POETICAL TERMS

AESTHETICISM	A movement of the late nineteenth-century emphasising the supreme importance of beauty in art, literature and music
ALLEGORY	Poem or narrative in which the characters and events symbolise a deeper moral or spiritual meaning
BALLAD	A narrative poem, originally of traditional origin
BLANK VERSE	Unrhymed verse
CANTO	Main division of a long poem
COUPLET	Two successive lines of poetry usually rhymed and of the same metre
DACTYL	Metrical foot of three syllables, one long followed by two short
DECADENCE	A period style of the late nineteenth century stemming from such so-called decadent French poets as Baudelaire and Mallarmé who explored sexual behaviour
DICTION	Choice and use of words

231

DRAMATIC MONOLOGUE	A long statement made by one person revealing his character
ELEGY	Reflective, mournful poem, usually lamenting the dead
EPIC	A long narrative poem recounting heroic deeds
EPILOGUE	A short postcript to a poem or other literary work
FOOT	A group of two or more syllables in a line of poetry in which one syllable has the major stress
GENRE	A kind or category of literary work
GEORGIAN	A term applied to poets of the early years of the reign of George V from 1910, indicating verse of a pastoral or escapist nature
GOTHIC	Literary style characterised by the macabre, fantastic and the supernatural
HEROIC COUPLET	Two rhyming lines of poetry in iambic pentameter
HOMERIC SIMILE	An extended simile, as employed in the epic poetry of Homer
HYPERBOLE	Deliberate exaggeration used for effect
IAMB	Metrical foot of two syllables, the first short and the second long
IAMBIC PENTAMETER	Line of poetry consisting of five iambs

IMAGISM	A movement of English and American poets led by Ezra Pound in revolt against Romanticism through concentration, exact and simple language. It flourished during the decade from 1910 onwards
IRONY	Humorous or satirical use of words implying the opposite of what is meant
LYRIC POEM	Poem expressing the poet's personal feelings and thoughts
METIER	Writer's strong point or speciality
METRE	Rhythmic arrangements of syllables in a poem
MODERNISM	Early twentieth-century tendency in poetry, associated particularly with the work of T S Eliot and Ezra Pound, indicating awareness of the irrational and the unconscious
MUSE	Mythological goddess who inspires a creative artist, especially a poet
ODE	Lyric poem addressed to a particular object
PARODY	Mimicry of someone's style in a humorous or satirical way
PENTAMETER	Verse line consisting of five metrical feet or measures
POESY	Archaic word for the art of poetry

233

PRE-RAPHAELITES	Association of painters and writers founded in 1848 with the aim of producing serious works of art faithful to nature
PROSODY	The study of poetic metre and the art of versification
RHYME	Poetry having corresponding sounds at the end of lines
RHYTHM	The arrangement of words in a regular sequence of stressed or unstressed or long and short syllables
ROMANTIC MOVEMENT	Movement in European art, music and literature in the late eighteenth and early nineteenth century characterised by an emphasis on individuality and passionate feeling
ROUNDEL	A poem of three verses of three lines each, the first and third verse being followed by a brief refrain
SATIRE	Literature in which contemporary events and issues are held up to ridicule
SIMILE	A figure of speech expressing the resemblance of one thing to another of a different kind
SOLILOQUY	The act of speaking alone or to oneself in a stage play
SONNET	Poem of fourteen lines, generally in iambic pentameter, with rhymes arranged to a fixed scheme

234

SYMBOLISM   A movement associated with a group
                           of French writers in the second half
                           of the nineteenth century. They
                           stressed the priority in poetry of
                           suggestion and evocation over direct
                           description. T S Eliot in particular
                           was much influenced by them

SYNTAX   The grammatical arrangement of
                           words in sentences

TROCHEE   Metrical foot of two syllables, the first
                           long and the second short

STANZA   A fixed number of lines in a definite
                           metrical pattern, forming a unit of a
                           poem

VERSE   Short sub-divison of a poem; or
                           another name for poetry

NOTABLE PERSONS REFERRED TO IN THE TEXT

ACHILLES	Mythical Greek hero whose body was invulnerable except for the heel of one foot
AESCHYLUS	Ancient Greek dramatist; father of Greek tragedy
ARTEMIS	Ancient Greek goddess; virgin huntress associated with animals
APHRODITE	Ancient Greek goddess of beauty, love and reproduction. Known to the Romans as Venus
ARNOLD, Matthew	Nineteenth-century English poet and essayist
AUGUSTINE, Saint	Fourth-century divine; one of the fathers of the Christian church
BADEN-POWELL, Baron	Founder of the Boy Scout movement
BALDWIN, Lord Stanley	Three times British Prime Minister in the 1920s and 30s
BARRIE, Sir James	Scottish writer and dramatist (1860-1937); author of *Peter Pan*
BAUDELAIRE, Charles	Nineteenth-century French poet; a leader of the Decadent movement

237

BOTHWELL, Earl	Scottish nobleman; third husband of Mary Queen of Scots
BRIDGES, Robert	English poet and essayist; Poet Laureate, 1913-30
BROWN, Ford Madox	Nineteenth-century English painter; member of the Pre-Raphaelite Brotherhood
BROWNING, Robert	Major nineteenth-century English poet; author of *Men and Women* and *The Ring and the Book*
BUNYAN, John	English preacher and writer (1628-88); author of *The Pilgrim's Progress*
BURNE-JONES, Edward	Nineteenth-century English Pre-Raphaelite artist (1833-98)
BURTON, Richard Francis	English explorer, writer and orientalist (1821-90)
CAMPBELL, Mrs Patrick	Actress: creator of role of Eliza Doolittle in Shaw's *Pygmalion*
CARLYLE, Thomas	Nineteenth-century Scottish essayist and historian
CATULLUS, Gaius Valerius	First-century BC Roman poet, noted for his love poems
CHASTELARD	A lover of Mary Queen of Scots
DANTE (Dante Alighieri)	Great Italian poet (1265-1321); author of *The Divine Comedy*
DE' MEDICI, Catherine	Sixtenth-century queen of Henry II of France; Regent of France, 1560-74

de SADE, Marquis	Eighteenth/nineteenth-century French author. His writing on sexual perversions gave rise to the term sadism
DEMETER	Ancient Greek corn goddess; mother of Persephone
DICKENS, Charles	Celebrated English novelist (1812-70); author of *David Copperfield, Oliver Twist, Great Expectations*
DICKINSON, Emily	Nineteenth-century American poetess
DODGSON, Charles (Lewis Carroll)	Nineteenth-century English author of *Alice in Wonderland*
DUNS Scotus, John	Thirteenth-century Scottish scholar and divine
ELIOT, Thomas Stearns	US-born poet and dramatist; a major figure in English literature from 1920 onwards; author of *The Waste Land, Four Quartets, Murder in the Cathedral*
ERECTHEUS	King of Athens; worshipped as a god in ancient Greece
FIELDING, Henry	English novelist and dramatist (1707-54); author of *Tom Jones*
GEORGE V	King of Great Britain and Northern Ireland, 1910-36
GAUTIER, Théophile	French poet and novelist (1811-72); leader, with Baudelaire, of the Decadent movement
GLADSTONE, William Ewart	English Liberal statesman (1809-1898); Prime Minister four times

GOSSE, Sir Edmund	English man of letters (1849-1928); author of *Father and Son*
HAGGARD, Sir Henry Rider	1856-1925; author of adventure novels such as *King Solomon's Mines*, and *She*
HECTOR	Son of King Priam of Troy; killed by Achilles
HENRY V	King of England, 1412-22
HORACE (Quintus Horatius Flaccus)	Celebrated first-century BC Roman poet
HUGO, Victor	Great French novelist, poet and dramatist (1802-85); central figure of the Romantic movement; author of *Les Misérables*
HUNT, William Holman	Nineteenth-century English Pre-Raphaelite artist
INGELOW, Jean	English poetess (1820-97)
JOHNSON, Dr Samuel	Eminent eighteenth-century English essayist, lexicographer and man of letters
JOWETT, Benjamin	Renowned nineteenth-century classical scholar; Master of Balliol, Oxford
KEBLE, John	Nineteenth-century Anglican churchman; inspirer of Anglo-Catholic Oxford Movement
KRUGER, Paul	Boer leader in the Boer war; President of the Transvaal
LANDOR, William Savage	English poet (1775-1864)

LOYOLA, Saint Ignatius	Sixteenth-century Spanish divine. Founder of the Society of Jesus (Jesuits) in 1534
MALLARME, Stéphane	French Symbolist poet (1842-98)
MAZZINI, Giuseppe	Chief architect of Italian independence in nineteenth century
MEREDITH, George	English novelist and poet (1828-1909)
MILLAIS, John Everett	Nineteenth-century English artist and member of the Pre-Raphaelite Brotherhood
MILNER, Sir Alfred	British High Commissioner in South Africa at the time of the Boer War
MORRIS, William	English artist and poet (1834-96); member of the Pre-Raphaelite Brotherhood
NAPOLEON I (Napoleon Bonaparte)	Emperor of the French 1804-14
NAPOLEON III	Nephew of Napoleon I; Emperor of the French, 1852-1870
NEWMAN, John	Nineteenth-century English theologian; an Anglican minister who became a Roman Catholic and was eventually made a Cardinal
ORIGEN	Second-century Christian theologian
ORWELL, George	Essayist and novelist (1903-50); author of *1984* and *Animal Farm*

PALGRAVE, Francis	Nineteenth-century English literary figure who edited the anthology *The Golden Treasury* (1861)
PATER, Walter	Essayist and critic (1839-94)
PATMORE, Coventry	English Catholic poet (1823-96)
PLATO	Ancient Greek philosopher; founder of Western philosophy
POUND, Ezra	Prominent American poet and critic (1885-1972); founder of Imagism; author of the *Cantos*
PROSERPINE	Ancient Roman goddess, popularly worshipped in Rome before the conversion to Christianity. According to ancient Greek myth she was the daugher of Zeus
PUSEY, Edward	Anglican churchman (1800-82); leader, with John Keble, of the Oxford Movement
RAPHAEL (Raffaello Sanzio)	Italian painter and architext (1483-1520)
RHODES, Cecil	English financier and statesman in South Africa; Prime Minister of Cape Colony, 1890-96; founder of Rhodesia
ROSSETTI, Dante Gabriel	English-born painter and poet; leader of the Pre-Raphaelite Brotherhood; older brother of Christina Rossetti
ROSSETTI, William	English-born writer and critic (1829-1919); younger brother of Christina Rossetti

242

RUSKIN, John	Leading nineteenth-century English art critic and social reformer
SAPPHO	Sixth-century BC Greek poetess who lived on the Greek island of Lesbos. She was the centre of a group of young women, and from her affection for them the term Lesbian originates
SCOTT, William Bell	Scottish artist and writer (1811-90)
SAVONAROLA, Girolamo	Florentine religious and political reformer burnt as a heretic in 1498
SHAKESPEARE, William	English dramatist and poet (1564-1616), recognised as the country's greatest playwright
SHELLEY, Percy Bysshe	Major early nineteenth-century English lyric poet
SIDDAL, Elizabeth	Artist model and wife of Dante Gabriel Rossetti
STUART, Mary	Queen of Scots, 1542-67
TENNYSON, Lord Alfred	Major English poet (1809-92); author of *Morte d'Arthur, The Charge of the Light Brigade* and *In Memoriam*
THACKERY, William	Eminent nineteenth-century novelist; author of *Vanity Fair*
TYNAN, Katharine	Irish poet and novelist (1861-1931)
VENUS	Ancient Roman goddess of love; known to the ancient Greeks as Aphrodite
VICTORIA, Queen	Queen of Great Britain and Ireland, 1837-1901

VIRGIL *(Publius Vergilius Maro)*	First-century BC Roman poet; author of *The Aeneid*
WATTS-DUNTON, Theodore	English solicitor and man of letters (1832-1914)
WHISTLER, *James Abbott McNeill*	Eminent American painter who studied in Paris before settling in London (1834-1903)
WORDSWORTH, William	Major English poet of the Romantic movement (1770-1850); author of *The Prelude*, and *Lyrical Ballads*
ZEUS	Father of the ancient Greek gods; known to the Romans as Jupiter

SELECT BIBLIOGRAPHY

There are many books on these poets, ranging from the popular to the severely academic. I have listed below a few which are both informative and enjoyable to read.

ROSSETTI   *Christina Rossetti: A Dvided Life,* Georgina Battiscombe, Constable, 1981; *A Choice of Christina Rossetti's Verse,* ed. Elizabeth Jennings, Faber 1989; *Learning Not to be First: The life of Christina Rossetti,* Kathleen Jones, Windrush Press, 1991; *Christina Rossetti: Poems and Prose,* ed. Jan Marsh, Everyman, 1995

SWINBURNE   *Algernon Charles Swinburne: Selected Poems,* ed. L M Findley, Fyfield Books 1987; *Swinburne: The Portrait of a Poet,* Philip Henderson, Routledge 1974; *Swinburne: The Poet in His World,* Donald Thomas, Weidenfeld 1979; *The Works of Algernon Charles Swinburne,* ed. Lawrence Binyon, Wordsworth, 1995

HOPKINS   *Gerard Manley Hopkins: A Selection Of His Poems and Prose,* ed. W H Gardner, Penguin 1982;

Gerard Manley Hopkins: A Life, Paddy Kitchen, Carcanet 1989;
The Poetry of Gerard Manley Hopkins, ed. J R Watson, Penguin 1989;
Gerard Manley Hopkins: A Very Private Life, Robert Bernard Martin, Harper Collins 1991

HARDY

Young Thomas Hardy, Robert Gittings, Penguin 1978;
The Older Hardy, Robert Gittings, Penguin 1980;
The Oxford Authors: Thomas Hardy, ed. Samuel Hynes, OUP 1984;
Thomas Hardy: A Biography, Michael Millgate, OUP 1982;
Hardy, Martin Seymour-Smith, Bloomsbury 1994

KIPLING

Something Of Myself, Rudyard Kipling, Penguin 1988;
A Choice of Kipling's Verse, ed. T S Eliot, Faber 1990;
Rudyard Kipling: The Complete Verse, foreword by M M Kaye, Kyle Cathie 1992;
Kipling The Poet, Peter Keating, Secker 1994